IMAGES OF THE DISABLED,
DISABLING IMAGES

IMAGES OF THE DISABLED, DISABLING IMAGES

Edited by
Alan Gartner and Tom Joe

PRAEGER

New York
Westport, Connecticut
London

Library of Congress Cataloging-in-Publication Data

Images of the disabled, disabling images.

Includes bibliographical references.
1. Handicapped in mass media—United States.
2. Handicapped—United States. 3. Attitude (Psychology)
I. Gartner, Alan. II. Joe, Tom.
HV1553.I43   1986   362.4'0973   86-15153
ISBN 0-275-92178-6 (alk. paper)

Library of Congress Catalog Card Number: 86-15153
ISBN: 0-275-92178-6

First published in 1987

Praeger Publishers, 521 Fifth Avenue, New York, NY 10175
A division of Greenwood Press, Inc.

Printed in the United States of America

The paper used in this book complies with the
Permanent Paper Standard issued by the National
Information Standards Organization (Z39.48-1984).

10 9   8   7   6   5   4   3   2   1

In honor of Jacobus tenBroek and
George Wiley, soldiers in the army.

CONTENTS

Acknowledgments   ix

Introduction
Alan Gartner and Tom Joe   1

, 1   Disability Rights: From Caste to Class in the
       Context of Civil Rights
       Robert Funk   7

  2   The Cripple in Literature
       Leonard Kriegel   31

  3   Disabled Women: Portraits in Fiction and Drama
       Deborah Kent   47

  4   Screening Stereotypes: Images of Disabled People
       in Television and Motion Pictures
       Paul K. Longmore   65

  5   Framed: Print Journalism's Treatment of Disability Issues
       Douglas Biklen   79

  6   Procedural Rights in the Wrong System:
       Special Education is Not Enough
       Lisa J. Walker   97

  7   The Employment Dilemma for Disabled Persons
       Cheryl Rogers   117

  8   The Application of Technology in the Classroom
       and Workplace: Unvoiced Premises and Ethical Issues
       Al Cavalier   129

  9   Easing Everyday Living: Technology for the
       Physically Disabled
       Georgia L. McMurray   143

10   The Awful Privacy of Baby Doe
       Nat Hentoff   161

11   Civil Rights for Disabled Americans: The Foundation
       of a Political Agenda
       Harlan Hahn   181

12   Conclusions
       Alan Gartner and Tom Joe   205

Index   209

About the Editors and Contributors   217

ACKNOWLEDGMENTS

In producing a book such as this one incurs many debts. We first thank Frank J. Macchiarola, then chancellor of the New York City Public Schools, for bringing us together. A decade earlier, the late George Wiley nearly did so.

Dorothy K. Lipsky helped greatly in the initial framing of the ideas, while the attendees at a conference at the Johnson Foundation's Wingspread Center refined them. The foundation was both generous and helpful in sponsoring that conference and in supporting the development of this book. We hope they find a good return on their investment, both in the work here and in the ramps which now make Frank Lloyd Wright's magnificent building accessible. And at a point when help was quickly needed, Colin Greer at the New World Foundation provided it.

Of course, the book is the reflection of the authors' efforts. We are grateful to each of them, and to Audrey Gartner who helped to shape their manuscripts.

The dedication reflects the editors' recognition that one's work builds upon that which has come before and that the highest reward of work, both intellectual and social action, is to provide the base for future efforts. In that spirit, the royalties from this book will be contributed to support the work of five organizations, to promote the rights of the disabled, through litigation, research, social action, and publications. The organizations are the American Civil Liberties Union, The Center for the Study of Social Policy, the Disability Rights Education and Defense Fund, *Disability Rag* and *Social Policy* magazine.

You see, we are confronted with a vast ignorance in the world about the handicapped, and they would not understand if we acted like normal people.

Ved Mehta, Personal History, *The New Yorker,* vol. 61, no. 39 (November 18, 1985), p. 64.

Introduction

Alan Gartner and Tom Joe

"Incompetent Persons—Persons convicted of certain infamous offenses . . . ,
persons of unsound mind, persons not in the full possession of their senses of
hearing and seeing, and habitual drunkards are incompetent to act as jurors"
(State of Tennessee Code, Section 22-1-102).

"[T]he city explained that under the zoning regulations applicable to the site, a
special use of a permit, renewable annually was required for the construction of
'[h]ospitals for the insane or feeble-minded, or alcoholic [sic] or drug addicts, or
penal or correctional institutions'" (cited in the U.S. Supreme Court's decision,
Cleburne v. *Cleburne Living Center*, 1984, p. 2).

Laws both guide and reflect the public's consensus, taking shape
from and giving form to public attitudes. These two citations, culled
from literally thousands of state and local statutes which affect persons
with disabilities, all too accurately reflect the public's attitudes toward the
more than 35 million people with disabilities in the United States.

It is the contention of this book that the characterization of persons
with disabilities as invalid—pronounced either way—is more a function
of the images, the "disabling images," held by both so-called able-bodied
and disabled individuals alike, than of the actual conditions of the individuals. Or, more precisely, this characterization is a function of the
interaction between the individuals' conditions and the environments—
both physical and attitudinal—in which they live.

Something of our sense of the importance of the handicapping condition is expressed in the presidential address delivered by Kenneth

1

Jernigan, at the 1985 annual convention of the National Federation of the Blind.

> Sight is enjoyable; it is useful; it is convenient. But that is all that it is— enjoyable, useful, convenient. Except in imagination and mythology it is not the single key to happiness, the road to knowledge, or the window to the soul. Like the other senses, it is a channel of communication, a source of pleasure, and a tool—nothing less, nothing more. It is alternative, not exclusive. It is certainly not the essential component of human freedom.[1]

Jernigan captures several important points here. One is that a person is many things. Sight, or its absence, is not the whole of the person. Yet, too often, we substitute the disabled part for the whole person. The images are so powerful they overwhelm all else.

Images of the disabled as either less or more than merely human can be found throughout recorded history. There is the blind soothsayer of ancient Greece, the early Christian belief in demonic possession of the insane, the persistent theme in Judeo-Christian tradition that disability signifies a special relationship with God. The disabled are blessed or damned but never wholly human. As Erving Goffman notes, "By definition, of course, we believe the person with a stigma is not quite human."[2]

While differing conditions—in the jargon of the field, sensory impairments, orthopedic impairments, neurological impairments, language and speech disabilities, emotional disturbances—have particular consequences for the individuals involved, in each instance it is the interplay between the condition and the environment which determines the extent to which a disability becomes a handicap. A building without ramps or elevators becomes closed to those who use wheelchairs, the absence of ballots in braille disenfranchises those who are blind, the refusal of a school system to catheterize a student with spina bifida excludes him from education with his peers. Of course, the installation of ramps does not give the person who had polio use of his legs, nor does the presence of a braille ballot give sight to the blind woman, nor does school-provided catheterization close the open spinal cord of the student with spina bifida. What they do is to mitigate the effect of the disability.

But even more than the physical environment it is the attitudinal milieu which affects those with disabilities. Attitudes are immediate, as expressed in the treatment of persons with disabilities and the bases for decisions about the environment—both built and social. Thus, for example, it is the belief that students with handicapping conditions are incapable of learning or behaving appropriately that leads state education departments, school systems, and courts to excuse them across the board from the expectations held for other students; it is an all or nothing concept of disability which requires a person to prove total incapacity in order to gain entitlement to various benefit programs; it is a skewed sense of the "place" of the disabled in the society which permits the maintenance of public and private facilities that in effect establish a system of separation not far distant from South Africa's apartheid; it is the inculcation in the belief system of the disabled themselves which encourages attitudes of acquiesence, looking for sympathy and understanding rather than mobilizing for liberation and entitlement.

The sources of these images, for both the able-bodied and disabled (or as the disability rights movement says, "the temporarily able-bodied") are varied. They include literature and the movies; telethons with their infantalized portrayal of the disabled, and the news presentations; the print media, which like TV news, rarely include the disabled and then most often as a human interest feature—not news; the textbooks used in training those who work with the disabled, which focus on the disabled person's limits and abnormality and generally portray those disabled who are children or elderly, but not those in midlife. It is not only the particular portrayal nor the inclusion or exclusion of people with disabilities that is the issue here. Rather, it is the way we see what is presented; what Thomas Kuhn has called the function of paradigms—the theories of how the world works, which emphasize certain aspects of experience and ignore others.[3]

Analyses of depictions of people with disabilities in literature, popular entertainment, textbooks, the print and electronic media illuminate both the obvious and, more often, the subtle images of disability which are both cause and effect of handicapping public and private responses to the disabled. Indeed, it was our observation of the media portrayals of and public response to "Baby Jane Doe" and Elizabeth Bouvia which provided the impetus for this book. It was not only that we felt that the portrayals were wrong; describing "Baby Jane's" condition, spina bifida, and the prognosis of her life, inaccurately, and failing to see in the reports of Elizabeth Bouvia's attempt at suicide descriptions of the social context of her life. It was the common assumptions behind these descriptions, as to the value of life and who should make decisions for people, which disturbed us. And, as we thought about the treatment in the media, we reflected upon the ways in which the assumptions made, or paradigms used, undergirded so much of our public policy. So it is that we felt it useful both to examine the ways in which disability and the disabled are portrayed and how these portrayals affect, and are affected, by public policy.

There is a pernicious reciprocal relationship between image and policy. The way out of the conundrum of the "disabling image" cycle is to use the power of government to force society-wide changes in behavior affecting the disabled. As we have learned in race relations, it is changes in behavior that ultimately effect changes in attitudes and beliefs.

It is especially important at the present time, we believe, to develop a critical awareness of the roles of images of disability in shaping the lives and (limiting the) opportunities of persons with disabilities. Currently, there is greater attention to issues of disability and the disabled, and while the attention is positive, this is a time when regressive social policies hold sway.

Even were this not the case, policy advocates are confused as to the appropriate direction to take. While the disability rights movement has been extraordinarily successful in the short span of less than a quarter of a century in both challenging disabling images and enlisting government support of equal rights for persons with disabilities, the image of disability reflected in at least some of these victories is contradictory, even regressive. For example, advocacy for double person income tax exemptions or reduced public transportation fares is in reality a demand for preferential treatment. While it may be argued that these are only fair (and temporary) compensation for a disabling society, in fact this undercuts the simultaneous effort to gain equal treatment of job applicants solely on their merits, without regard to impairment. In effect, preferential tax treatment or lower bus fares on the basis of impairment (or age for that matter), without reference to individual income, conveys an image of pathetic figures who need charity. Dignity seems a high price to pay for a cheap bus ticket!

In the past, the dominant view of disability has been a medical model. In Talcott Parsons's classic formulation, the sick role has four main characteristics: 1) the patent is exempted from normal role obligations and 2) is not held responsible for being sick; 3) the state of being sick is considered legitimate if 4) the patient cooperates with the legitimate sources of help and works toward recovery.[4] When the sick person's condition is chronic, as in the case of disability, an otherwise fair exchange is transformed "into a restatement in scientific and apparently objective terms of the most oppressive traditional stereotypes about the social ability of handicapped people. . . ."[5] The sick person's grant of temporary exemption from normal role obligations thus becomes a permanent exclusion from normal opportunities. In addition, exclusion of patient responsibility becomes a generalized unwillingness to take seriously the handicapped person's self-assertion; instead, this is viewed as symptoms of maladjustment. The sick role's insistence that the patient cooperate with the help giver and work toward recovery becomes an acceptance of the permanent tutelage of those whose ministration too often, in John McKnight's acute phrase, is in the form of "disabling help."

While the emergence of new views has tamed some of the extremes of the medical model, it still holds sway, particularly in the training of the "helping professions." Old views continue to make possible the exclusion of persons with disabilities from full participation in society. They perpetuate public policies and private practices which make disability a true handicap, rather than mitigating its effects.

The following chapters look at both the portrayal of images of the disabled and the ways in which these play themselves out in the lives of people with disabilities and the public policies and programs that affect them. Robert Funk sets the stage in an historic overview, tracing the move from the attic to the public warehouse, from viewing the disabled as sick to an emerging civil rights focus.

Leonard Kriegel and Deborah Kent look at portrayals in Western literature and with rare exception find only variations of the cripple—in Kriegel's schema the demonic cripple, the charity cripple, and the survivor cripple. Themselves disabled, both Kriegel and Kent describe how as readers and writers the image and the reality of disability affect their lives.

Paul Longmore looks to television, noting that contrary to conventional wisdom there have been hundreds of disabled characters and, yet, they are overlooked. He asks both why they are so frequently portrayed and why we screen them out of our consciousness.

Douglas Biklen examines the newspapers' treatment of two major stories about persons with disabilities: "Baby Jane Doe" and Elizabeth Bouvia. He pays particular attention to the ways these stories are framed, arguing that it is in this process that the reader is taught how to construe the meaning of disability.

Turning from these media portrayals, we examine various arenas— education, employment, everyday living, and the treatment of the high-risk newborn. Lisa Walker, one of the key authors of the major special education law, hails its inclusion of those who previously had been barred from school but questions its failure both in terms of the quality of education provided and the lack of effect upon the general school system.

Cheryl Rogers describes how the system of employment programs for the disabled results in most people being unemployed, and others underemployed, all at huge public and private expense, satisfying no one—not the disabled, not employers, not the taxpayer.

Al Cavalier and Georgia McMurray, in separate chapters, look at the effect of technology, he in education and employment, she in everyday living. Cavalier suggests the image of the disabled as "broken," needing a technological "fix," as characterizing much of the development here, while McMurray questions the substitution of technology for human relationships in the lives of the disabled.

Nat Hentoff examines the reaction to the birth and treatment of "Baby Jane Doe," pointing to the tension between the assertion of parental "privacy" rights and the child's life and liberty interests. In the process, he skewers traditional liberals for ignoring the rights of the handicapped.

In a far-ranging piece, Harlan Hahn, having examined the ways in which disability has been conceptualized, calls for a new paradigm, one which rejects the victim-blaming features of the current medical and economic models. And the editors conclude with a brief set of programmatic principles and a discussion of the challenges disability group activists must meet if they are to have long-term success in the political arena.

NOTES

1. *Braille Monitor* (August-September 1985), p. 387.
2. Erving Goffman, *Stigma: Notes on the Management of Spoiled Identity* (Englewood Cliffs, N.J.: Prentice-Hall, 1963), p. 5.
3. Thomas S. Kuhn, *The Structure of Scientific Revolutions,* 2nd ed. (Chicago: University of Chicago Press, 1970).
4. Talcott Parsons, *The Social System* (Glencoe, Ill.: Free Press, 1951), pp. 439-47.
5. John Gliedman and William Roth, *The Unexpected Minority: Handicapped Children in America* (New York: Harcourt Brace Jovanovich, 1980), p. 41.

1

Disability Rights: From Caste to Class in the Context of Civil Rights

Robert Funk

The general public does not associate the word "discrimination" with the segregation and exclusion of disabled people. Most people assume that disabled children are excluded from school or segregated from non-disabled peers because they cannot learn or because they need special protection. So, too, the absence of the disabled coworkers is simply considered confirmation of the obvious fact that disabled people can't work. These assumptions are deeply rooted in history. Historically, the inferior economic and social status of disabled people has been viewed as the inevitable consequence of the physical and mental differences imposed by disability. Over the years, this assumption has been challenged by policy makers, professionals, disabled citizens, the courts, and by Congress. Public policy has begun to recognize that many of the barriers to integration faced by disabled people are not inevitable, but instead are the result of discriminatory policies and practices based on unfounded, outmoded stereotypes and perceptions and deeply rooted prejudices toward disabled people.

Increasingly, disabled people have begun to perceive themselves as a minority group who have been denied basic civil liberties such as the

This chapter initiated as an unpublished statement reflecting the Disability Rights Education and Defense Fund, Inc. (DREDF) point of view as a civil rights legal defense fund run by and for disabled people. The ideas contained in the chapter have been used for background in training materials, briefs, and related work DREDF has undertaken since its inception in 1979. This existing chapter reflects the ideas and involvement of the entire DREDF organization; however; the author is responsible for the analysis and opinions expressed herein.

right to vote, to marry and bear children, to attend school, and to obtain employment. This new movement resembles, in method and legal theory, movements by other disadvantaged and disenfranchised groups in American politics. Disabled people and advocates have started to call on the same clauses of the U.S. Constitution for court victories and legislative mandates—specifically, those requiring due process before life, liberty, and property may be infringed upon, and those mandating equal protection of the law.

This chapter makes no pretense of discussing the important distinctions among disabled people, including disability-specific needs, nor their varied levels of political activity. Rather, it is a look at the history of disability from a civil rights perspective, in order to develop a basis for understanding the concept of equal opportunity and integration as it applies to disabled people as a class.

Over the last 15 years, there has been the recognition that disabled people are generally treated as a dependent caste. New laws and policies recognize the existence of this caste and the resulting special-political-minority status. Further, it is recognized that the thread that ties this class together is discrimination, segregation, and denial of equal opportunity. The key to understanding disability in the context of civil rights is to focus upon the common goal of integration in the society. Disabled people want to be treated with dignity and respect and given the opportunity to achieve and fail. Thus, the purpose of specific civil rights legislation is to assist individual disabled people to achieve a normal life experience as a citizen, not to create a nearly normal person as has been the focus of human service providers. This is not a focus upon equal results. It is not a requirement that society guarantee an ideal end. It is the provision of the means (that is, equipment, transportation, housing, health care) to ensure a meaningful opportunity to achieve the level of integration that is appropriate to the individual's ambition, abilities, and potential.[1]

A CHANGING IMAGE: THE HUMANIZATION OF DISABLED PEOPLE

The evolution of disability history and policy in the United Staes can be described as the increasing humanization of disabled people: humanization is defined as a recognition that disabled people have human needs and characteristics, and public policy must be designed to reflect and further this human potential.

People who are disabled have historically been treated as objects of pity and fear—individuals who are incapable and neither expected nor willing to participate in or contribute to organized society. Thus, a societal attitude developed that this class of persons, viewed as unhealthy, defective, and deviant, required special institutions, services, care, and attention in order to survive. This social construct has been supported by national welfare policies to care for the deserving poor, charitable programs to help the unfortunate, the continued application of the medical model to disability, and rehabilation services provided in a manner that undermines self-initiative and self-respect and perpetuates stereotypical education and employment avenues. This has resulted in discriminatory programs, policies, and laws designed to deny disabled people's participation in organized society. These discriminatory policies and practices affect all classes of disabled people in virtually every aspect of their lives.

Phase 1, 1700-1920: From the Attic to the Warehouse

The unwritten law of primitive society that the crippled and disabled were to be sacrificed for the good of the group was carried over into written laws, and for many centuries determined the treatment of disabled persons. In the early years of the United States, the responsibility for assisting disabled persons fell on the extended family. If the disabled person was a pauper or without family support, local communities assumed responsibility, and in many cases contracted out to the lowest bidder for provision of care.[2] This system of societal indifference was so subject to abuse that public sentiment compelled reforms, which resulted in state-funded institutions to house indigent disabled citizens. A further level of specialization occurred in time, with the establishment of institutions for specific categories of disabled persons such as deaf and blind children, the mentally ill, feeble-minded, and retarded.

These special-care institutions and county poor farms represented a move from total indifference by organized society to a recognition of the need for at least minimum care. But this reform was closely followed by a long period of neglect. The institutions charged with custodial care became known more for the horrors committed against the inmates than for the extent of care.[3]

Apart from the move to institutionalize and warehouse disabled people, a second level of reform grew out of the era. Included were reforms providing assistance to disabled persons deemed "deserving," because of government service-related injuries (veterans), or industrial-related accidents. Such policies were the forerunners of the U.S. rehabilitation structure of the twentieth century.

By the 1920s, disability policy was characterized by a pattern of total-care institutions set up to house the indigent dependent, and specialized institutions for classes of disabled persons. Additionally, minimum medical care and/or rehabilitation services were provided to the few "deserving" disabled to help them achieve gainful employment.[4]

Phase 2, 1920-60: Segregation and Charitable Care

The next four decades saw increased numbers of people placed in institutions and continued massive neglect in those settings, and increases in welfare and entitlement programs to low-income disabled persons with a new goal of providing alternatives to total-care institutions. After World War II and the Korean War, the range of rehabilitation services and the classes of disabled persons covered increased, with programs established to minimize the effects of a disability such as vocational training leading to gainful employment.

This period was also marked by a growth in the number and type of occupations available to professionals in the disability services arena, especially in the areas of physical medicine and rehabilitation, physical therapy, occupational therapy, nursing, rehabilitation counselling, and disability research. The rapid growth of medical-science technology and rehabilitative medicine had a positive impact on the number of people surviving disease, accidents, and injuries and significantly increased the ability of disabled people to be more physically mobile and more involved in life decisions.[5]

Special interest organizations such as the National Spinal Cord Injury Foundation, Muscular Dystrophy Association, Easter Seal Society, National Association of Retarded Citizens, and United Cerebral Palsy, also grew in numbers, size, and importance. Medical and rehabilitation research, recreation training, and work programs provided avenues for socializing and expanding skills, albeit in segregated and sheltered settings. While most, if not all, of the special organizations were run by nondisabled individuals, they had increasing impact in educating the general public as well as policy makers on the needs of disabled people. This resulted in increased legislation and programs designed to provide services to meet the needs of many disabled people.

By the end of the 1950s, disability policy from the human rights perspective was reflected in the following eight general points.

1. Existence of massive total-care institutions to house disabled persons deemed unable to function in organized society. The initial hope that institutional care would provide "villages of the simple, made up of the warped, twisted, and the incorrigible, happily contributing to their own and the support of those more lowly—'cities of refuge' in truth, havens in which all shall live contentedly, because no longer misunderstood nor taxed with expectations beyond their mental or moral capacity," became in fact destructive, dehabilitating, and dehumanizing warehouses. "The institution became not a paradise, but a purgatory, not a Garden of Eden but an agency of dehumanization; to this day, residents are subjected to physical and medical abuse, to neglect and inadequate care and services, to environmental deprivation and to restriction of the most basic rights and dignities of a human."[6]

2. Board, care, training, and work institutions to house specific groups of disabled persons who were deemed trainable or educable, but also considered in need of segregated and structured settings because it was believed that their handicap would not permit them to compete or function in society.

Sheltered workshops and training institutions grew out of special schools for the blind in the middle of the nineteenth century. They developed on the assumption that if disabled persons could master a trade, they would be accepted into competitive employment. However, it became apparent that the general public would not abandon prejudice and stereotypes and accept the concept that blind and other disabled workers could be contributing members of organized society. Instead of pressuring for placement in public schools to emphasize the positive effects of integration, educators accepted the public judgment that blind and disabled workers were unable to compete, and relegated education and employment programs to the status of "a retreat where bread can be earned; their [handicapped persons'] morals protected, and a just estimate put upon their talents."[7]

3. Provision of public entitlements to persons with severe disabilities in order to provide an alternative to total-care institutions (generally minimum care institutions, home-bound settings, or group-care arrangements). Beginning with the Social Security Act of 1935, Congress has passed a wide array of public assistance programs to provide minimum protection against insecurities imposed by old age, unemployment, and

disability. The 1956 amendments to the Social Security Act undertook a fundamental revision of public assistance programs by incorporating provisions for self-support and self-care, as well as minimum income to meet current needs. Thus, Congress recognized that along with food, shelter, and clothing, self-support and self-care are basic necessities of life.[8]

Programs initiated during this era, which continue to be essential to the survival of low-income disabled persons living outside total-care institutions, include income assistance, nutrition, health care, personal care, and homemaker services.[9]

4. Provision of rehabilitation benefits to a larger and more varied population of disabled persons, including veterans, with the primary goal of assisting those who were deemed capable of obtaining gainful employment. The massive industrialization of the economy, the increase in industrial accidents and war-related injuries, and an increased recognition of social responsibility mandated development of a national rehabilitation policy. Programs in training, physical restoration, auxiliary aids, and placement became the keystones necessary to reach the ultimate objective of establishing "eligible" clients in a suitable vocation.

But there were basic weaknesses in the programs which perpetuated the second-class status of disabled persons. The primary effort was to place the greatest number of clients in employment. Little effort was given to place people in competitive employment or to remove the legal, administrative, and related obstacles to employment.

5. Massive increases in number, size, and power of disability-specific medical research and charitable organizations to aid disabled people. Organizations such as the Muscular Dystrophy Association, Easter Seal Society, American Cancer Society, American Heart Association, and United Cerebral Palsy were founded to assist in medical research to find a "cure" for the medical nature of the disability in question, as well as to provide recreation and therapy programs. The organizations had major impact on research funding and public image, and were characterized by the common tendency to perpetuate the charity approach of helping poor unfortunate people "who can't help themselves."

6. Increased numbers and sophistication of a broad range of medical and rehabilitation professionals. Industrialization of the economy, industrial accidents, and war injuries, as well as congenital and disease-related disabilities increased in society over this period. The role and expertise of varied disability professionals became preeminent as more and more disabled people survived and became "medicalized," requiring medical and rehabilitation intervention.

The "medical model" and resulting role of the "patient" has been the subject of numerous studies.[10] The negative impact of the medical/rehabilitation model lies in its perpetuation of the dependent and nonparticipatory role expected of a "patient" in regard to decisions about "illness" and its negative impact in defining the role of disabled people in virtually every aspect of life, from education and employment to transportation and voting. (Chapters 6, 7, 8, and 9 describe how this occurs.)

7. Increasing activity by disability-specified advocacy and education organizations involved in networking among their constituency and instrumental in developing state and federal legislation and policy to aid membership needs. Numerous disability-specified organizations and coalitions were formed in this period, including the National Federation of the Blind, National Association of the Deaf, and the Congress of Physically Handicapped Organizations.

The organizations had varied roots. Some were formed out of the charitable recreation and social programs and others from educational institutions and employment workshops. All were unique in that they were founded and directed by their constituency, and all worked on creation of legislation and policy that would further their special needs.

8. Early development of legislation and policy, primarily on the part of disability professionals, to expand the provision of rehabilitation services to disabled individuals for whom employment was deemed not to be an obtainable objective. In the late 1950s rehabilitation and related professionals became concerned about the number of disabled people for whom services were not available because employment was not considered an obtainable objective. In 1959, legislation was introduced that would provide independent living services as an alternative to vocational goals. This legislation failed, and while distinct from later independent living legislation, it was the forerunner of provisions of the Rehabilitation Act of 1973 and the 1978 amendments. These laws resulted in the provision of services to those individuals "for whom a vocational goal is not possible," mandating services as a first priority for those who were most severely disabled, as well as independent living program legislation.[11]

There are many ways to view this 40-year period, from 1920 to 1960, and its impact on disabled people. From a broad disability/human rights perspective, the era reflects an increasing humanization of certain classes of disabled people based on qualities of "deservedness" and "normalcy" and "employability," and a move from total societal indifference to a recognition that the remaining "unfortunates" must receive some level of minimum care.

However, the handicapped still retained their caste status in the public mind as dependent, unhealthy deviants, who would, in the great majority, always require segregated care and protection. The charity, rehabilitation, and medical professionals ruled the day, providing better care and better services to a people who would, it appeared, retain their childlike dependent status in perpetuity.

Phase 3, 1960-75: Social Movements and Civil Rights

The 1960s was a watershed era in U.S. civil rights reform. The pressures of history coalesced in mounting demands for equality of opportunity for a major segment of the population who were disenfranchised and disadvantaged because of discrimination based on poverty, racial, or ethnic background or gender.

Disability law and disability as a social movement was profoundly affected by this era. Disabled people began to question the tradition of limited options, exclusions, and dependency. Advocates began to attack, on behalf of disabled clients, the dehumanizing policies and practices in terms of denial of constitutional, civil, and human rights.

Organizing for Social Reform

The disability rights movement's overall development was profoundly influenced by the social and political activity of the period. The concepts of right to integration and meaningful equality of opportunity, as well as method and tactics utilized by other civil rights groups, began to be employed in disability rights work. Other movements of the 1960s including consumerism, self-help, demedicalization/self-care, and deinstitutionalization also had an impact on disabled people and their advocates. Each supported the growing comprehension by disabled people that they had rights, could choose, belong, and participate as full and equal members of society.

The coalitions and organizations of disabled persons that evolved in these decades cut across medical-based disability distinctions to focus upon issues of common concern, and ran counter to the specialization and diffusion of energy and resources that was the inevitable result of the period 1920-60.

Disabled student programs at the University of Illinois at Champaign-Urbana (1950) and the University of California, Berkeley (1964), were among the first to facilitate community living for disabled students. In

1972, the independent living movement began to gain great momentum and credibility with the incorporation of the Center for Independent Living in Berkeley, California. The Berkeley CIL was founded by seven severely disabled persons, including former University of California students who had participated in the university's disabled student program.[12]

The Berkeley CIL had impact far beyond its local community. It was the first and ultimately the largest center of its type. It was nonresidential and provided a wide range of services to the community. It was, perhaps more importantly, created by disabled people and designed to serve their needs as they saw them. As a result, it became the model and symbol of what individual disabled people could achieve given the opportunity. It offered hope and dignity and had profound influence on disability professionals, Congress, and disabled people throughout the United States.[13]

The movement was not limited to centers for independent living. The special interest organizations and coalitions that developed during the period 1920 to 1960 became increasingly active, advocating and lobbying for change. Local and statewide coalitions formed to press on special issues, along with broad social change. In 1974, the organizations joined to create the American Coalition of Citizens with Disabilities, the first national cross-disability forum to coordinate policy actions.

It should be noted that, unlike other civil and human rights movements in U.S. history, the mandated legislative protection for disabled people occurred before there was an active movement. Racial minorities, women, labor, and other progressive reform movements, were actively advocating for policy change and were instrumental in its creation and implementation. Disability policy reform and the resulting civil rights focus grew out of the concern and indignation of advocates, attorneys, and a sympathetic Congress during a progressive social era. This is not to vitiate or undermine the contributions of the individuals involved, many of whom continue to provide strong and instrumental support. Rather, it is indicative of the fact that in our society, no social reform, regardless of how well-intentioned, can be adequately implemented or maintained without the active involvement and continued effort by the beneficiaries of the reform.

Law Reform—The Constitutional Basis

The 1960s and early 1970s not only saw major change and growth in the organizing and advocacy efforts by disabled people and parents of disabled children, but also saw the legal basis for major disability policy evolve to a civil rights focus. Traditional programs, policies, and stereo-typed assumptions about the disabled persons were attacked in the courts and the legislatures in terms of constitutional rights and liberties. Attorneys utilized due process and equal protection challenges to attack dehumanizing institutions and segregated schools. Congress passed legislation to include the handicapped as a class protected by civil rights statutes. Disabled adults and children began to be perceived as a class of people denied civil liberties, not merely a dependent caste society must house and protect.

Institutions came under increasing attack for denial of basic human rights. In theory, institutionalized persons had the same basic rights as others, but in practice these rights were abrogated without due process or without inquiry into individual needs and capabilities. In journal articles and legislative hearings, professionals and advocates attacked the institutions for dehabilitating and dehumanizing conditions and the denial of basic constitutional liberties. Advocates quickly turned to the courts and legislature for individualized treatment and community-based living alternatives. By 1979, there were sweeping class action challenges of institutional settings in 17 states. Legislative and administrative reform occurred so rapidly that "no state could regard its mental disability laws as wholly updated."[14]

While the early twentieth century saw the introduction and expansion of day schools and educational programs for disabled children, virtually all education was delivered in segregated, institutional settings, and services were, at best, second class. Over 15 years after *Brown* v. *Board of Education,* equal protection arguments were made with respect to disabled children in Pennsylvania litigation.[15] The consent decree in that case established the right of each mentally retarded school-age child in the state to an appropriate and integrated education. The same rights were extended to all disabled children in the District of Columbia, regardless of the nature of severity of their disability.[16]

Federal Statutory Reform

Congressional reform occurred at a rapid pace. Integration and equality of opportunity mandates were enacted to provide for access to public facilities and transportation.[17] The Rehabilitation Act of 1973 was passed, and later amended, to develop and implement, through research, training, services, and the guarantee of equal opportunity, comprehensive and coordinated programs of vocational rehabilitation and independent living.[18] The act included provisions under Title V creating a federal board to coordinate and monitor access to public buildings and public transportation,[19] prohibiting discrimination in employment, and requiring affirmative action by federal agencies[20] and federal contractors.[21] It also included the key national mandate prohibiting discrimination against the handicapped by recipients of federal assistance (Section 504).[22]

Congress mandated an end to separate and unequal educational opportunities by requiring that "to the maximum extent appropriate, handicapped children [shall be] educated with children who are not handicapped. . . .;"[23] and passed legislation containing a bill of rights for persons with developmental disabilities with the primary goal of providing services that would further the individual potential to become a participating member of the community.[24]

The congressional reforms of the 1970s were enacted to attack the roots of historical prejudice and stereotypes that had isolated disabled people from organized society as a caste of inferior dependent beings. As Congress stated in 1974:

> The Congress finds that. . . . it is essential . . . to assure that all individuals with handicaps are able to live their lives independently and with dignity, and that the complete integration of all individuals with handicaps into normal community living, working and service patterns be held as the final objective.[25]

Phase 4, A Changing Society: 1976-85

The passage of federal legislation, however, is not sufficient within the U.S. political system to realize the reforms that impact on the lives of the constituency for which the legislation is intended. Adequate methods of implementation and enforcement must be defined and redefined by the courts and must be reinforced by a broad base of support at the state and local community level.

The late 1970s saw the rapid development of disability as a civil rights movement and the rise of a restrictive and conservative political climate. Both developments began to achieve rapid impact during the Carter administration (1977-81) resulting in changes in the federal arena.

The notable features of the disability activism during the Carter years were the key roles played by disabled people and coalitions of people with different disabilities. Disabled people were the leaders and disabled people formed the forces that pressed for reform. The individuals were disabled people from the new community-based independent living programs and from the programs and communities of deaf, blind, mentally retarded, and mentally ill people.

In April 1977, an event occurred that illustrated this process in relation to the development of federal policy. In the four years since the enactment of section 504 of the Rehabilitation Act of 1973, a set of compromise regulations had emerged from the evaluation of over 30 hearings and over 1,200 written comments. However, Health, Education, and Welfare Secretary Joseph Califano failed to sign regulations implementing section 504. In response to Secretary Califano's refusal to issue the regulations, demonstrations took place throughout the United States. In San Francisco, disabled activists occupied the office of the Department of Health, Education, and Welfare for 28 days until the regulations were signed. Protest activities were also staged in other major cities—including Washington, D.C.—to bring public attention and political pressure to bear on the enactment of the section 504 regulations. These demonstrations, for the first time, showed the nation and policy makers that the growing grass-roots disability rights movement was a significant political force.

The grass-roots groups continued to evolve in numbers and form and had increasing impact in defining federal disability policy. In 1978, Congress authorized support for community-based independent living centers;[26] the Rehabilitation Act of 1973 was amended to add Title VII, Comprehensive Services for Independent Living. Title VII established a major change in federal disability policy, and in doing so reflected the growing influence of the community-based independent living disability rights movement through specific legislation drawing on the experience of disabled people in the local communities.

The community groups not only had impact on federal policy in social services but spawned the formation of new advocacy groups to push the civil rights reform at the city, county, state, and federal levels. The reforms included provision of sidewalk curb cuts for wheelchairs; active roles in city, county, and state agencies; affirmative action in hiring and promoting disabled people for employment; and the integration of disabled adults and children into educational programs.

There is continuing development of coalitions and advocacy organizations created by and designed to educate and advocate on behalf of disabled adults and disabled children. The focus of the organizations vary. They include increasing numbers of community-based independent living centers that provide support services to their community, as well as state focused advocacy and community organizing groups working to increase access to programs and policy setting arenas for parents and disabled adults. Political action committees and disability law and policy agencies are rapidly evolving. They focus upon broader policy issues

and pursue their goals through programs in education, research, advocacy, networking, and leadership development, particularly of disabled people. And, in recent years, a large number of parent groups have formed to work on issues regarding disabled children.[27]

Disability rights organizations began because there was a recognized need. The leadership became aware that, as independent living programs assisted an increasing number of disabled people to pursue lives with greater freedom of choice, true integration would occur only by increasing the involvement of disabled adults and parents of disabled children in the broader social and political arena.

The changing political climate resulted in the 1980 election of a conservative administration and brought changes in Congress, the executive agencies, and the courts. This election also signaled a conservative social and fiscal period in the federal arena particularly in the area of individual rights. This change represented the resurgence of the view that resents federal intrusion into what are considered private or state and local matters.

One example that displays the convergence of the increasing grassroots political activism of disabled people and the changing federal role is reflected in attempts by the Reagan administration to change federal civil rights regulations that forbid state and local governments, universities, hospitals, and a wide variety of recipients of federal financial aid from discriminating against disabled people, racial minorities, women, and older persons.[28]

The administration first attempted to redraft the regulations that implement section 504 in the deregulation process. Over a 15-month period a grass-roots effort by disabled people and parents of disabled children organized and responded with over 40,000 letters to numerous attempts to weaken these key regulations. In March 1983, Vice-President Bush announced the administration had decided not to change the regulations. A May 28, 1983, article in the *National Journal* noted that "the disability rights community engaged in one of the most effective and sophisticated lobbying efforts ever seen to get the 504 regulations withdrawn."[29]

The changes wrought by the new view of the federal role in civil rights is also seen in civil rights cases decided by the U.S. Supreme Court, which has, since 1975, issued at lease 26 decisions directly affecting the interests of disabled persons. Section 504 and Pub. L. No. 94-142, the key statements of the integration and equality opportunity mandate, have been subject to scrutiny by the Court, resulting in what is recognized as a generally restrictive interpretation of disability civil rights law.

The first 504 case to be reviewed by the Supreme Court was the landmark *Southern Community College* v. *Davis,* 442 U.S. 397 (1976). In a unanimous decision the Court overturned a Fourth Circuit decision by holding that Ms. Davis, a deaf applicant to nursing school was not "otherwise qualified" because her participation would require a full-time personal aide and/or waiver of the clinical portion of the program, thus resulting in a fundamental alteration in the nature of the program.

More significant was the tone of the opinion and the dicta that the unanimous Court issued with the decision. In an incorrect analysis of 504, the Court stated that while 501 (nondiscrimination in federal employment) and 503 (nondiscrimination in employment by federal contractors) require affirmative action, 504 contains no such concept or requirement. Thus the Court in its first 504 decision incorrectly equated reasonable accommodation with "affirmative action" and legitimized the restrictive use of the "undue financial and administrative burden" standard.

Disability rights advocates immediately reacted to the Court's decision by calling for a nationwide civil rights day to show their extreme displeasure at the Court's specific restrictive language that indicated the Court was not sensitive to disability rights issues. Looking back with six years of hindsight we can see that the disability community's reaction was prophetic because the terms "undue financial and administrative burden" and "no affirmative action" became the key terms used in many lower court decisions, administrative decisions, and implementing regulations (for example, regulations recently issued by the Department of Justice for federally conducted programs) to deny disabled people access to federally funded programs.

In 1984 the Court issued another landmark decision interpreting section 504 in *Consolidated Rail Corporation* v. *Darrone,* 104 S.Ct. 1248 (1984). The case both strengthened and weakened 504.

In *Darrone* the Court overturned a majority of circuit court decisions that held that 504 did not provide broad coverage for nondiscrimination in employment. The Court stated that the language of the statute, the legislative history, and the executive agency interpretation of 504 in the regulations did not support the narrow construction issued by a majority of the circuit courts. Further the Court, while not addressing the private cause of action issue directly, held that 504 allowed an employee to sue under 504 for intentional discrimination by recipients of federal financial assistance.

The *Darrone* decision also weakened 504. The Court found that, based upon a Title IX (nondiscrimination based on sex in education) ruling issued the same day as *Darrone,* the ban against discrimination on the basis of handicap is limited to the specific program that received federal funds. In *Darrone*, Consolidated Rail received large amounts of funds that were distributed broadly throughout the corporation. Therefore the "program or activity" receiving federal financial assistance was the entire entity. However, the Title IX case, *Grove City College* v. *Bell*, 104 S.Ct. 1211 (1984), clarified the full impact of the narrow view held by the Court, when it defined "program or activity." It held that even if the college gets federal funds, this fact alone is not sufficient reason for concluding that the entire institution is the recipient and therefore, subject to civil rights coverage. The Court concluded that only the specific office receiving federal funds is covered and in the *Grove* case this limited coverage to the financial aid office.

Another 504 case decided by the Court is *Choate* v. *Alexander,* 53 U.S. Law Week 4072 (Jan. 8, 1985). In this unanimous decision the Court held that the method used by Tennessee in administering its Medicaid program did not violate 504, even though the State decisions resulting in reductions of Medicaid disproportionately affected poor, disabled persons. The Court concluded that nothing in 504 indicated that Congress required 504 to serve as a "National Environmental Policy Act" for disabled people and the state's reduction of the number of days of care beneficiaries received due to budget reasons was valid.

While the case lost on the merits, in following its previous ruling in *Darrone,* the Court decided that 504, though based upon Title VI, may not be limited by the restrictions that are imposed upon Title VI. Specifically, the Court found that 504 was enacted by Congress to prohibit not only 'intentional/purposeful" discrimination, but also discrimination resulting from the "effects" of recipient actions. The Court recognized a distinct difference in discrimination on the basis of race from that based on handicap; it said that the majority of disability discrimination was the result of benign neglect based on a history of dependency, charity, segregation, and invisibility and was not generally based on invidious animus. Further, the Court clarified the troublesome language in *Davis* regarding affirmative action by stating that its previous ruling that 504 did not impose affirmative action obligations was not intended to preclude a requirement of reasonable accommodation to ensure non-discrimination.

Along with the enactment of section 504 in the 1970s, Congress passed The Education for All Handicapped Children Act (Pub. L. No. 94-142), a major civil rights landmark. In it Congress required that each disabled child be provided a free appropriate education in the least restrictive environment. The law was also a radical departure from tradition by providing rights to parents to be involved in the process of deciding the type and nature of their child's education through an individualized educational plan and establishing due process provisions.

The Supreme Court has decided two important cases that interpret the language and scope of 94-142, *Board of Education of the Hendrich Hudson School District* v. *Rowley,* 50 U.S. Law Week 4925 (June 28, 1982) and *Irving Independent School District* v. *Tatro,* 104 S.Ct. 3371 (1984).

In *Rowley* the Court held, among other items, that a free appropriate public education requires that educational jurisdictions provide individualized instruction with adequate support services to ensure that all children benefit from education. However, the Court stated, the law does not require services that enable a child to obtain the maximum benefit and that the determination of what method is to be used to achieve a beneficial and appropriate education is left to the states.

In *Tatro,* the Court decided that a special procedure known as clean intermittent catheterization was a related service under 94-142. The Court held that without the service the child could not attend public school. The Court concluded the service was necessary for the child to benefit from his/or her education and therefore it is a related service. The Court provided a narrow exemption for those services that by their nature require the assistance of a physician.

As with the *Darrone* decision, where the Court on one hand provided for broad coverage under 504 for employment but limited the scope of the act to the specific program or activity that receives federal financial assistance, the Court in *Tatro* and a companion case *(Smith* v. *Robinson)* limited access to the legal system under both 94-142 and 504 in the area of public education.

The practical effect of the *Smith* decision is to limit severely the access to the courts for all but wealthy parents on issues concerning their disabled child's right to a public education.

The review of the history of disability and the evolution of disability law and policy in the United States from a civil rights perspective leads to several important points. First, it is important to recognize that the disabled are viewed by the general public as a class. Regardless of the distinctions among disabled individuals, they are socially and legally a people oppressed by attitudes and images that perpetuate the caste of the handicapped.

> The disabled—like all other minority groups—tend to be evaluated more on the basis of their categorical membership than on their individual characteristics. . . . And the fact that [a person] is disabled will color all his activities and potentialities in the eyes of the non-disabled in such a pervasive way that he will either be considered weak and inferior, incapable of doing anything, or

possessed of exceptional capacities and abilities. Very seldom will he be evaluated on the basis of his knowledge, abilities, skills, strengths, and weaknesses. And since stereotypes are often attached to categories of people singled out because of one"negative" attribute in common, those belonging to a category (a minority group) are evaluated on the basis of these stereotypes. Thus, the disabled are assessed by the nondisabled on the bases of the overall stereotype attached to all disabled as well on the bases of the particular stereotype attached to their specific disability. And since these stereotypes are usually negative, most of the time the disabled are discriminated against by the nondisabled because the assessment stops at the recognition of the presence of disability.[30]

Second, it is important to recognize that the key federal legislation enacted since 1970 recognizes disabled people as a protected class and focuses upon a goal. The terms of art vary from statute to statute but in each case the key underlying concept and goal is integration through the provision of meaningful equal opportunity.

EQUAL CITIZENSHIP AND DISABILITY RIGHTS: A CONFLICT IN IMAGES

There are several threads that can be pursued given the history of disabled people and disability rights in our society. This can range from an analysis of the movement by disabled people to gain control of their lives; to a study of the impact of the courts and litigation; a review of the impact of the disability rights movement on policy and policy developments; or, a look at the implication of disability rights and the evolving social-political model of disability on the broad area of civil rights law, welfare, and entitlements and on social policy in general. Discussion can continue to focus on history, undertake an analysis of the present, or look at the possible future of disabled people and society.

For our purposes, we shall pursue the general thread of the relationship of civil rights policy and disability as a minority status: defining the key concepts of integration and equal opportunity in the present-day context of disability as a sociopolitical movement.

The thesis of this thread of thought is that organized society, its decision makers, and program and policy implementors do not understand the concepts of integration and equal opportunity as it relates to the inclusion and participation of disabled adults and children in the social, political, and economic mainstream. This unwillingness or inability to understand and utilize these concepts as they apply to disabled adults and children is rooted in the overriding influence of the persisting images of disabled people as deviant, incompetent, unhealthy objects of fear who are perpetually dependent upon the welfare and charity of others; and, the resulting inability of society to view the confirmed exclusion, segregation, and denial of equal opportunity as unlawful and harmful discrimination.

The first question to be addressed (and the key to understanding the disability rights movement) is: "What is the goal of disability civil rights?" For individual disabled people, it is accessible public transportation, community-based independent living support services, sign language interpreters, mobility aids and skills training, adequate housing, appropriate medical care, communications access and aids, and appropriate and adequate employment.

For all disabled persons, however, the ultimate goal is the freedom to choose, to belong, to participate, to have dignity, and the opportunity to achieve. It is the end of the caste of the handicapped and the stereotypes and prejudices that persons of disabilities lack essential human attributes necessary to be considered a part of organized society.

The existence of a caste status coupled with stereotypes and prejudices have led to an organized society that was designed without consideration of the human potential of disabled people and without disabled people's participation.[31] It is a society that is segregated and discriminatory in law and in fact.

The myriad of disability-specific programs and policies, the segregation of disabled people, the inability to gain access to organized society, to experience an integrated and adequate education, to obtain meaningful employment, and to socially interact and participate has resulted in a politically powerless and diffuse class of people who are unable to coalesce with other groups of disabled people on common issues, to vote, to be seen or heard. This class has accepted the stigma and caste of second-hand citizenship and the incorrect judgment of social inferiority.

The goal for a disability rights movement can be stated as the mandated application of the principle of equal citizenship to all programs and policies that affect disabled people.

> The principle of equal citizenship presumptively insists that organized society treat each individual as a person, one who is worthy of respect and who "belongs." Stated negatively, the principle presumptively forbids the organized society to treat an individual either as a member of an inferior or dependent caste or as a non-participant.[32]

Disabled people have the constitutional and human right to equal citizenship, that is, the right to be treated as a person worthy of dignity and respect. Thus, policy and legal mandates to further integration, equality of opportunity, and nondiscrimination must evolve sufficiently so the caste and stigma of the handicapped is no longer tolerated; where individual freedom of choice and the individual's right to participate and belong are recognized as absolute; an affirmative duty is mandated to overcome the effects of a history of segregation and discriminatory policies and practices and to ensure the existence of meaningful equality of opportunity in the future.

The test of social thought and public policy for disabled people, in accordance with this belief, is whether it meets or deters meeting these needs: whether it presupposes the human potential and equality of disabled persons or presumes their abnormality and inferiority; whether it recognizes both their right and competence to govern their lives or seeks to impose a protective custody and perpetuates a dependent child-like status; and, whether it creates meaningful equal opportunity and encourages growth and integration into organized society, or erects artificial handicaps and arbitrary barriers.[33]

Disability as a protected class presents unique conceptual problems for the authors of legislation, regulatory policy, and judicial decisions. The "handicapped" are conceptually a minority class of persons who suffer similar isolation and categorical discrimination based upon their membership in the class. However, disabled people do not constitute a homogeneous minority group who share the characteristics that bring about discrimination in the same way that members of racial or ethnic groups or women share discriminative characteristics. There is a continuum of severity and visibility of the handicap and stigmatization among disabled people that determines the nature and intensity of discrimination by organized society.[34]

The majority of policy and environmental barriers that deny disabled individuals the equal opportunity to participate are based on historical tradition, social preference, and stereotyped presumptions about the class.[35] This can be seen in two basic areas.

First, the vast majority of environmental and policy barriers have a direct connection to a tradition of exclusion of disabled people from organized society. For example, multi-storied educational facilities lacking either ramps or elevators prevent use of the educational facilities by persons in wheelchairs or others with ambulatory disabilities, including the temporarily disabled and elderly. The facilities were designed and continue to be designed on the assumption that disabled individuals will not participate in the offered educational services, be they primary, secondary, or postsecondary, or adult programs.

In employment, we see the same stereotypical assumptions and barriers. Architecture barriers and communication barriers[36] are manifest and of predominant concern not only in employment but in all areas of life for many disabled persons. Further, traditional policy and practice barriers exist that prevent an individual from being offered employment or receiving a promotion, regardless of the individual's qualifications. These barriers include pre-employment medical standards and standard job descriptions and job structuring that prevent employment or promotions.[37]

The second area where we see the interplay of historical tradition, social preference, and stereotyped presumptions is in the area of discriminatory attitudes and prejudice regarding the class of handicapped persons.[38] This manifests itself, for example, in both segregated schools and limited educational programs (see Chapter 6, "Procedural Rights in the Wrong System: Special Education is not Enough") as well as in limited and sheltered employment, based on the unwillingness to accept a disabled coworker and low expectations of the disabled individual's skill, capability, health, safety, and potential (see Chapter 7, "The Employment Dilemma for Disabled Persons").

To achieve the potential goal of equal citizenship that we believe is mandated under our constitutional system, we must alter our perception of the role of civil rights policy in achieving integration and equal opportunity.

The issue of prejudicial treatment of disabled persons is analogous to confronting discrimination on the basis of race and sex. It is direct and subject to class remedies. But the analogy fails when we focus on the actual disability. In the vast majority of cases, one must provide for an individualized[39] remedy that addresses a disabled individual's specific needs and disability (or a subclass of disabled people) to ensure meaningful equal protection of the law.

This issue can be best understood when we contrast two very early cases involving access to public transportation brought under section 504 of the Rehabilitation Act of 1973:[40] *Snowdon* v. *Birmingham Jefferson County Transit Authority* and *Lloyd* v. *Regional Transportation Authority*. Both cases were filed on behalf of mobility-impaired persons and, in both instances, the plaintiffs alleged that the respective authorities were violating section 504 by continuing to purchase unmodified, physically inaccessible buses.[41]

In *Snowden,* the Fifth Circuit affirmed the district court, which had ruled that the transit authority was not violating section 504 by purchasing inaccessible buses. The court declared that the transit authority was not discriminating on the basis of disability providing that it allowed mobility-impaired persons the opportunity to board buses in any way they can. Unless it ordered its bus drivers to slam the doors of buses in the faces of mobility-impaired persons, the transit authority would not be discriminating.

In *Lloyd,* the Seventh Circuit reached an opposite conclusion. The district court merely ruled that Lloyd did not have a private right of action under section 504, and refused to try the case. The circuit court reversed that decision, ruling that the plaintiff did have a private right of action, and remanded the case to the district court for reconsideration on its merits. The circuit court continued its analysis of the issue, and declared that section 504 imposes an "affirmative duty" on recipients to ensure facilities are accessible, not merely a passive duty to allow mobility-impaired persons the opportunity to use such facilities, if they can.

The Seventh Circuit relied on the similarity between section 504 and Title VI to impose an affirmative duty.[42] The court then quoted from a civil rights case in education which recognized that equal treatment does not always provide equal opportunity, substituting "handicapped" for Chinese-speaking students.

> There is no equality of treatment merely by providing [the handicapped] with the same facilities [as ambulatory persons]. . . . [for handicapped persons] who [can] not [gain access to such facilities] are effectively foreclosed from any meaningful [public transportation].[43]

The application of nondiscrimination law to public transportation for disabled people is not the issue to be addressed here. The *Snowden* and *Lloyd* cases, however, clearly point out the basic issue in achieving non-discrimination and equal citizenship. Adequate assurance of equal protection of the laws and integration requires an understanding of disability, disability discrimination, the role of civil rights policy in our society, and the development of solutions that recognize the differences among disabled people and include provision of a duty to modify, accommodate, or adapt to the actual physical or mental disability of the beneficiary or beneficiary population.[44]

To achieve the goal of integration we must recognize the role that historical stereotypes and prejudices play in society's perception and treatment of disabled people. We must recognize that disabled people are a disenfranchised class denied equal opportunity because of the persistent image of disabled people as a class of incompetent people perpetually dependent upon welfare and charity.

The concepts of equal opportunity and integration must be based on the reality of the differing needs and potential of people who are disabled. Thus equal opportunity must be defined as providing each individual with the chance to achieve, to develop their abilities and potential to the fullest. As a corollary, integration must be defined as permitting each individual the freedom of choice, control, and participation that is necessary and appropriate to the individual's skills and potential.

NOTES

1. *Disabled People:* The class of persons who are the focus of civil rights law encompasses 30 to 40 million persons who suffer varying degrees of discrimination, segregation, and social stigmatization because they are perceived as handicapped. As a legal term of art, a "handicapped individual" means any person who (i) has a physical or mental impairment which substantially limits one or more of such person's major life activities, (ii) has a record of such an impairment, or (iii) is regarded as having such an impairment. 29 U.S.C. Section 706 (1978).

This definition overlaps many of the social programs and policies our society has developed for the varied distinctions among the class of disabled persons. Projects and policies abound designed for groups of specific diseases, classes of disabled persons, age distinctions, educability distinctions, sex and human potential determinations. Only in the last 15 years has the law and policy focus become class-oriented to "the handicapped" with the development of broad statutory mandates and case law that attacks erroneous social constructions and provides for basic human rights and liberties for people who are disabled.

2. "The Elizabethan poor laws inherited virtually intact by the American colonies, which made them the basis for early laws concerning 'paupers' and the poor. . . ." Every person who because of poverty, sickness, or other misfortune, was a "miserable and proper object of public charity. . . ." Jacobus tenBroek and Floyd W. Matson, *Hope Deferred: Public Welfare and the Blind.* (Berkeley: University of California Press, 1959), p. 43. See also D. Kaplan, "Deinstitutionalization: Freedom from Confinement; The Road to Self-Determination," vol. 2, *Law Reform in Disability Rights, Articles and Concept Papers,* DREDF (1981).

3. See W. Wolfensberger, *The Principal of Normalization in Human Services,* Toronto: National Institute of Mental Retardation, 1972.

4. See Burton, *Federal Assistance for Disabled Persons: Law and Policy in Uncertain Transition,* 15 CLEARING HOUSE REV. 753 (1982).

5. Id.

6. Wolfensberger, *supra* note 3 at 29, 60.

7. tenBroek and Matson, *supra* note 2 at 252.

8. Id., Chap. 7, "The Amendments of 1956: A New Departure."

9. 42 U.S.C. Section 401 *et seq.* (1973); 42 U.S.C. Section 1381 *et seq.* (1973 and Supp. 1980; 7 U.S.C. Section 2011 *et seq.* (1979 and Supp. 1980); 42 U.S.C. Section 1395 *et seq.* (1973 and Supp. 1980); 42 U.S.C. Section 1396 *et seq.* (1973 and Supp. 1980); 42 U.S.C. Section 1397 *et seq.* (Supp. 1980).

10. G. de Jong, "Independent Living: From Social Movement to Analytic Paradigm," 60 *Archives of Physical Medicine and Rehabilitation* (October 1979) p. 435. "Medicalized" refers to the tendency for increasing varieties of behavior to be considered illnesses with the resulting medical approach to cure and care.

11. de Jong, *supra* note 10 at 437, in vol. 2.

12. For an overview of the movement, see R. Funk, *Challenges of Emerging Leadership: Community Based Independent Living Programs and the Disability Rights Movement* (Washington, D.C.: Institute for Educational Leadership, 1984).

13. See "Oversight Hearings on the Rehabilitation Act of 1973: before Sub-committee on Select Education of the House Committee on Education and Labor, January 5, 1978, at Center for Independent Living, Inc., Berkeley, Ca.

14. For a discussion of law reform attacks on institutions, see S. Hern, "The New Clients: Legal Services for Mentally Retarded Persons," Legal Services Corporations (1979).

15. *Pennsylvania Aid to Retarded Citizens (PARC)* v. *Commonwealth of Pennsylvania,* 334 F. Supp. 1257 (E.D. Pa. 1971).

16. *Mills* v. *Board of Education of the District of Columbia,* 348 F. Supp. 866 (D.D.C. 1972). See also A. Mayerson, "Equal Educational Opportunity of Disabled Children," vol. 2 *Law Reform in Disability Rights: Articles and Concepts Papers,* DREDF (1981).

17. Architectural Barriers Act of 1978, 42 U.S.C. Section 4151 *et seq.;* Urban Mass Transportation Act of 1964, as amended, 49 U.S.C. 1612; Federal Aid Highway Act of 1973, 29 U.S.C. 142.

18. Pub. L. No. 93-112, Pub L. No. 93-602; 29 U.S.C. Section 702 (Supp. II 1978), "Declaration of Purpose."

19. 29 U.S.C. Section 792 (Supp. II 1978).

20. 29 U.S.C. Section 791 (Supp. II 1978).

21. 29 U.S.C. Section 793 (Supp. II 1978).

22. 29 U.S.C. Section 794 (Supp. II 1978).

23. The Education Acts of 1974 and 1975, 20 U.S.C. Section *et seq.*

24. Developmentally Disabled Assistance and Bill of Rights Act of 1975, 42 U.S.C. Section 6001 *et seq.*

25. White House Conference on Handicapped Individuals Act, 29, U.S.C. Section 701 (December 7, 1974).

26. The 1978 amendments to the Rehabilitation Act created Title VII, Comprehensive Services for Independent Living, 29 U.S.C. 706.

Title VII established a major change in federal disability policy, and in doing so reflected the growing influence of the community-based independent living/disability rights movement through specific legislation drawing on the experience of disabled people in the community.

27. See *Challenges, supra* note 12 for a further discussion.

28. See, for example, "Handicapped Policy Undergoing a Rewrite," *Washington Post,* March 4, 1982; "How Handicapped Won Access Rule Fight," April 12, 1983.

29. *National Journal,* "Reagan Courting Women, Minorities, But It May Be Too Late To Win Them," May 28, 1983 at 1,121.

30. Safilios-Rothschild, *The Sociology and Social Psychology of Disability and Rehabilitation* (New York: Random House, 1970) p. 111.

31. See F. Bowe, *Handicapping America: Barriers to People* (New York: Harper & Row, 1978).

32. K. Karst, The Supreme Court, 1976 Term-Forward: "Equal Citizenship Under the Fourteenth Amendment," 91 Harv. L. Rev. 1 (1977). The term "equal citizenship" is not, in the context of Professor Karst's work, limited to a legal status. ". . . this Forward's main thesis is that equal citizenship, far from being trivial, is a constitutional principle of central importance. Although the two ideas are connected historically, . . . I do not contend that the narrow legal status of citizenship is, . . . by itself, the source of the rights here discussed" at 5 fn 21. "The essence of equal citizenship is the dignity of full membership in the society" at 5.

33. tenBroek and Matson, *supra* note 2, p. 2.

34. See *The Unexpected Minority*, John Gliedman and William Roth (New York: Harcourt Brace Javonovich, 1980), chap. 1.

35. Bowe, *supra* note 31.

36. Communication barriers include those that deny effective access to programs or activities for individuals who are deaf or hard of hearing, blind or visually impaired or individuals who have difficulty speaking because of disability.

37. That is, pre-employment screening devices utilized by employers to select prospective employees on medical grounds. Many are arbitrary and not job related and thus exclude many disabled persons from consideration for employment.

38. See Safilios-Rothschild, *supra* note 30 at 59 and Gleidman, *supra* note 34 at 13-30.

39. The concept of individualized remedies to ensure equal protection of the law may relate to a single disabled person or a subclass of disabled persons within the class (for example, blind individuals or persons who utilize manual wheelchairs).

40. 29 U.S.C. Section 794 (Supp. II 1978).

41. The plaintiffs did not request retrofitting of existing buses, but requested prospective relief relating to future purchases.

42. The standard parallels the one established under Title VI of the Civil Rights Act of 1964 with respect to the provision of educational services to students whose primary language is not English. See *Lau* v. *Nichols,* 414 U.S. 563 (1974). "To be equally effective, however, an aid, benefit or service need not produce equal results; it merely must afford an equal opportunity to achieve equal results"; 548 F. 2d 1277, 1279 (7th Cir. 1977).

43. 548 F.2d 1277, 1279 (7th Cir. 1977).

44. In cases of disability discrimination that necessitate provision of a substantive duty to modify, accommodate, or adapt to the actual disability of the beneficiary or beneficiary population in order to provide meaningful equal protection, the degree of duty to be mandated will turn on a balancing of competing interests. These include the nature of the right(s) being infringed, the size of the class, and the degree of financial and administrative burdens the duty will impose. In each instance, the burden should be on the defending party to prove the duty would be extraordinary.

2

The Cripple in Literature

Leonard Kriegel

One of the hits of last year's theater season in England was the Royal Shakespeare Company's new production of *Richard III*. Anthony Sher's Richard has been hailed as one of the more memorable performances of a role that must seem, to us, the embodiment of the passion of the crippled and disabled. A friend of mine, a noted Shakespearean scholar, saw the performance at Stratford and described the play's opening as follows: The lights go up and we hear Sher, speaking quietly but firmly, establishing Richard's crippled presence, "But I, that am not framed for sportive tricks." As he concludes "the winter of our discontent" soliloquy, he advances menacingly on the audience, swinging on two crutches that propel his body as if it were being hurled at the audience. He bounds like some threatening animal across the stage. Throughout the performance the crutches emerge as a statement of Richard's presence, both a prop for Sher and a weapon with which he seems to flail away at the audience's sense of well being.

Contemporary Shakespearean criticism tends to stress the play in performance. Its purpose is to liberate the dramatist from the constrictions of the text by viewing the play as something to be seen. In this view of Shakespeare, Anthony Sher transforms Richard into the quintessential literary cripple. Everything in the drama that unfolds can be traced back to Richard's consciousness of himself as a "deformed, unfinished" man. How had Sher arrived at his conception of Richard? It was this question that Sher was asked after the performance. And why the crutches? A year or so earlier, it turned out, Sher had snapped an Achilles tendon and had been forced to walk on crutches for about two months. The result was that he found himself encountering that same sense of displacement that any crutchwalker encounters virtually every day of his life. Casual passersby would stare at him; he found himself the object of a curiosity that was as unabashed as it was depersonalized and he felt within himself a growing rage at the manner in which what he could and could not do was defined by others, a growing irritability and impatience with the world-at-large. At what specific point he seized upon his own experience on crutches as the source for his interpretation of Richard is not particularly important. What is important is that Anthony Sher saw in Richard a character who was first cripple and then man, and whose relationship to the world derived in large part, from the inadequacy of his body.

Act I concludes with Richard's coronation. In the production at Stratford, Anthony Sher is carried on stage in a sedan chair. This is the only time in the entire performance when he is seen without his crutches. Wearing a flowing red cape, he ascends the stairs to the coronation throne, literally crawling up the steps with a hunger and rage that are both helpless and intimidating. Sher brings to the image a "serpentine terror" that transforms his body as surely as the crutches do. And in these two images—the crutches used as weapons to propel the protagonist across the stage even as they intimidate the audience and the legless serpentine ascent of the steps to make legitimate a crown for which he has murdered—Shakespeare provides us with the two fundamental images that cripples are accorded in Western literature. The accoutrements of being crippled, Richard's crutches, are transformed into a weapon, almost a primal force, designed to impose the crippled king's presence upon both his world and the audience watching the drama unfold; in the ascent, the red-caped figure crawls up steps, like some gigantic insect, to take that which he has cheated others of. Imposing its limitations to rob legitimacy, the broken body begs for compassion. In the history of Western literature, both before and after Shakespeare, there is little to be added to these two images, although there are a significant number of variations upon them. The cripple is threat and recipient of compassion, both to be damned and to be pitied—and frequently to be damned as he is pitied.

In the past, when I have been asked to discuss the image of the cripple, my focus has been on different images of disability as they have been projected in literature. Over this last decade, a number of critics have turned their attention to the role and function of image in Western culture in the depiction of disease and disability. The seminal essay for this remains Edmund Wilson's discussion of the literary adaptability of the myth of Philoctetes, an essay which gave its name to Wilson's *The*

Wound and the Bow, published in 1941. Wilson's concern was the artist as the bearer of the wound. More recent however, we have begun to pay attention to the social and psychological consequences of images of disease and disability, to discuss both how they help create society's conception of the cripple and the cripple's conception of himself.[1]

This chapter focuses on two areas: the categories into which images of the crippled and disabled tend to fall and how the world outside appears to the writer who is himself crippled. The second part will, hopefully, turn the tables and look at those whom the late Erving Goffman called the "normals" as they appear to the stigmatized.[2] For if anything can be said about the ways in which *literature*—the separation between creative, imaginative work and ordinary discourse—looks at the crippled and disabled, it is that the diseased and afflicted impose their presence on the "normals." In showing themselves, they call attention primarily to their wounds. At its most gripping and perhaps memorable, this is done in a wild, sustained manner such as Shakespeare's Richard and Melville's Ahab. But the Demonic Cripple as embodied in Richard and Ahab is only one corner of the box. Along with him, we have the cripple as victim, or the Charity Cripple (Dickens's Tiny Tim and Melville's Black Guineau are the examples that come most readily to mind here); the cripple whose wound is merely a part of his overall sense of selfhood—the Realistic Cripple (Tennessee Williams's Laura in *The Glass Menagerie* and the German anarchist, Berthold Lindau, in Howells's novel, *A Hazard of New Fortunes*); and the cripple who triumphs not over but against misfortune by outlasting the effects of his wound until those effects have been incorporated into his way of dealing with the world—the Survivor Cripple (Saul Bellow's poolroom entrepreneur, William Einhorn of Chicago, can best serve as our model here).

It is important to point out that writers, by and large, view the world from the vantage point of the "normals." Writers like to think of themselves as rebels, but the rebellions they are interested in usually reinforce society's conception of what is and is not desirable. And most writers look at the cripple and the wounds he bears with the same suspicion and distaste that are found in other "normals." The image exists in literature because the reality exists in life. The world of the crippled and disabled is strange and dark, and it is held up to judgment by those who live in fear of it.

The cripple is the creature who has been deprived of his ability to create a self. If others cry, like God from the burning bush, "I am that I am," the cripple in literature is expected to submit to the cries of others, to say, "I am what you tell me I am." He is the other, if for no other reason than that only by being the other will he be allowed to presume upon the society of the "normals." He must accept definition from outside the boundaries of his own existence. In his role as demon, his wound is not only the visible manifestation of his condition, it is also the symbolic correlative of that existence. Without it, he does not exist—indeed, he cannot exist. Accident is essence, where the cripple in literature is concerned. And his accident claims not only the totality of his condition as a man but the attention of the audience.

Melville's Captain Ahab is dominated by his sense of absence, of physical insufficiency. Psychoanalysts like to point to this as his castration complex; those who give *Moby Dick* a religious reading speak of it as the absence of God. But the complex is in many respects beside the point. What we can say with surety is that the absent leg is Ahab's mark, the brand of his permanent insufficiency. Ahab cannot live with his ivory leg. Obviously, he cannot live without it either. His injury becomes his selfhood, and his selfhood is the leg ripped from him by Moby Dick. His rage is directed against the white whale, but his argument is with the very idea of victimization.

Something has been done—*and it has been done to him!* He is demonic because, like Shakespeare's crippled king, he must now spend his remaining life resisting categorization. His existence is predicated on the need not to become what he believes the world demands he become. As a result, he has no choice but to enact the role of the Demonic Cripple. "For this Ahab, the question of whether the white whale represents principle or accident is less important than the ever-present knowledge that what has happened has happened to *him*. It is *his* leg that has been ripped away by Moby Dick; it is *he* who must hobble through the world on an ivory substitute; it is *he* who lives in a world in which accident has been imposed by something outside the self. And that something is a constant affliction to his consciousness."[3] From the world of the "normals," he demands not compassion but allegience. He cares nothing for what they care for—wife, home, children—all are readily sacrificed to Ahab's quest for vengeance. Like Shakespeare's Richard, he cannot help but see accident as victimization and he is enraged by victimization. Indeed, for Richard, the accident is uncovered in the very fact of his birth: from the beginning, he has been "rudely stamped," "cheated of feature," "deformed, unfinished," a man "sent into this breathing world, scarce half made up."

A man's character is his fate, insisted Heraclitus. Few better examples can be offered as proof of that assertion than the Demonic Cripple. His existence testifies to that truth. Both Ahab and Richard are what they are because they have been crippled. A pervasive sense of absence forces each of them to plot and scheme and burn with the need for revenge. Each finds himself trying to bend the world's will to his own. Each assumes—as demonic characters inevitably assume—the perogatives of that very God their existence challenges. In this, they resemble the father of demonism, the devil himself. Blake accused Milton of unconsciously being of the devil's party for just this reason—that he recognized that Milton, like so many men, secretly sympathized with Satan's rebellion. A fallen angel is still an angel. His anguish becomes what men can identify with. His defiance is purposeful and single-minded. His example is that of the nay-sayer. When Richard dedicates himself to evil in order to right the balance with a malignant nature, a part of each of us must sympathize with him. He refuses to accept what has been meted out to him without voicing his defiance, his determination, his resistance to acquiescence. In this, he is admirable, even as we recognize that his purpose is evil. He challenges the very principles of Nature by insisting that man must not accept what has been given. Interestingly enough, he sees himself—and he shares this with Ahab—as a man surrounded by children, a warrior in a world of weaklings.

> Why I, in this weak piping time of peace,
> Have no delight to pass away the time,
> Unless to see my shadow in the sun
> And descant on mine own deformity.

Do we not usually admire the individual who sets out to rectify injustice? Richard calls Nature itself to account. And so does Ahab, who insists that the world recognize how singular his frustrated potency had made him. "Ahab stands alone among all the millions of the peopled earth, nor gods nor men his neighbors."

The Demonic Cripple burns with his need for vengeance. Because of this, he frightens the "normals." He is too singular, too focused on his wound and the needs that wound has created within him. As a consequence, he threatens to unleash a rage so powerful that it will bring everything down in its wake. The visible fact of his infirmity offers no solace to other men, because he himself is quite willing to accept the idea that his accident is his essence. His image becomes, both for him and the "normals," the very center of the threat he embodies. His accident gnaws at his insides, leaves him no peace, consumes his every breathing moment, so that he cuts himself off from ordinary pursuits and ordinary men. Indeed, he despises their values, questions their successes, holds fast to the center of his own existence, the wound he so visibly bears.

The Charity Cripple is far easier for the "normals" to handle. At least as an image, he is. What he is remains the shadow of how he is seen.

He exists in order to soothe. As Melville's Black Guineau in *The Confidence Man,* he is "a grotesque Negro cripple" complete with tambourine and begging cup. His existence is seen by his fellow passengers on Melville's Ship of Fools as a "singular temptation to *diversion* and charity." He is an acceptable image, even if he turns out to be a con artist, because he projects the image of the cripple the world feels at home with. "Where Ahab commands, Black Guineau begs; where Ahab cries out for vengeance, Black Guineau whimpers after love and affection; where Ahab's wounds add to his physical presence, Black Guineau has been "cut down 'to the stature of a Newfoundland dog.'"[4]

Characters such as Black Guineau and Tiny Tim are intended to draw out the charitable impulses of a middle-class audience. They enthrall because they relieve both guilt and the need to look directly at the other. Black Guineau is a master of disguises and manipulation, in actuality, a confidence man, who plays the heartstrings of his fellow passengers on board the *Fidelé* by donning a variety of disguises. As the black cripple, the sole threat he possesses is his color, not his condition. As a black man, he is a lineal brother to the black slave, Babo, leader of the slave insurrection in *Benito Cereno.* Like Babo, he manipulates through his appearance. He transforms himself into an object other passengers on the *Fidelé* can look at with charity and disgust. And it is charity which nominally controls his life. In this, he anticipates one of the roles that cripples are expected to assume in American life today. He is authentic only because his incapacity is designed visibly to affect others. In some ways, he reminds us, as he catches pennies in his mouth, of the ways in which crippled children are today paraded before viewers of television marathons. There is something totemistic about this kind of thing, but there is something that offers relief to the giver, too. His goodness is absorbed into the public spectacle. Ahab's wound makes him maniacal; Richard's makes him cunning and murderous; but Black Guineau feeds the sense of superiority his fellow passengers assume in his presence. As a totem, he allows them to believe that they will escape his fate. In *A Christmas Carol,* Tiny Tim is Scrooge's totem. One almost senses that Dickens, in his heart of hearts, had designed a scene in which Scrooge would be transformed into kindly Uncle Ebenezer by rubbing his hands on Tiny Tim's crutches. Where Anthony Sher uses crutches to force his audience to confront Richard on terms Richard himself chooses Tiny Tim's crutches seem an intended offering to middle-class sentimentality. They embody the miraculous conversion even before the conversion takes place.[5]

The Charity Cripple soothes middle-class society because he refuses to accept his wound as the source of his rage. Indeed, he refuses to acknowledge rage. His purpose is never to make "normals" either uncomfortable or guilty. He inspires pity, but not fear. He plays with the heartstrings of his world. Or rather he plays on them. In updated versions, on telethons and billboards and letters appealing for alms from the American public, his picture is intended to destroy the isolation of the giver. He enables the audience to avoid the coldness of its own potential fate by becoming givers of alms. Of course, Dickens is offering a Christian message. And the giving he is so enamored of springs from a specifically Christian sentimentality about the poor and maimed. (Tiny Tim is, of course, *both* poor and maimed.) For the poor and halt and lame are not only forever with us, they can also be called upon—and called upon consistently—to help the middle-class justify its own virtue.

The most difficult of these types for the critic to handle is the Realistic Cripple. On one level, literary realism sees all men as potential victims and sees their victimization as more or less equally interesting. The Realistic Cripple can make little of his wound, because his wound is neither his essence nor the reflection of his glory. It is simply there, like the clothes he wears or the food he eats. Society cannot view him as the object of its fear or the object of its charity. It will not turn from him in disgust and bewilderment, for he is neither approved nor condemned. If he possesses a center, it is not a center than can be defined in terms of his wound. The fact that he is crippled is never allowed to be the chief element in his fate. His audience does not have to pity him for the wound he carries, because the wound is as much design as substance. In Tennessee Williams's *The Glass Menagerie,* Laura limps. But the limp is merely part of a southern girl's softness, her shriveled braced leg merely one of the ingredients that make her unsuited for the kind of life her mother Amanda envisions for her. The fact that she is crippled contributes to her shyness as well as to her lack of experience with other men and women. But it is not primary, not her essence. She cannot achieve a will through its exploitation nor is it ever presented as a possible means of her survival. Her life, one senses, would not have been different had her leg been sound. (For a different view of Laura, see Chapter 3, "Disabled Women: Portraits in Fiction and Drama.")

As an aesthetic approach to the world, literary realism portrayed the crippled and disabled as it portrayed the rest of humanity. The cripple's problems were neither singular nor symbolic. Rather, they were viewed as human problems. And if there were solutions available, they were human solutions. Had Melville been a realist, Ahab would simply have been a ship's captain with an amputated leg. The realist cannot really believe that a part can stand for the whole, that a wound can claim a character's essence.

In William Dean Howells's *A Hazard of New Fortunes,* a German anarchist, Berthold Lindau, loses a hand while fighting against slavery in the Civil War. But the lost hand has little if anything to do with Lindau's socialist and anarchist views. It is a very small piece in the puzzle that makes up his character. It doesn't even work as an indictment of war. Lindau could never conceive of Ahab's self-dramatization, and he would contemptuously look at the ways in which Tiny Tim's Christian sentimentality makes his condition the world's debt. With or without the hand, he is Lindau. Can we claim that Richard would be Richard if his body were not misshapen, "cheated of feature by dissembling Nature"? The reader is never allowed to forget that Tiny Tim's angelic face is wed to that frail indictment of a body. Tiny Tim's goodness is the direct result of his having been cheated by Nature, just as Richard's evil is. And if Richard entraps an entire country in his wound, then Tiny Tim converts Scrooge to goodness through his. The body dictates the terms under which they encounter their fates. But what we react to in Laura or Berthold Lindau is their very ordinariness. Neither offers catharsis, because neither is wounded enough to inflict that wound on the audience.

In the twentieth century, the image undergoes an interesting metamorphosis. In a world that possesses surety and optimism, the maimed figure creates discomfort. His wound intrudes, his figure disturbs. But for all of our scientific and technological progress, the history of our century bears witness to the growth of chaos. We lack surety, we lack belief, we lack meaningful traditions. It can be said that modern literature lacks heroic figures; its protagonists are notable for their "ordinariness." Even evil in the twentieth century has been deemed "banal." Kafka, Beckett, Joyce, and Proust all lack what once was known as the tragic sense of life.

The image of the cripple our times offer is the man who endures and in his endurance discovers survival as a cause in itself: the Survivor Cripple. By definition, any man with a wound is an outsider; but in our century he discovers that he is an outsider in a world that possesses growing doubts about its insiders. His condition exemplifies what has become the human condition. The Survivor Cripple is not demonic and he is not the object of charity. At the same time, he assumes that his wound has given him certain prerogatives, has set him apart, has denied his "ordinariness." His endurance is attractive, both to himself and to the audience, for it is constructed around his understanding of the limitations it has imposed on him.

Of course, our century has produced its literary portraits of more traditional cripples. Foremost among them, I suppose, is the extension of the idea of demonism to industrial soullessness. What else is D. H.

Lawrence's Clifford Chatterley but a Richard enslaved to the machine, a Richard in whom evil is no longer capable of poetry. An impotent (for all of his deformity, Shakespeare's Richard possesses a harsh, bitter sexuality) industrialist into whom Lawrence poured everything he despised about modern industrial society, Chatterley is set up as a target for Lawrence's runty little gamekeeper, Mellors. In Clifford Chatterley, Lawrence loads not only the dice but the gun, too. Mellors may bring the bliss of orgasm to Constance Chatterley, but he is bound to bring a sense of inviolable rage to anyone who has spent time in a wheelchair. Indeed, it is difficult to determine whether Clifford Chatterley or Tiny Tim has done more harm to the cripple's conception of himself.[6]

Like Faulkner's negroes and like Malamud's Jews, the cripple who is a survivor has an instinctive appeal to modern audiences. He has been ennobled not by his condition but by his willingness to accept the condition as his own. To endure is to outlast circumstance, to step into if not beyond the pain of one's existence. It is as if his presence announces to the reader, "This is what I must live with. And if I *must,* then you *can.* For are we not brothers beneath the wound?" His image has been made more attractive to modern man, for endurance is a virtue in itself. And modern man does not wish to shield himself from endurance; he wishes, instead, to embrace it, even if in embracing it he must embrace the cripple's wounded body, too. No longer as isolated as he once was, the cripple now discovers that he does not have to claim a singularity beyond the comprehension of other men. After Auschwitz and Treblinka, after Hiroshima and Dresden, even demonism begins to seem a trifle puerile. Like the heroic, the demonic is too absorbed by selfhood. What the modern world wants are images of its own facelessness. For the modern world has been so battered by cataclysm and the fear of cataclysm that its literature has become more and more a literature of outcasts. Our world, one suspects, is more comfortable with the outcast than with the "normal."

In modern literature, we usually face protagonists who themselves lack a sense of wholeness. And for the modern writer, all men are victimized by the limitation of humanity itself. In Proust, man is neurasthenic, of so delicate a constitution that sickness threatens him at every turn; in Kafka, man is alien even to himself, a homeless wanderer moving through the inevitability of a life he neither truly understands nor wants; in Joyce, man is rebel and artist, but even in his passionate embrace of art he finds himself sniffing at the shabby bourgeoise gentility of everyday life, and discovering behind the tedious morality of that life the smell of pain and death.

Endurance in the face of an indifferent universe is the sole meaningful defiance man can claim. And in this picture, the cripple discovers that he is well-equipped to "run" the race as any other victim of time or circumstance. His credentials have been validated by the fact that he exists. Endurance is as much his trademark as it is the trademark of anyone else.

My model for the Survivor Cripple is not the central character of the novel in which he appears. But he is one of the teachers of the central character. William Einhorn is a wheelchair-bound poolroom sage and clubhouse politician in Saul Bellow's *The Adventures of Augie March* (New York: Penguin, 1984). But if, like Lawrence's Clifford Chatterley, Einhorn occupies a wheelchair, his vision of existence is neither impotent nor sterile nor industrial. He lives in day-to-day confrontation with life itself. He lives, too, with the sensuality of his own anger. And he lives, finally, because he does not wish to die, and because he is conscious of what staying alive has cost him.

> He wouldn't stay a cripple, Einhorn; he couldn't hold his soul in it. Sometimes, it was dreadful, this; he'd lose everything he'd thought through uncountable times to reconcile himself to it, and be like the wolf in the pit in the zoo who keeps putting his muzzle to the corners of the walls, back and forth, in his exhibition jail. It didn't happen often; probably not oftener than ordinary people get a shove of the demon. But it happened. Touch him when he was off his feed, or he had a cold or a little fever, or when there was a rift in the organization, or his position didn't feel so eminent and he wasn't getting the volume of homage and mail he needed—or when it was the turn of a feared truth to come up unseen through the multitude of elements out of which he composed his life, and then he'd say, "I used to think I'd either walk or swallow iodine, and I'd have massages and exercises, and drills when I'd concentrate on a single muscle and think I was building it up by my will, and it was all the bulk, Augie, the Coue theory, et cetera. For the birds. And *It Can Be Done* and the sort of stuff that bigshot Teddy Roosevelt wrote in his books. Nobody'll every know all the things I tried before I finally decided it was no go. I couldn't take it, and I took it. And I *can't* take it, yet I do take it (Bellows, p. 79).

On the one hand, this speaks to the cripple's condition; on the other, it speaks to the condition of all men conscious of the limitations of modernity. "Einhorn is the mediator between Black Guineau and Ahab, a man who looks at the table and takes whatever he finds that is worth taking. He binds himself to the life of the cripple because he never allows himself to deny what might have been if he had not been crippled. He is dependent, but he is also stronger than those he is dependent upon. And he is aware, as the cripple must be aware, that self-creation is limited by the very accidents that give it shape . . . Einhorn schemes, plots, lies, uses people—but rarely does he lie to himself about what he faces. For Bellow, he is an attractive individual of dubious repute; for me, he is a knowledgeable hero, the cripple's living contradiction."[7]

There is nothing grandiose about Einhorn. But there is something grand about him. He does not exist beyond the reach of ordinary men, but he himself is out of the ordinary. This is no Ahab swearing to bring the universe itself to its knees or else die in the attempt; this is no crippled prince scheming to seize a throne to which he has no right other than the legacy of a misshapen body that has bred a misshapen ambition; and this is no religious sentimentalist seeking the world's sufferance, asking for alms in exchange for allowing a harsh humanity to see itself as softer than it is. Einhorn does not tell us that life in a wheelchair is no different from the trials other men and women face. It is different. And he knows what the difference is. Because he is not demonic, he is not sentimental; and because he is not sentimental, he is realistic; and because he is realistic, he is a survivor. He can't take it, but he takes it. And he gets by, because he has no choice but to get by.

At one point, Einhorn tells Augie that the day inevitably comes when "you feel like the stinking fly in the first cold snap." At such moments, the cripple knows nothing better than the price he must pay for survival. Having managed to come through, he discovers that his triumph in the eyes of the world is that he will be able to count his days. Getting by is the only reward he can offer himself. In the final analysis, madness lurks for Einhorn, too.

How then, one must ask, does the writer who is himself crippled deal with the Einhorn in his own bones? His singular condition is the condition of the writer. But for the writer *who writes consciously* out of his existence as a cripple, the passion that sets him apart sets him apart from his fellow writers, too. The language, the images, the tenor of his work must be adequate to that which has been taken—his wound, his handicap. For he writes out of a pain that is distinctly his alone. He is not Bellow creating Einhorn or Shakespeare creating Richard or Melville creating Ahab. The loss he is writing about is specifically *his,* that which *he* has been denied. And all of his work springs from that sense of absence.

In a well-known essay entitled "Why I Write," George Orwell noted that the realities of our century made him into a political writer. His desire became to change the way men lived together. Were I to write an essay entitled "Why I Write," I would speak far more selfishly than Orwell. For the truth is that every word I have written has been written to rectify the *what is* of my life with the *what should have been.* In autobiography, in fiction, even, I suspect, in literary criticism, I have been seeking the legs that were taken from me when, as I wrote in my very first book, *The Long Walk Home,* "the knife of virus severed legs from will at the age of eleven." In such singlemindedness, the crippled writer embodies Ahab's monomaniacal quest. And yet, I am not demonic, I am not mad, and I claim for my own the hard-earned balance of Mr. William Einhorn of Chicago. Had I written the script of my life, I wouldn't have taken it. But I didn't write it. And I do take it. What Ahab never learned is what Einhorn instinctively knows. Because one cannot, one does.

But how does one go about creating the balance? How does the writer measure that self that should have been against the self that is? I'm not certain I can answer these questions, but books I wrote at three different periods in my life dealt, in one way or another, not with cripples but with the self as cripple.

When I sat down to write *The Long Walk Home* my intention seemed to me obvious. To begin with, I sensed that I would never write anything else until I had written about my war with the virus. My stated purpose was to write a book about my encounter with polio, a book that would be simple and unsentimental and totally honest. I consciously chose to view myself neither demonically nor charitably. My unstated purpose was to create the thing as it had created me, a realistic narrative about polio and its consequences. I recognized that I had survived fairly well, at least as such things are measured by the world at large. But I was determined not to credit my rehabilitation to God or society or whatever generally received credit for such things. Indeed, I took my epigraph from Agee's remarkable book about tenant farmers in the South during the Depression, *Let Us Now Praise Famous Men* (Boston: Houghton Mifflin, 1960). "A piece of the body torn out by the roots might be more to the point," wrote Agee.

However embarrassing it may be today, I remember thinking that what I wanted to do was to pull my body out by its roots and force the reader to pay attention to its existence. The *what is* of one crippled writer's life would reflect the *what should have been* of the life he had never lived.

Now it has long been recognized that all autobiographies are fictions, where the writer chooses how and when he wants to show himself to others. His life appears to him in remembered glimpses and he proceeds to select those glimpses he will use and those he will not use. In writing *The Long Walk Home,* I became quite intimate with the condition that had claimed me—both as writer and man. The guiding reality behind the book was that *I, my* first-person singular, had lost part of its substance. What conspires with the time prior to the appearance of the virus could easily be dismissed. The cripple was born again, only his rebirth would itself be an accident. All experience before the virus could be dismissed. Life ends so that the new life can begin.

Implicitly, the writer who writes out of consciousness of his own wound creates images in which the life lived is measured against the life he never had a chance to live. And is this not what Ahab demands? Is this not the essence of Richard III's scheming? And if they are mad, is there not something ultimately ennobling in such madness?

And yet, the very act of writing an autobiography demands that the writer not be overwhelmed by what has been taken away. After all, in "real life," one cannot live as Ahab or Richard III do. So intense a focus on what has been taken away would drive one literally mad. Still, one can address one's own accidents with empathy, with the recognition that to put the life of a cripple down on paper is to challenge accident, perhaps even to sustain a temporary triumph over it. There is something romantic about holding one's own battered self up to the mirror because there is something rebellious about it. The condition addressed in the autobiography of a cripple is a denial of the life one had originally envisioned for himself. No matter how matter-of-factly I traced my own evolution from lying paralyzed in a small country hospital in upstate New York to assuming the actual dimensions of the life I had been called upon to live, I spoke as a rebel. When I wrote *The Long Walk Home,* I knew that I could no longer live with the virus, but I also knew that in writing it I had condemned myself to never living without it, too.

Notes for the Two-Dollar Window, published 12 years after *The Long Walk Home,* was not about what polio had done to me but what time and memory had done to the Bronx neighborhood in which I came of age. All good writing, Hemingway wrote, begins with a sense of geography. But as I once again approached my old Bronx neighborhood, both in literal returns to it and in sketching it out in my imagination and memory, I discovered that the self also exists within the geography it inhabits, a geography in which a sense of place and a sense of time are so intertwined that it is virtually impossible to distinguish one from the other. To speak autobiographically is to speak from the center of one's own selfhood. And if what a virus did to one's body and soul at the age of eleven is the heart of one's heart, then that is where the voice is going to come from. The self and its habitat prove indistinguishable.

My neighborhood was where I had watched myself, first as a *normal* and then as a *cripple.* In *Notes,* I found myself dredging up both memories. The book's protagonist was not to be me but those landmarks of the mind that go to make up a neighborhood—the lots, the streets, the parks, the alleys that mark boundaries which are as intimate as they are familiar. My consciousness of the neighborhood had been formed while I lived in the world of the "normals," between the time I moved there at the age of four and the time I left for camp at the age of eleven, where the virus and I struck our peculiar bargain. When I returned to the neighborhood two years later, I was no longer a *normal:* instead, I was now a *cripple.* The streets, the lots, the parks, the alleys, all had changed because I had changed. Here, in the schoolyard at P.S. 80, I had hit a baseball from home plate to the fence, the first fourth grader to accomplish that feat. Now, encased in steel prostheses and crutches, it took me 15 minutes to maneuver that same distance. Change in the self dictated change in the neighborhood; where geography should have shrunk with age, it expanded, ballooned, as I tried to capture the depth of a past that was in reality as itself, dead as my legs.

A writer observing a neighborhood in which he came of age cannot afford to be either demonic or passive. The center of his world suddenly exists beyond him, and he must be realistic in order to accept this. I was no longer even the sum total of my own existence, because I was forced to deal with conflicting selves: the normal and the cripple, each addressing my past, each laying claim to it.

Like most other American men, I had been watching with increasing fascination the growth of the women's movement during the 1960s and 1970s. The result was a book entitled *On Men and Manhood,* published early in 1980. I had no intention, when I began working on this book, of using the figure of the cripple to examine American men in a time of siege. But I quickly discovered that the book would be, at least in part, autobiographical, for I had to use the lives of men with whom I was familiar. And I was most familiar with my own life. Of course, I knew that cripples were no more representative of men than were blacks or homosexuals or left-handed baseball players. But as I examined the confusions and aspirations of men in America, it occurred to me that they were facing a situation similar to the situation any handicapped individual faces all his life. They were being asked to accept their wounds, survive, and learn how to function all over again.

I knew what I wanted to say in this book, perhaps more clearly than I have ever known what I wanted to say in any book I sat down to write. But I had a good deal of trouble in finding a beginning. And then, what struck me quite suddenly, was an image from my own life, an image anchored to being a cripple and being a father. What I discovered, both from that image and from extending the condition of the cripple so that it might become a metaphor for the condition of men in our time, was that we are bound to our lives as they have to be lived. "I couldn't take it, and I took it. And I *can't* take it, yet I do take it." Not, I confess, a very satisfying condition and not, I suspect, a very coherent metaphor—but the best we have. We American men live in a country in which manhood is flashed before us as a series of cosmetic images. In such an America, all one can demand is to get through. And that demand must be made on the self. The issue had become one of survival. And what better image of survival than the cripple, Einhorn figuring out the world's angles in his Chicago poolroom? In our time, madness is not really a possibility. And charity is increasingly offensive. Even Shakespeare's demonic king or Melville's mad Ahab would be transformed into another poor Richard. After all, how can the demonic exist in the presence of structured inquiry?

But the Survivor Cripple does what he must in order to survive. And in surviving, he cauterizes his wound, his visible stigma, into the source of his existence. Not that he is better than others—simply that he is more experienced at doing because he can't, at winning because he loses. "Here I am," he acknowledges like Abraham standing before the God whose existence he has uncovered. Knowing that he must ultimately lose, he knows, too, that his existence is his defiance. He is the self created out of necessity.

The cripple can hold up the ragged ends of his own existence and ask others to match his honesty with their own. Courage, cunning, patience, resourcefulness—out of these Einhorn created a self. Disease, accident, rage—out of these he recognized that a man is condemned to live with what he has been given by fate. In the last analysis, what makes Einhorn the image of the survivor is his consciousness of the prices he has paid. To survive is to condemn oneself to taking it. And he does.

NOTES

1. The past decade has seen a number of essays and books about literature dealing with disease and disability. Indeed, the entire area of writing about images of disease and disability seems in need of a good bibliographical essay at this point. Let me call particular attention to my own essay entitled "The Wolf in the Pit in the Zoo," *Social Policy* (Fall 1982), from which some of this present essay has been taken; Susan Sontag's *Illness as Metaphor* (New York: Random House, 1979), a brilliant if sometimes wrongheaded book; and Leslie Fiedler's *Freaks* (New York: Simon & Schuster, 1984).

2. See Erving Goffman's remarkable little study, *Stigma: Notes on the Management of Spoiled Identity* (Englewood Cliffs, NJ: Prentice-Hall, 1963).

3. Kriegel, "The Wolf in the Pit in the Zoo," p. 18.

4. Ibid.

5. In the summer of 1977, I was traveling through New Mexico. At one point in my travels, I visited a small sanctuary church and found in an ante room discarded

wooden crutches, worn trusses, broken prostheses, tokens sacrificed to incapacity and dread. Had I discovered a worn copy of Dicken's *A Christmas Carol,* the symbolism would have been complete.

6. Let me give Lawrence his due and acknowledge that in his short story, "The Blind Man," he created one of the more intriguing portraits of disability our literature offers. Of course, Lawrence is dealing with blindness in this story, and blindness in Western culture is a traditional metaphor for the acquisition of deeper, often more mystical, insight than the "normal" can claim. We have only to recall Sophocles's Oedipus, Milton's Samson, and Shakespeare's Gloucester to note the extent to which Maurice Pervin is an extension of this quasi-mystical attitude toward blindness. But we should also note that Maurice possesses a certain physical magnetism as a result of his blindness; he is as "sexual" as Chatterley is impotent. Charlotte Bronté's Rochester, of course, is another English blind literary protagonist. He is particularly interesting to us since in his case blindness is combined with a lost hand and a mutilated arm. On the surface, one might assume that Miss Bronté loaded the dice against Rochester. But in her own mind, apparently, such wounds were ennobling. Before Rochester and Jane marry, he insists on showing her his arm. Her response is interesting, particularly in light of what I have written here and elsewhere about society's reaction to the Charity Cripple. Rochester's helplessness appeals to Jane. And when she sees the mangled arm, she says, "One is in danger of loving you too well for all this." The mangled arm is a gift to their love as well as a curious legitimization of that love. Because they are not social equals, Rochester's wound and Jane's social position (she is a governness) make their marriage acceptable. After all, the crippled Rochester needs someone to take care of him.

7. Kriegel, "The Wolf in the Pit in the Zoo," p. 22.

3

Disabled Women: Portraits in Fiction and Drama

Deborah Kent

> If anyone therefore thinks that a cripple makes an indifferent heroine, now is
> the time to close these pages and desist from reading. For you will never see
> me wed the man I love, nor become the mother of his children. But you will
> see how that love never faltered, for all its strange vicissitudes . . . And you
> will learn also how, for all my helplessness, I took the leading part in the
> drama that unfolded, my very immobility sharpening my senses, quickening
> my perception, and chance itself forcing me to my role of judge and witness
> (du Maurier, p. 51).

Thus begins the chronicle of Honor Harris, the narrator of Daphne du
Maurier's historical novel, *The King's General* (New York: Avon,
1978). Honor is, indeed, an unusual heroine. The heroine of fiction
and drama is nearly always slender, graceful, and unblemished, meeting
all the traditional criteria of physical attractiveness. She is a prize for
men to covet and pursue. Yet, when Honor is 18 her legs are shattered
in a riding accident, and she is never able to walk again. In her own esti-
mation and that of most of the other characters in the book, she is no
longer worthy of a man's desire.

Disabled since birth, I was in my teens when I began to realize that
most novelists and playwrights agree that "a cripple makes an indifferent
heroine." In the hunger for role models that seems to compel so much
adolescent questing, I searched everything I read for the woman I might
some day hope to become. Over and over again, I read of graceful,
dexterous, bright-eyed girls, dazzling dancers with flashing repartee,
girls whose physical perfection was never questioned. They agonized

over which of their numerous suitors to accept, or, if the drive for independence ran strong, they spurned all of their admirers and found fulfillment in high adventure or a challenging career.

What would have happened, I wondered, if Juliet had been blind? Would Romeo still have deemed her worthy of his love? Would Darcy have appreciated Elizabeth Bennett's wit if she had had a disfigured face? Would Emma Bovary have chafed under the yoke of married life if she had walked with a limp?

I longed to find proof that disability need not bar me from all of the pleasures and perils that other girls regarded as their birthright. I needed confirmation that somehow, despite society's prevailing negative attitudes, I could manage to hold onto good feelings about myself and explore a full range of options in life. Relatives and counsellors mouthed reassurance, but the few disabled women I met frightened me, with their narrow, isolated lives. And the disabled women I encountered in my reading, when I found them at all, were little consolation. To me they belonged to another time, to an age when education and employment, physical mobility and emotional expression were luxuries that no disabled woman could hope to afford.

My awareness of and concern about the place of disabled women in literature deepened in the succeeding years. As I undertook to write this chapter, I found myself wondering if my original impression had distorted and exaggerated the disabled woman's negative literary image. If I reread some of the books from my past, and perhaps discovered some new ones as well, might I find hidden virtues I had hitherto overlooked?

How, precisely, do writers view the woman who has a disability? Is she ever shown to have healthy, rewarding friendships with other women, or is she always a lonely outsider? Is she automatically judged unattractive due to her impairment, or can she, like other heroines, be a prize for men to pursue? Even if she encounters social obstacles, can she still feel strong and whole within herself?

And why do writers ever use disabled women as characters in the first place? Does the disabled woman, in a work of fiction or drama, emerge as a fully developed character, or is she merely exploited as a metaphor, a bloodless vehicle to transport the author's ideas?

An assessment of the disabled woman's place in literature may serve as a barometer to measure how she is perceived by society. Conversely, the literary image of the disabled woman may influence the way disabled women are seen and judged in real life.

Since an individual's acceptance or rejection by others is a critical factor in how she regards herself, I will begin with a discussion of the friendships disabled women in plays and novels have with other female characters. As women in literature are largely defined by the way in which they relate to and are perceived by males, I will explore at length the relationships between disabled women and both disabled and non-disabled men. In conclusion, I will discuss the disabled woman's attitude toward herself and the writers' attitudes toward her.

WOMEN FRIENDS

"I had enough confidence and strength not to fear letting each new person I met feel superior to me. It was a price worth paying, and paying it I made friends."[1]

Although friendships between female peers are vital in helping a woman gain a sense of herself, they do not receive much attention in literature. Generally, the female protagonist's friends are minor characters, cast in the role of confidante. They are far overshadowed by the men in her life.

Disabled woman may have particular difficulties making friends. Friendships with women peers are strikingly absent from the lives of many of the disabled women in literature. In a few instances, the author simply makes no reference to friends, and the possibility remains that they hover somewhere offstage. But far more often the disabled woman is clearly isolated. She is cut off from normal interactions with other women by emotional barricades erected by herself and by the people around her.

Bertha Plummer, who is blind (Dickens, *Cricket on the Hearth,* Dunwood, GA: Genesis, 1981), is visited by other young women, not as a peer but as the object of charity. She is humbly grateful for even this small attention. Her sweetness and naiveté are almost saintly. She never envies her friends for their greater freedom and their romantic involvements. Bertha is delighted when her friend May's long-lost lover returns, though lovers are distinctly absent from her own life, existing for her only in fantasy.

At the opposite pole, Gertie McDowell, in James Joyce's *Ulysses* (New York: Random House, 1974), who is lame, is bitterly jealous of her nondisabled friends. Watching her friend Sissy run gracefully down the beach past a man she, Gertie, has been admiring, she thinks: "It was a wonder she didn't rip up her skirt at the sides, it was too tight on her. ... Would have served her just right if she had tripped up over something accidentally on purpose with her high crooked French heels on her to make her look tall and got a fine tumble" (Joyce, p. 359). Gertie senses that Sissy has all of the advantages when it comes to pursuing a mate. And in her view of the world, nothing else really matters.

Intimate friendships between women are seldom crucial in these books and plays. But in a few instances the close ties between woman and woman prove more important than any relationship the disabled woman has with a man.

In *Memoirs of a Midget* by Walter de la Mare (New York: Oxford University Press, 1982) Miss M. is captivated by her landlady's mercureal daughter Fanny Bowater. Fanny is all that Miss M. feels she is not: physically perfect, bold, worldly wise, and so confident of her desirability that she can be contemptuous of those who love her. Idolizing Fanny, living for her smallest attention, Miss M. gives Fanny all of her meager savings, schemes with her to deceive others, and thoroughly demeans herself. Ultimately she earns nothing but Fanny's scorn and her own self-loathing. In this novel, de la Mare has drawn an extremely complex relationship. It is difficult to assess how much of Miss M.'s enthrallment with Fanny derives from her own disability. But, while other factors come into play, Fanny's physical attractiveness is one of her most compelling attributes. "Whatever her mood, or her treatment of me, or her lapses into a kind of commonness to which I deliberately shut my eyes, her beauty remained" (de la Mare, p. 107).

Gibson's play *Monday After the Miracle* focuses upon the symbolic relationship between Helen Keller and her teacher, Annie Sullivan. Throughout the play Annie calls Helen "Baby." On one level this can be interpreted as simple infantilization—Annie's inability to let Helen grow up. At the same time, her persistent use of the term "Baby" reveals that Annie (who is unable to bear biological children) regards Helen as her offspring, her personal creation. Relentlessly she works to improve Helen's speech, tirelessly polishing a work of art which is never fully complete.

Helen is almost totally dependent upon Annie, both physically and emotionally. She is jealous and terrified when Annie takes a lover and plans to marry. Gibson implies that Helen's achievements could only come about through the sacrifice of Annie's private life. Both women are nourished by their friendship, yet suffocated by it as well. Ultimately Annie's marriage crumbles as her dedication to Helen overshadows her love for her husband.

The friendship depicted in Margaret Kennedy's novel *Not in the Calendar* (New York: Macmillan, 1964) provides a striking contrast. Carrie Knevett, who can hear, and Wyn Harper, who is deaf, meet as small children, each of them regarded as a misfit by her family. The novel traces their friendship throughout their lives and careers—Wyn becomes a world-famous painter, and Carrie helps to establish a school for the deaf. Carrie is literally the only person Wyn can talk to; to everyone else her speech is unintelligible. Yet, unlike Helen Keller, Wyn refuses to become unduly dependent upon Carrie. She cultivates other friends and hires her own interpreter. She insists that Carrie lead her own life, though separation from her is at times exquisitely painful. Wyn and Carrie are so close that in rare moments their communication supersedes words or signs; they simply feel one another's thoughts and emotions.

Wyn has concluded that, because of her disability, she will never have any but platonic relationships with men. Carrie, too, has eschewed marriage, preferring the freedom of life as a single woman. Perhaps it is the absence of men in their lives which permits their friendship to thrive and deepen with the years.

Not in the Calendar is remarkable in portraying an enduring friendship between a nondisabled woman and a woman who is disabled, a friendship based wholly upon mutual respect and the deepest affection. Such friendships may not often be paralleled in real life. Carrie and Wyn are certainly unique in literature.

WAITING FOR THE PRINCE

> Alone until she dies, Bessie Bighead, hired help, born in the work-house, smelling of the cowshed, . . . picks a posy of daisies in Sunday Meadow to put on the grave of Gomer Owen, who kissed her once by the pigsty when she wasn't looking, and never kissed her again, although she was looking all the time.[2]

Traditionally the woman is expected to be passive, to make herself pretty and wait patiently until a man pursues and wins her. If the woman who is physically different, however, waits passively for a suitor to come to her, she may wait in vain. On the other hand, she may commit a grievous social error if she pursues a man aggressively.

Bessie Bighead is not alone among disabled women characters, dreaming of the only man who, in a casual, soon-forgotten moment, made her feel desirable and womanly. After seven years Laura Wingfield (Williams, *The Glass Menagerie*) still dreams of the boy in her high school music class who teasingly nicknamed her "Blue Roses." When he appears at last, Jim O'Connor barely remembers her at all.

Laura's physical lameness is the foundation for her withdrawal from the world to an introverted existence which revolves around her collection of tiny glass animals. Throughout the play Laura's mother,

Amanda, lives on the glorified memories of her own girlhood as a southern belle, and fantasizes about the gentleman caller who may some day rescue Laura from her isolation. At last the gentleman caller arrives in the form of Jim O'Connor, an emissary from the world outside the Wingfield apartment. He is sensitive to Laura's shyness; he talks to her reassuringly; he dances with her, and in a moment of tenderness he kisses her. Then he tells her that he is already engaged to be married. Laura gives him her glass unicorn, a symbol of her differentness and fragility. In parting Jim takes away the last tenuous hope that Laura will ever break free of her fears and self-doubts to face the world of work, people, and challenges.

Sitting on the beach, Joyce's Gertie McDowell gazes at Leopold Bloom and fantasizes that he will be the man to appreciate her, to love and marry her. Keenly aware that Bloom is watching her, too, she slowly leans back, enticingly revealing more and more of her legs and petticoats. Bloom is properly entranced. He indulges his own fantasies about Gertie as he masturbates. Later, when he realizes that Gertie walks with a limp, Bloom reflects: "The defect is ten times worse in a woman, but it makes them polite. Glad I didn't know it when she was on show" (Joyce, p. 368). Gertie has a pretty face, lovely hair, and a slender figure; she has cultivated all the charms of the day. Yet she is a travesty of womanhood. Because of her disability, her efforts to lure a man are cruelly doomed.

Some of the women in these works do not even fantasize about men. Miss Sampson (Trevor, *Elizabeth Alone*), whose face is dominated by an enormous birthmark, concludes at the age of 13 that romance will have no place in her life. Years later her gratitude toward the man who employs and shelters her deepens into a feeling she cannot name. Only after Mr. Ibbs's death does she come to the shocking realization that her secret feeling toward him was real love.

Wyn Harper accepts her teacher's statement that "for most decent men, they were nuns. Their affliction placed a gulf between them and other people in which desire was likely to flounder" (Kennedy, p. 83). Coolly Wyn decides that "she was never likely to get a man worth having, and she preferred to be a nun" (ibid.).

Marriage is the ultimate goal for the unmarried woman in most works. For women like Laura Wingfield and Gertie McDowell, to be single is to be an old maid—economically dependent, socially ostracized, and emotionally unfulfilled.

In a number of novels and plays, the disabled women do develop relationships with men. Ironically, the woman herself often strives to raise doubts in the mind of her lover. If she truly loves him, she must protect her man from taking on an intolerable burden. At the same time, in testing a man's commitment she is attempting to protect herself from the pain of future rejection.

Though Richard Grenville begs her repeatedly to marry him, even after she can no longer walk, Honor Harris steadfastly refuses. She remains his unshakeably loyal friend, she nurses him back to health after he receives a near-fatal wound in battle. But she never wavers in her decision to keep their friendship strictly platonic. She is among the most articulate of these characters in expressing her reasons. "The sense of helplessness, of ugly inferiority, would have worked like a maggot in my mind, and even when he was most gentle and most tender I should have felt, with some devil flash of intuition, 'This is not what he is wanting'" (du Maurier, p. 211).

Like Leopold Bloom, many nondisabled men in these works feel pity and revulsion at their initial meeting with the disabled woman. One of the most clear-cut examples of this reaction appears in Charlton Ogburn's *Winespring Mountain* (New York: Morrow, 1973). Wick Carter has been admiring Letty from afar, until he realizes that she is blind.

> He had been overwhelmed with embarrassment and with pity, repelled, frightened. From that moment he had been unable to think of the emotions he had nursed about her without an intense desire to hide from himself. He had been duped, not by her, of course—though deep inside he held it against her that, disqualified as she was, she had stirred such thoughts in him—but by fate. He had been made a fool of (Ogburn, p. 49).

Wick and Letty do become friends, but their relationship remains platonic until Letty's sight is miraculously restored. Suddenly she is besieged by friends and admirers, a modeling career is proposed for her— and at last she and Wick discuss a shared future. Only as a fully sighted woman can Wick accept her as a potential partner for life.

Yet revulsion and avoidance are not the total picture. Perversely, the same men who are repelled by a disabled woman are at times attracted by the disability as well. Though he pities Gertie and feels dismayed that he had fantasized about her, Leopold Bloom goes on to reflect: "Hot little devil all the same, wouldn't mind. Curiosity, like a nun or a Negress or a girl with glasses" (Joyce, p. 368). In Susan Sontag's *Death Kit*, Dalton, who has just recovered from a suicide attempt, is drawn to Hester because of her blindness. Consciously he admires what he perceives as her bravery in the face of her affliction, and he believes that she must possess an inner vision which can somehow help him to see himself more clearly. Yet on another level Hester's blindness represents for him a physical and spiritual darkness, the darkness of oblivion which he sought when he attempted to take his life. Gradually he sinks into this darkness himself, closing out the visible world, growing steadily weaker, courting death.

The narrator of Coetzee's *Waiting for the Barbarians* (New York: Penguin, 1982) is likewise repulsed and attracted by the disabilities of the barbarian girl. He is the commander of a frontier outpost in an unnamed country. The girl, belonging to one of the barbarian tribes suspected of plotting an uprising, is blinded and lamed by torturers under the narrator's jurisdiction. He employs her in his kitchen and takes her into his bed at night. For months he bathes and massages her each evening, though he never has sexual relations with her and is repelled when she attempts to seduce him. He is aghast at his attraction to her: "The thought of the strange ecstasies I have approached through the means of her incomplete body fills me with a dry revulsion, as if I had spent nights copulating with a dummy of straw and leather" (Coetzee, p. 4).

Yet through the girl, he desperately hopes to grasp some essential understanding of the relationship between his people, the ruling class, and hers, the dominated and tortured. He asks himself: "Is it then the case that it is the whole woman I want, that my pleasure in her is spoiled until these marks on her are erased and she is restored to herself? Or is it the case ... that it is the marks on her which drew me to her but which, to my disappointment, I find do not go deep enough? ... Is it she I want, or the traces of a history her body bears?" (ibid., p. 64). For this man, the disabled woman is a living symbol of the brutality acted against her people, not a total human being to be loved or hated on the strength of her personal merits.

Coetzee, however, carries the narrator's introspection an important step farther. He reflects:

> While I have not ceased to see her as a body maimed, scarred, harmed, she has perhaps now grown into and become that new, deficient body, feeling no more deformed than a cat feels deformed for having claws instead of fingers ... More ordinary than I like to think, she may have ways of finding me ordinary, too (ibid., p. 56).

At the core, then, he is fleetingly aware that she possesses a wholeness he has never touched in all his seeking.

The most extreme instance I have discovered of the nondisabled man's desire for the disabled woman appears in Marilyn French's *The Bleeding Heart* (New York: Ballantine, 1981). Dolores, resolutely independent and constantly questioning, spends a year thrashing out a relationship with Victor Morisey while they are both working abroad. The details of Victor's unhappy marriage back home emerge late in the novel. On the night of a bitter argument his wife Edith had set out in the car, so wild with rage that she neither knew nor cared where she went. Her car crashed into a concrete wall, and as a result Edith lost the use of her legs. While she was in the hospital she underwent a face lift, so she now has the countenance of a young girl.

When their year in England comes to an end, Victor chooses to leave Dolores and return to Edith. As a former lover of Victor remarks, "Oh, how nice! You have what you've always wanted, a woman with a child's face and a child's dependency. You don't have to worry about her running around because she's numb, and you don't have to worry about her running away because she has no legs. She's utterly house-bound, utterly subject, and utterly passive. Just what you wanted. How nice to get what you want. Just what you deserve" (French, pp. 264-65). Edith's paraplegia is symbolic of the dependency which, according to French, most men secretly want from their wives and lovers.

Perhaps the most probing exploration of the relationship between a disabled woman and a nondisabled man appears in Medoff's play *Children of a Lesser God*. Sarah Norman, profoundly deaf since birth and unable to speak, marries her speech teacher, James Leeds. To Sarah at their first meeting James is just one more hearing person who wants her to be like him, to speak. In sign she expresses her hostility through her scathing wit. James is drawn to her from the very beginning: "You know, I hate to say this, but you're the most mysterious, attractive, angry person I've ever met" (Medoff, act I).

Sarah readily yields to his warmth and spontaneity, but she still has reservations about their budding relationship. "Sarah: Don't hate me for not learning to speak. James: Hate you? No, I love you for having the strength to be yourself" (act I).

Her defenses down at last, Sarah agrees that they should marry. Yet James is eager to make a new woman of her. When Sarah's mother and the director of the school for the deaf come for an evening of bridge, they are astonished by Sarah's "progress," and credit James with working wonders. Not only can she now play bridge, she can even cook a quiche, just like any normal housewife. And, despite his protestations, Sarah senses that James still cherishes a dream of accomplishing the ultimate miracle—teaching her to speak.

Gradually Sarah comes to resent that it is always she who must change, must try to enter her husband's world. Sarah entreats him to come into her world too, to join her in her silence so that he may truly know and understand her. In one shattering scene, James accuses her of refusing to speak as a means of manipulating people. "You want to talk to me?" he cries. "Then you learn my language! . . . Now come on! I want you to speak to me! Let me hear it. Speak! Speak! Speak!" For the only time in the play Sarah speaks, her hands at her sides, and her voice is grotesque, almost unintelligible as she screams: "Speech! Speech! Is that it? No! You want me to be your child! You want me to be like you. How do you like my voice? Am I beautiful? Am I what you want me to be? What about me, what I want?" (act II).

At the play's close, Sarah has left James and he seeks her out, imploring her to come home. Sarah refuses, explaining that she would only keep trying to change him, as he has tried to change her. "We would have to meet in another place, not in silence or in sound but somewhere else. I don't know where that is now. I have to go it alone" (act II).

The problem depicted in this play is not unique to marriages between disabled women and nondisabled men. The struggle for true communication across existing differences is the fabric of any close human relationship. But in *Children of a Lesser God,* Sarah's deafness is the focus of tension. On one level, James wants her to learn to speak so that she can be more independent, so that she need not rely upon an interpreter as her intermediary. Yet, representing the larger society, he seeks to hone down Sarah's differentness so that she will blend unnoticed into the world of hearing people.

When Esther Summerson (Dickens, *Bleak House*) becomes facially disfigured after an attack of smallpox, she concludes that she must free her lover, Allen Woodcourt, from any obligation toward her. But Allen loved her before she became disfigured, and the change in her appearance has no bearing upon his feeling for her. When she realizes that his love is unshaken, Esther joyfully agrees to marry him. Their marriage is part of a typically Dickensian happy ending. It is never explored in any depth, but it is one of the few happy unions portrayed in any of the works I have examined.

Nearly all of the relationships I have described turn upon the woman's disability. If she is an isolate, deemed unqualified by men, it is because she is disabled. Potential mates doubt her competence to tend to a family. Frequently the man feels he will be diminished in the eyes of others if he can only acquire a substandard partner. If on the other hand a man finds the disabled woman attractive, it is because her disability draws him to her, making her mysterious, heroic, or appealingly vulnerable. In either case, disability looms as an overwhelming issue for the men in most of these works. They may be repelled or attracted to the disabled woman, or struggle with both feelings at once. But the woman's disability is nearly always seen as her first and most salient attribute.

COUPLES WITH DISABILITIES

Thus far, I have referred only to relationships between disabled women and nondisabled men. But five of the women in the works under discussion have relationships with men who are themselves disabled. Janice and Abel Ryder (Greenberg, *In This Sign*) are both deaf. Rosie Celli (Twersky) marries Ken Werner, who, like herself, is blind. In both of these instances, the couples live very much within the bounds of a disabled community, and for both the men and the women intimacy with nondisabled peers seems out of the question. The outside world is perceived as hostile and alien, and security rests wholly within the community of people who share a like disability.

In contrast, Clare Thompson (Twersky, *Face of the Deep*) has had far broader experience among nondisabled people, and identifies strongly with the larger community. Her tortured relationship with Fred Harris dramatically illustrates the painful struggle of a disabled woman who longs for total acceptance in a nondisabled society. Both Clare and Fred are blind, but both have moved beyond the sheltered blind community. Their jobs are not connected with blindness agencies, they have sighted friends, and they have dated some sighted people. Each of them yearns to find a sighted mate, the ultimate symbol of acceptance by the world which has so often been cruelly rejecting. Ashamed of her deepening involvement with Fred, Clare avoids introducing him to her mother or to her friends, but she is hurt and angry when Fred shows a similar reluctance to bring her into his life. Having been the victims of prejudice themselves, they victimize each other in their turn. Ultimately they reject one another, simply because neither of them wants a partner who is blind.

Yet it is Clare who suffers most. Fred rejects her first, moving on to a series of relationships with sighted women who accept him because of his money and position. Clare is left with no one. She can only salvage a shred of dignity, refusing to open the door to Fred when he returns unexpectedly after an absence of many months. As a man, Fred appears to have opportunities and alternatives which are barred to Clare. In keeping with the feminine role, she is expected to make herself attractive, to be passive, to wait.

THE WOMAN HERSELF

> Sarah: I want to be joined to other people, but for all my life people have spoken for me: *she* says, *she* wants, as if there were no *I*, as if there were no one in here who could understand. Until you let me be an individual, an I just as you are, you will never truly be able to come inside my silence and know me. And until you do that I will never let myself know you. Until that time we cannot be joined. We cannot share a relationship (Medoff, act II).

For Sarah Norman, deafness is not a cruel affliction, a cross to bear, but a social stigma which permits the majority of the human race to set her aside. In the impassioned speech quoted above, she defies the forces in society which pressure her to conform. She pleads instead for the right to be accepted as herself, a deaf person, a woman, a human being.

Sarah's self-acceptance, her struggle to win the respect and acceptance of others are remarkable when one contrasts her with most of the other disabled women in literature. The majority feel that their disabilities make them inferior to nondisabled people. They believe that they deserve little from life, and they seldom dare to make demands of anyone else. Moments of self-loathing are frequent. "Even a gypsy in the hedges, a beggar woman in the gutters had more dignity than I!" (du Maurier, *The King's General*, p. 211). "Sometimes it's so shaming! So shaming! . . . You know that being blind I'm not much good to anyone" (Ogburn, *Winespring Mountain*, p. 213).

In Marsha Norman's Pulitzer Prize-winning play *Night Mother*, Jessie Case carries out the first truly self-directed act of her life when she commits suicide. Epileptic since childhood, she has always existed on the fringes. She has never successfully held a job; her marriage (arranged by her mother) ended in failure; she is estranged from her teenage son. At the time of the play Jessie has been seizure-free for a year, but she has never learned how to relate to other people, and she still perceives herself as an outcast. The only sensible thing to do with such a blighted life, she concludes, is to blot it out altogether.

Inge in Hamsun's *The Growth of the Soil* does not commit suicide, but infanticide, murdering the newborn daughter who, like herself, has a harelip. Gazing down at the baby she is appalled by its ugliness, which she considers especially devastating because the child is a girl. Hamsun implies, without furnishing details, that Inge suffered intolerable misery as a young girl because of her disfigurement. But by the time this baby is born she is happily married and the mother of two lively sons. It is the anguish she remembers, not the hope that her daughter might also have a fulfilling life in the end. It is her own ugliness she sees in the child's face, and her self-loathing drives her to obliterate the being which seems to be her own reflection. Some of the characters define themselves almost exclusively in terms of their disabilities. In *Death Kit* (New York: New American Library, 1967), when Dalton asks Hester to tell him about herself she replies, "There isn't much to tell. When you're blind it's all inside . . . People wait on me. They have to. And I think a lot, listen to music. I'm fond of flowers" (Sontag, p. 45).

In sharp contrast, a few of the women in these works, like Sarah Norman, strive to break free of the disabled stereotype. They perceive themselves, and yearn to be seen by others, as women with many facets and capacities, deserving a place in the nondisabled world. Clare Thompson (Twersky) avoids association with other blind people in an effort to escape being stereotyped; she does not resent her blindness itself or feel that it renders her inferior to others. Society's discrimination, and not her disability, has restricted her and prevented her from realizing her fullest potential. Ironically, by rejecting contact with other blind people, she re-enacts the very prejudice which has injured her, and denies an essential part of who she is.

Similarly, for years Wyn Harper (Kennedy) refuses to endorse the cause of education for deaf children, because she does not want the public to learn that she herself is deaf. She fears that, if she is categorized as a deaf artist, she will never compete with other painters on their own terms. Wyn is perhaps the only one of these characters who ultimately achieves a balanced, healthy attitude toward herself. She is in her late fifties when, with her lifelong friend Carrie, she revisits the scene of her early childhood and suddenly is confronted with the long-suppressed memory of those agonizing years when she was regarded by her own family as worthy only of pity. By reliving the misery of that time in her life she recognizes that she has indeed put the past behind her. She is no longer an outcast, but a woman with friends, an artist with an international reputation. At last, without feeling threatened or compromised, she is able to lend her support to the cause of deaf people everywhere.

THE MEANS TO A WRITER'S ENDS

"Under her shapeless dress her body kept its limp immobility, and her dark eyes had the bright witchlike stare that disease of the spine sometimes gives."[3]

It is interesting to speculate how much these characters' attitudes toward themselves express the attitudes of the writers who have created them. In some instances, the disabled woman unquestionably embodies the writer's negative feelings. Edith Wharton, in describing Mattie

Silver, portrays her as a demonic creature, daily wreaking vengeance upon her former lover and his wife. Wharton uses Mattie's paraplegia as a divine punishment, impartially meted out to Mattie and Ethan for their forbidden love and to Ethan's wife Zenobia for cruelly standing in their way. For Wharton, disability is literally a fate worse than death. The disabled woman is often seen from the outset as a victim. She is not acted upon by random circumstance, but is physically damaged by someone in her life, most commonly by a man. This image of the disabled woman as victim serves to heighten the sense that she is inadequate and helpless, more vulnerable than her nondisabled peers.

In actuality there is seldom anyone to blame for a disability. Disabilities most often occur as the result of natural causes—illnesses or genetic conditions—and they become markedly more prevalent with advancing age. But this gradual, random onset lacks the dramatic impact which most writers and readers seem to feel makes an engrossing story.

Only a few of the novels examined here are written wholly or in part from the disabled woman's point of view. Most of the women are seen from the outside, commonly through the perceptions of a man. Thus the writer, identifying more closely with his or her nondisabled characters, does not attempt to show the real complexity of the disabled woman's being. The disabled woman's purpose in the book is to reveal the effect which she and her impairment have upon others.

A clear example of this use of disability occurs in Rosellen Brown's *Tender Mercies*. Laura Courser becomes quadriplegic in a boating accident which is directly caused by her husband Tom's carelessness. Although Brown gives brief and sometimes very moving glimpses into Laura's thoughts, the novel is essentially Tom's story, a study in guilt and atonement. While Laura remains passive, locked into herself by depression and barely suppressed rage, Tom struggles to conquer his guilt and rebuild their life together. Brown gives no hint about what Laura must feel.

In many instances, the disabled woman is little more than a metaphor through which the writer hopes to address some broader theme. Her disability may stand for helplessness, innocence, or blighted opportunity. As mentioned earlier, Gertie McDowell's lameness (Joyce) renders her a mocking travesty of all that is feminine. For Gide in *Pastoral Symphony* (New York: Knopf, 1931), Gertrude's blindness represents virginal purity, freedom from contamination by the world's ugliness. For Sontag, on the other hand, Hester's blindness is a devouring, malevolent force of darkness and death.

Meridian, in Alice Walker's novel by the same name (New York: Pocket Books, 1976), is a relentless fighter for the civil rights of blacks in the south. For Walker Meridian's strange falling sickness embodies all the suffering of the black race. It lifts her to an almost Christlike stature; in one scene her roommate, watching over her on her sickbed, "glanced at Meridian's head in shock, for all around it was a soft full light as if her head, the spikes of her natural, had learned to glow" (Walker, p. 120).

de la Mare uses Miss M.'s diminutive stature as a means for exploring the dimensions and boundaries of the self. In a delightful debate with her rather humorless physician over the merits of being small she comments, "There is indeed [a norm]. But why, I ask myself, so vast a number of examples of it! . . . And yet, do you know, I have watched, and they [normal-sized people] really seem to enjoy being the same as one another. . . . And if on the outside, I suppose on the inside, too. . . . One wouldn't so much mind the monotonous packages, if the contents were different" (de la Mare, *Memoirs of a Midget,* p. 85). It is not Miss M.'s physical size which wakens her self-contempt at last, but the small-mindedness of her stubborn pride and her willingness to sacrifice her integrity in an effort to please others.

Though he explores the metaphorical significance of being a little person, de la Mare never loses contact with Miss M. as a human being. He creates a sensitive, complex woman endlessly seeking self-realization. de la Mare is one of the few writers in this group who manages to use disability in a symbolic sense, yet to treat the disabled woman as a full-fledged individual. He demonstrates that works involving disabled women, like all serious literature, can and should strike universal themes.

Despite the tendency for writers to exploit disability as a metaphorical tool, several, like de la Mare, do a remarkable job of depicting realistic, believable women who are disabled. Medoff, Twersky, Greenberg, and Kennedy are especially effective in entering the minds and hearts of the women they portray and bringing them fully to life. I am left wondering why these few writers are so successful, while so many others seem unable to break free of their own limiting view of disability.

To my knowledge, only two of these writers have intimate personal experience with disability. Twersky is blind, and Medoff is married to a deaf woman. Women from other minority groups have brought their unique point of view to fiction and drama, sharing with the world a glimpse of life as a woman who is black, Hispanic, Native American, or gay. But not one of the works discussed in this chapter is written by a woman who is herself disabled.

Perhaps disabled women, plagued by feelings of inferiority and self-contempt, fear that others will not wish to read about their lives. Or, like

Clare Thompson, those who have achieved some degree of assimilation into the nondisabled community may wish to divorce themselves from disability and all that it represents. Whatever the reason, disabled women have made little attempt to shape their experiences into works of fiction or drama. Thus they leave the field open for writers with little real knowledge to make guesses and draw wild inferences, to conjure the disabled woman from imagination and set her down on paper as truth.

Does art imitate life, or does life imitate art? In the case of the disabled woman, both seem to be true. Even at their best, most of these writers focus chiefly upon the most negative aspects of life as a disabled woman—the helplessness and isolation, the sense of inferiority. For many women with disabilities such a portrait is all too accurate. Yet a great number of disabled women do not fit this picture at all. Those who lead satisfying lives, thoroughly integrated into the community, are rarely found in literature. By failing to offer more positive images, these writers help to perpetuate the negative stereotypes they present. The nondisabled reader comes away from most of these works with awe and pity. The disabled woman, searching as I did through my growing-up years, will find few positive role models in their pages. Instead, most of these novels and plays confirm our most deep-seated fears about how we appear to others and what our lives may hold. There aren't many of these characters I would like to get to know in real life; there are even fewer I would ever want to become.[4]

CONCLUSIONS

I wrote this chapter to survey the ways disabled women are portrayed in a varied group of plays and novels, to determine whether my sense that the image which literature conveys is overwhelmingly negative. I wondered if disabled women would be portrayed as capable of establishing meaningful friendships with other women. I questioned whether they would be seen as possessed of physical and mental qualities which would make them attractive to men. I sought to determine how these characters are ascribed to feel toward themselves, and to infer how the authors feel toward the disabled women they have created.

When one examines the interpersonal relationships shown in these works, the disabled woman is at a severe disadvantage. She is hampered in forming friendships with other women, who perceive her as different, unable to share their overriding interest in men. Men are often repelled by her disability, though at times they find it draws them to her, meeting their own unhealthy needs.

In all of these instances, disability sets the tone for the woman's interactions with others. Her competence at homemaking chores, her educational attainments, or her personality have little effect upon the attitudes of others toward her. As other characters react to her disability they are not concerned about her competence, but something much deeper and harder to define. Disability seems to undermine the very roots of her womanhood.

Not surprisingly, therefore, the disabled women in these works frequently feel inferior to others and regard themselves with loathing. Only a rare few accept themselves, disability and all, and seek a place in the nondisabled world.

Writers, like most other people in the society, seem to see the disability before anything else when they contemplate a disabled woman. Few of them grant her a self beyond her impairment. Yet some writers have managed to create books and plays which show disabled women as total persons, capable of love and hatred, joy and anguish, the full range of human experience and emotion. Perhaps these works can open the way for an understanding of disabled women based upon awareness and respect.

de la Mare expresses this hope eloquently, in the voice of Miss M. at the close of her memoirs:

> And this tale itself? . . . What is it but once more to have drifted into being on show again—in a book? That is so; and so I must leave it, hoping against hope that one friend at any rate will consent in his love and wisdom to take me seriously, and to remember me, not with scorn or even with pity, but as if, life for life, we had shared the world on equal terms (de la Mare, *Memoirs of a Midget*, p. 379).

NOTES

1. Jacob Twersky, *The Face of the Deep* (New York: World Publishing, 1953), p. 221.

2. Dylan Thomas, *Under Milkwood* (New York: New Directions, 1954), p. 21.

3. Edith Wharton, *Ethan Frome* (New York: Scribners, 1970), p. 174.

4. Since this chapter was written, two collections of writings by women with disabilities have appeared: *With the Power of Each Breath: A Disabled Women's Anthology*, edited by Susan E. Browne et al. (Pittsburgh: Cleis Press, 1985) and *Disabled Women*, edited by Michelle Fine and Adrienne Asch (Philadelphia: Temple University Press, in press).

4

Screening Stereotypes: Images of Disabled People in Television and Motion Pictures

Paul K. Longmore

In examining images of people with disabilities in television and film, one encounters two striking facts. First, there are hundreds of characters with all sorts of disabilities: handicapped horror "monsters"; "crippled" criminals; disabled war veterans, from *The Big Parade* (1925) to *The Best Years of Our Lives* (1946) to *Coming Home* (1978); central characters of television series temporarily disabled for one episode: blind detectives; disabled victims of villains; animated characters like stuttering Porky Pig, speech-impaired Elmer Fudd, near-sighted Mr. Magoo, and mentally retarded Dopey. The second striking fact is how much we overlook the prevalence of disability and the frequent presence of disabled characters. Why do television and film so frequently screen disabled characters for us to see, and why do we usually screen them out of our consciousness even as we absorb those images?

The critic Michael Wood has some useful observations that apply here.

All movies mirror reality in some way or other. There are no escapes, even in the most escapist pictures. . . . Movies bring out [our] worries without forcing us to look at them too closely . . . it doesn't appear to be necessary for a movie to solve anything, however fictitiously. It seems to be enough for us if a movie simply dramatizes our semi-secret concerns and contradictions in a story, allows them their brief, thinly disguised parade. . . . Entertainment is not, as we often think, a full-scale flight from our problems, not a means of forgetting them completely, but rather a rearrangement of our problems into shapes which tame them, which disperse them to the margins of our attention.[1]

Often, as Wood says, film and television programs touch upon our areas of concern without explicitly acknowledging or exploring them. At other times, for instance, in the "social problem" dramas popular in the 1970s and 1980s, the subjects of our worries were addressed but without a deep examination. In such cases, television and film supply quick and simple solutions. They tell us that the problem is not as painful or as overwhelming as we fear, that it is manageable, or that it is not really our problem at all, but someone else's.

Disability happens around us more often than we generally recognize or care to notice and we harbor unspoken anxieties about the possibility of disablement, to us or to someone close to us. What we fear, we often stigmatize and shun and sometimes seek to destroy. Popular entertainments depicting disabled characters allude to these fears and prejudices or address them obliquely or fragmentarily, seeking to reassure us about ourselves.

What follows is a brief consideration of the most common screen images of people with physical, sensory, and developmental disabilities and some thoughts about their underlying social and psychological meaning. This chapter by no means exhausts the range of images or their significance; although it concentrates on live-action fictional depictions, it also compares them to fictional images in order to illuminate the social and cultural attitudes and concerns they reflect and express. Further, it is important to show the connections between recent changes in those characterizations and the emergence of a new sociopolitical consciousness about disability, particularly among disabled people themselves.

DISABILITY AND CRIMINALITY

Disability has often been used as a melodramatic device not only in popular entertainments, but in literature as well. Among the most persistent is the association of disability with malevolence. Deformity of body symbolizes deformity of soul. Physical handicaps are made the emblems of evil.

As Kriegel describes, Richard III's hunchback and Captain Ahab's peg leg immediately come to mind. But "bad guys" still frequently have handicaps. Doctor No and Doctor Strangelove both have forearms and hands encased in black leather. The overpowering evil embodied in Strangelove's leather-wrapped hand nearly makes him strangle himself. He is also "confined to a wheelchair." The disabilities of both doctors apparently resulted from foul-ups in their nefarious experiments. They are "crippled" as a consequence of their evil.

One of the most popular adversaries of the TV adventure series "Wild Wild West" was the criminal genius—yet another doctor—Miguelito P. Loveless, a hunchbacked "dwarf." Michael Dunn, a marvelous and talented actor, spent much of his career relegated to such horrific roles. In one episode, Dr. Loveless says to the story's hero, "I grow weary of you, Mr. West. I weary of the sight of your strong, straight body." This brilliant villain repeatedly hatches grandiose schemes to wreak havoc and overthrow the U.S. government for an obvious motive: he wants revenge on the world, presumably the able-bodied world. Disabled villains, raging against their "fate" and hating those who have escaped such "affliction," often seek to retaliate against "normals."

Other criminal characters may operate on a less magnificent scale, but act from the same animus. In the "Hookman" (1973) episode of "Hawaii Five-O," a double-amputee sniper who had lost both hands in a foiled bank robbery blamed the series' hero and pledged to avenge his "maiming" by killing the police detective. Or consider the "one-armed man," the real murderer in one of the most popular series in television history, "The Fugitive." (Bill Raisch was another handicapped actor confined to criminal roles because of his disability.)

Another disabled villian—not a criminal, but a "bad guy" just the same—appeared in the popular British miniseries, "The Jewel in the Crown" (broadcast on American public television in 1984-85). This dramatization of the last years of British colonial rule in India revolved around one Ronald Merrick, a police investigator and army intelligence officer who is arrogant, deceitful, and viciously racist. Because of a battle injury, the left side of his face is disfigured and he loses his left arm. Like Doctor No, and Doctor Strangelove, and a number of other maimed or amputee bad guys, he acquires a black leather-covered prosthetic limb. This dramatic device recurs frequently enough that one begins to wonder about the psychosexual significance of the connection between blackness, badness, amputation, and artificial arms.

Giving disabilities to villainous characters reflects and reinforces, albeit in exaggerated fashion, three common prejudices against handicapped people: disability is a punishment for evil; disabled people are embittered by their "fate"; disabled people resent the nondisabled and would, if they could, destroy them. In historical and contemporary social fact, it is, of course, nondisabled people who have at times endeavored to destroy people with disabilities. As with popular portrayals of other minorities, the unacknowledged hostile fantasies of the stigmatizers are transferred to the stigmatized. The nondisabled audience is allowed to disown its fears and biases by "blaming the victims," making them responsible for their own ostracism and destruction.

Closely related to the criminal characterization, but distinct from it, is the depiction in horror stories of the disabled person as "monster." The subtext of many horror films is fear and loathing of people with disabilities. As with the equation of disability and criminality, the horrific characterization long antedates television and persists most frequently in horror films made for theatrical release. Still, television perpetuates the "monster" image not only by broadcasting these theatrical films, but also by producing new versions of horror classics such as *The Hunchback of Notre Dame* and *The Phantom of the Opera.*

The most obvious feature of "monster" characterizations is their extremism. The physical disabilities typically involve disfigurement of the face and head and gross deformity of the body. As with the criminal characterization, these visible traits express disfigurement of personality and deformity of soul. Once again, disability may be represented as the cause of evildoing, punishment for it, or both.

Further, the depiction of the disabled person as "monster" and the criminal characterization both express to varying degrees the notion that disability involves the loss of an essential part of one's humanity. Depending on the extent of disability, the individual is perceived as more or less subhuman. These images reflect what Erving Goffman describes as the fundamental nature of stigma: the stigmatized person is regarded as "somehow less than human." Such depictions also exemplify the "spread effect" of prejudice. The stigmatized trait assumedly taints every aspect of the person, pervasively spoiling social identity.[2]

That "spread effect" is evident in an extension of the notion of loss of humanity, the idea that disability results in loss of self-control. The disabled character is thus seen as endangering the rest of society. The dangerous disabled person is not necessarily a criminal or a malevolent monster, but may be a tragic victim of fate, as in the nonhorror story *Of Mice and Men.* Whatever the specific nature of the disability, it unleashes violent propensities that "normally" would be kept in check by internal mechanisms of self-control.

Violent loss of self-control results in the exclusion of the disabled person from the human community. Often in horror stories, and virtually always in criminal characterizations, it is the disability itself and the resultant dangerous behavior that separates and isolates the disabled character from the rest of society. But in some "monster" stories, for instance *The Hunchback of Notre Dame,* the disabled person is excluded because of the fear and contempt of the nondisabled majority. Still, even when the handicapped character is presented sympathetically as a victim of bigotry, it remains clear that severe disability makes social integration impossible. While viewers are urged to pity Quasimodo or Lennie, we are let off the hook by being shown that disability or bias or both must forever ostracize severely disabled persons from society.

For both monstrous and criminal disabled characters, the final and only possible solution is often death. In most cases, it is fitting and just punishment. For sympathetic "monsters," death is the tragic but inevitable, necessary, and merciful outcome. Again we can "sympathize" with the mentally retarded Lennie, while avoiding our fears and bias about him, and escape the dilemma of his social accommodation and integration.

During the 1970s and 1980s another depiction of persons with severe disabilities emerged: the severely physically disabled character who seeks suicide as a release from the living death of catastrophic disablement. This was the theme of the play and motion picture *Whose Life Is It, Anyway?*, the TV movie "An Act of Love," and the theatrical drama *Nevis Mountain Dew*. In the first two stories, recent spinal-cord-injured quadriplegics request assisted suicide, and in the last, a post-polio respiratory quadriplegic asks his family to unplug his iron lung. The ostensible subject of the first and second dramas is the arrogance and oppressive power of a medical establishment gone wild, which at exorbitant expense keeps alive suffering people who would be better off dead. But just beneath the surface of all of these tales runs a second unacknowledged theme, the horror of a presumed "vegetablelike" existence following severe disablement.

These stories present distinct parallels with the "monster" characterization. Disability again means loss of one's humanity. The witty, combative central character in *Whose Life is It, Anyway?* refers to himself as a "vegetable" and says that he is "not a man" anymore. The disabled persons in the other two dramas make similar statements of themselves. Severe disability also means loss of control. Unlike the criminal and "monster" characterizations, it does not mean loss of moral self-control, since the disabled would-be suicides clearly have a moral sensibility superior to those who would force them to live. Rather, disability means a total physical dependency that deprives the individual of autonomy and self-determination.

Disability again results in separation from the community. This exclusion is not presented as necessary to protect society from danger, as with the monstrous disabled character. Nor is it the result of discrimination or inaccessibility. It is portrayed as the inevitable consequence of a serious physical impairment that prevents normal functioning, normal relationships, and normal productivity. All of these dramas avoid considering what effects the enforcement of antidiscrimination and accessibility laws would have on the activities, identities, and sense of self-worth of disabled individuals.

Finally, as with the "monster" and criminal characterizations, these dramas present death as the only logical and humane solution. But instead of eliminating the disabled person who is a violent threat, it relieves both the individual viewer and society of the impossible emotional, moral, and financial burden of severe disability. The disabled characters choose death themselves, beg for it as release from their insupportable existence. The nondisabled characters resist this decision, but then reluctantly bow to it as necessary and merciful. Once again, the nondisabled audience is allowed to avoid confronting its own fears and prejudices. It is urged to compliment itself for its compassion in supporting death as the only sensible solution to the problems of people with severe disabilities. Even when bigotry is presented as a fundamental problem confronting severely disabled persons, as in *The Elephant Man* (1980), the final solution, the choice of the disabled character himself, is suicide. Whether because of prejudice or paralysis, disability makes membership in the community and meaningful life itself impossible, and death is preferable. Better dead than disabled.

PORTRAYALS OF ADJUSTMENT

The most prevalent image in film and especially in television during the past several decades has been the maladjusted disabled person. These stories involve characters with physical or sensory, rather than mental, handicaps. The plots follow a consistent pattern: The disabled central characters are bitter and self-pitying because, however long they have been disabled, they have never adjusted to their handicaps, and have never accepted themselves as they are. Consequently, they treat nondisabled family and friends angrily and manipulatively. At first, the nondisabled characters, feeling sorry for them, coddle them, but eventually they realize that in order to help the disabled individuals adjust and cope they must "get tough." The stories climax in a confrontation scene in which a nondisabled character gives the disabled individual an emotional "slap in the face" and tells him or her to stop feeling sorry for themselves. Accepting the rebuke, the disabled character quits complaining and becomes a well-adjusted adult.

These portrayals suggest that disability is a problem of psychological self-acceptance, of emotional adjustment. Social prejudice rarely intrudes. In fact, the nondisabled main characters have no trouble accepting the individuals with disabilities. Moreover, they understand better than the handicapped characters the true nature of the problem. Typically, disabled characters lack insight about themselves and other people, and require emotional education, usually by a nondisabled character. In the end, nondisabled persons supply the solution: they compel the disabled individuals to confront themselves.

The drama of adjustment seems to have developed in the aftermath of World War II, probably in response to the large numbers of disabled veterans returning from that conflict. Note, for instance, that two of the most powerful examples appeared in the films *The Best Years of Our Lives* (1946) and *The Men* (1950). This genre became a staple of television in the 1960s, 1970s, and 1980s.

Paradoxically, this depiction represents progress in the portrayal of disabled persons. The criminal and "monster" characterizations show that disability deprives its victims of an essential part of their humanity, separates them from the community, and ultimately requires that they be put to death. In contrast, the dramas of adjustment say that disability does not inherently prevent deaf, blind, or physically handicapped people from living meaningfully and productively and from having normal friendships and romantic relationships. But these stories put the responsibility for any problems squarely and almost exclusively on the disabled individual. If they are socially isolated, it is not because the disability inevitably has cut them off from the community or because society has rejected them. Refusing to accept themselves with their handicaps, they have chosen isolation.

A recurring secondary theme of many stories of adjustment is the idea of compensation. God or nature or life compensates handicapped people for their loss, and the compensation is spiritual, moral, mental, and emotional. In an episode of "Little House on the Prairie," "Town Party, Country Party" (1974), about a "lame" schoolgirl, Charles the father says that many "cripples" seem to have "special gifts." Laura, his daughter, asks if those gifts include "gumption." Yes, he answers, and goodness of heart, too. Other stories represent blind people with special insights into human nature (for instance, the blind, old, black man in "Boone," a short-lived 1983 TV series) or paraplegic detectives with superior skills ("Ironside"). Far from contradicting the image of the maladjusted disabled person, the notion of compensation reiterates it in yet another way. Compensation comes to those who cope. It is a "gift" to handicapped individuals who responsibly deal with their "afflictions."

Nonfictional television programs, particularly magazine shows such as "That's Incredible," "Real People," and "Ripley's Believe It Or Not," frequently present handicapped individuals who are the opposite of the fictional "maladjusted" disabled person. Repeatedly they recount stories of achievement and success, of heroic overcoming. Over and over they display inspiring blind carpenters, paraplegic physicians, and "handicapable" athletes. These "real-life" stories of striving and courage seem the antithesis of the bitter and self-pitying "cripples" in dramas of adjustment, but both stem from the same perception of the nature of disability: disability is primarily a problem of emotional coping, of personal acceptance. It is not a problem of social stigma and discrimination. It is a matter of individuals overcoming not only the physical impairments of their own bodies but more importantly the emotional consequences of such impairments. Both fictional and nonfictional stories convey the message that success or failure in living with a disability results almost solely from the emotional choices, courage, and character of the individual.

SEXUALITY AND DISABLED PEOPLE

Stigma and discrimination are still especially powerful regarding sexuality and romance. In a sexually supercharged culture that places almost obsessive emphasis on attractiveness, people with various disabilities are often perceived as sexually deviant and even dangerous, asexual, or sexually incapacitated either physically or emotionally. Film and television stereotypes reflect and reinforce this deviant sexual viewpoint.

Criminal disabled characters convey a kinky, leering lust for sex with gorgeous "normal" women. Dr. Loveless, the hunchbacked "dwarf" super-criminal in "Wild Wild West," surrounds himself with luscious women. The Nazi "dwarf" in the film comedy *The Black Bird* (1974) displays a voracious appetite for sex with statuesque beauties. Doctor Strangelove salivates over the prospect of having his share of nubile young women to perpetuate the human race in underground caverns following a nuclear holocaust. "Monster" disabled characters menace beautiful women who would ordinarily reject them. The disfigured *Phantom of the Opera* kidnaps a woman who reminds him of his dead wife. Quasimodo, the hunchback of Notre Dame, rescues and tenderly cares for a woman with whom he has obviously fallen in love. But there is always an undertone of sexual tension, of sexual danger. We are never quite sure what he might do to her. Sexual menace, deviancy, and danger stem from the loss of control often represented as inherent in the experience of disability.

In other stories, physical paralysis results in asexuality or sexual incapacitation. The quadriplegic characters in *Whose Life Is It, Anyway?*, "An Act of Love," and *Nevis Mountain Dew* opt for suicide partly because they believe they have lost the ability to function sexually. Neither of the first two films examines the reality of sexual physiology among people with spinal cord injuries, nor the possibilities of sexual rehabilitation. The latter play inaccurately represents sensory deprivation and sexual dysfunction as consequences of polio. But these individuals, and characters with less severe physical disabilities in other stories, have lost something more important than the physical capacity to function sexually. Disability has deprived them of an essential part of their humanness: their identities as sexual beings. More than one male character with a disability refers to himself as "only half a man."

Even when a disability does not limit sexual functioning, it may impair the person emotionally. Disabled characters may be quite capable of physical love making, but spurn opportunities for romance because of a lack of self-acceptance, disbelief that anyone could love him or her with their "imperfections." Nondisabled characters of the opposite sex have no trouble finding the disabled persons attractive or falling in love with them and have no difficulty in accepting them with their disabilities. From the double amputee veteran in *The Best Years of Our Lives* to a quadriplegic accountant in "Highway to Heaven" ("A Marriage Made in Heaven" 1985), disabled characters require convincing that they are lovable and that a romantic relationship is workable despite their disabilities. These depictions fly in the face of the real-life experiences of many handicapped men and women who find that even the most minor impairments result in romantic rejection. Once again, popular entertainments invert social reality and allow the nondisabled audience to disown its anxieties and prejudices about disabled people. The source of the "problem" is shifted to the stigmatized person himself or herself, in another version of blaming the victim.

In the past, most stories presenting a positive image of disabled people and romance have involved blind characters. Recently, a few productions have presented people with physical disabilities as attractive and sexual. Most prominent among these are Jon Voight's paraplegic Vietnam veteran in *Coming Home* and an episode of the TV situation comedy "Facts of Life" starring Geri Jewell, an actress with cerebral palsy. What distinguishes these and a handful of other portrayals is the self-assurance of the disabled characters regarding their own sexuality and romantic value. They enter relationships out of the strength of their own identities as persons with disabilities.

THE SOCIAL FUNCTION OF DISABILITY IMAGES

Both the dramas of adjustment and the nonfictional presentation of people with disabilities stem from the common notion that with the proper attitude one can cope with and conquer any situation or condition, turning it into a positive growth experience. Nothing can defeat us; only we can defeat ourselves. This belief in the power of a positive mental outlook so widely and successfully marketed in therapies, psychologies, and sects, not only currently but throughout American history, suggests a primary reason for the popularity of stories about disabled people adjusting and overcoming. It points to one of the social and cultural functions of that image and to one of the primary social roles expected of people with disabilities: In a culture that attributes success or failure primarily to individual character, "successful" handicapped people serve as models of personal adjustment, striving, and achievement. In the end, accomplishment or defeat depends only one one's attitude toward oneself and toward life. If someone so tragically "crippled" can overcome the obstacles confronting them, think what you, without a "handicap," can do.

Another obvious social function of the psychologized image of physical and sensory disability is to make it an individual rather than a social problem. Prejudice and discrimination rarely enter into either fictional or nonfictional stories, and then only as a secondary issue. In fictional productions, nondisabled persons usually treat disabled people badly, not because of bias, but out of insensitivity and lack of understanding. It becomes the responsibility of the disabled individual to "educate" them, to allay their anxieties and make them feel comfortable. For instance, in an episode of "Little House on the Prairie" ("No Beast So Fierce"; 1982), a boy who stutters is told that he must patiently help the other children to accept him and then they will stop ridiculing him.

Segments about disabled people on magazine shows and news broadcasts frequently focus on medical and technological advances. They often present "human interest" stories about individuals with disabilities performing some physical feat to demonstrate that they are not "handicapped," only "physically challenged." One could argue that these features demonstrate that medical and technological innovations are increasingly neutralizing physical impairments and that they and the "human interest" stories show that attitudes rather than disabilities limit people. But simultaneously they reinforce the notion that disability is fundamentally a physical problem requiring a medical or mechanical fix. They also suggest that disabled people can best prove their social acceptability, their worthiness of social integration, by displaying some physical capability. Finally, these features also reiterate, with the active complicity of the disabled participants themselves, the view that disability is a problem of individual emotional coping and physical overcoming, rather than an issue of social discrimination against a stigmatized minority.

The reactions of disabled people themselves to "human interest" stories are particularly illuminating. Some praise these features for showing that "physically inconvenienced" folks are as able as so-called "normals." Others criticize such "super crip" segments for continuing to portray handicapped people as "incredible," extraordinary, or freakish. Both responses, it would seem, stem from the same concern and aim: increasingly and in various ways, for instance in the debate over the language of disability,[3] people with disabilities are rejecting the stigmatized social identity imposed upon them. They are struggling to fashion for themselves a positive personal and public identity. Whether or not "human interest" stories in fact promote an alternative image, handicapped people themselves clearly intend to oppose stigma and discrimination.

CHANGING VIEWS OF DISABLED PEOPLE

New characterizations have slowly begun to appear, partly as a result of the increasing impact on casting and characterization of the Media Access Office of the California Foundation on Employment and Disability and other disability activist groups within the entertainment industry. Creation of these groups in turn reflects the emergence of the disability civil rights movement and the growing media awareness of the disability community. Even while previous stereotypes have persisted, a few productions have struggled to "read" these evolving events and to respond to a developing sociopolitical consciousness about disabled people. The resulting images are fascinatingly contradictory. Elements of a minority-group view of disabled people jostle uncomfortably with the themes of the drama of adjustment.

This complicated trend first appeared in *The Other Side of the Mountain* (1977) and *The Other Side of the Mountain, Part II* (1979). This film biography of Jill Kinmont turned her story into a traditional account of overcoming severe disability, while almost completely ignoring her struggle to combat discrimination in education and employment. However, one important scene showed her confronting prejudice when a professor praises her as an "inspiration" while declaring that she will never get a teaching job. Subsequently, the TV movie "The Ordeal of Bill Carney" (1981), dramatized the "real-life" landmark legal battle of a quadriplegic father to gain custody of his two sons. The characterization of Carney, according to Carney himself, distorted his personal life by fitting it into the stereotype of coping, showing him as frequently bitter and depressed, and particularly maladjusted in a sexual and romantic relationship. In contrast, his paraplegic lawyer was portrayed as having an emotionally and sexually healthy relationship with his wife. More importantly, the film showed the attorney militantly defending Carney's legal right to raise his children and the lawyer's own right of physical access to public places.

Contradictions of characterization and theme have also appeared in episodic television. A "T. J. Hooker" segment ("Blind Justice"; 1983), presented a blind woman in physical danger because she had witnessed a murder. Here is a recurring stereotype: a blind person, usually a woman, in jeopardy who tells of the terror of "living in darkness." But in this instance, the stereotype was mitigated and complicated because the woman was also presented as an advocate of the rights of handicapped people and Hooker was given a speech about the need to end bias against people with disabilities. Similarly, an episode of "Quincy" ("Give Me Your Weak"; 1983), showed hundreds of politically active disabled people demonstrating in favor of the Orphan Drugs Bill pending in Congress. But the story also followed the descent into self-pity of a woman who succumbed to her disability, until her husband rebuked her and demanded that she act responsible again. An installment of "Alice" (1984) focused on accessibility for wheelchair users, clearly a response to that pressing social and policy question. But it treated accessibility as an act of generosity that the nondisabled should perform to make things easier for "the handicapped," rather than an issue of the civil and legal rights of disabled people.

A few recent productions have directly dealt with the issue of prejudice. *The Elephant Man* showed the dehumanizing exploitation and bigotry inflicted on a severely disabled man; "Little Lou," an episode of "Little House on the Prairie" (1983), told of a short-statured man denied employment because of discrimination. Unfortunately, instead of showing such bias as widespread, this story had only one prejudiced character, the cartoonishly obnoxious and snobbish Mrs. Oleson. The weakness of both dramas was their indulgence in melodramatic sentimentality.

More realistic was the powerful "For Love of Joshua" on "Quincy" (1983), which examined the denial of medical treatment and nutrition to developmentally disabled newborns and showed the possibilities of independent living for intellectually handicapped people. The story climaxed with an eloquent courtroom speech by a teenager with Down's syndrome protesting prejudice against mentally retarded people. In the theatrical film *Mask* (1985), a teenager with a rare facially disfiguring disease confronts discrimination in education, social ostracism, and romantic rejection. He and his mother militantly resist prejudice. Unfortunately, as in *The Elephant Man,* the movie lets the audience off the hook when the youth dies. It is easier to regret prejudice if its victims won't be around.[4]

If stereotyping of handicapped persons has prevailed in both fictional and nonfictional television programming, the problem in TV commercials has been the total exclusion, until recently, of people with disabilities. Sponsors have feared that the presence of individuals with visible handicaps would alienate consumers from their products. They also have failed to recognize the substantial population of disabled Americans as potential customers. Additionally, they have asserted, not without reason, that by casting performers with disabilities in their commercials they would incur the charge of exploitation. As a result, past efforts to integrate commercials have met with massive resistance.

In 1983, 1984, and early 1985, commercials using handicapped performers began to appear. Departing significantly from past practices, these spots may signal a trend. In mid-1983, CBS broadcast a series of promos for its fall schedule. One showed a paraplegic wheelchair racer. Another had a deaf couple signing, "I love you"; "I love you too." Significantly, these commercials not only garnered praise from the disability community, but also criticism from at least one nondisabled TV critic who implied that CBS was exploiting handicapped people.

More important breakthroughs came in 1984. Levi's Jeans, a major sponsor of ABC's coverage of the 1984 Summer Olympics, presented jazzy spots showing hip young adults, including one with a beautiful woman walking next to a young man in a sports wheelchair who pops a wheelie and spins his chair around. Late in 1984, McDonald's "Handwarmin'" commercial featured its patrons one of whom is a young woman seated in a wheelchair—clapping rhythmically and enjoying its food, warmth, and conviviality. In May 1985, network commercials for Kodak and *People* magazine included wheelchair users, and, most importantly, a spot for the Plymouth Voyager prominently featured a middle-aged man on crutches praising the car.

These commercials represent a major departure in several ways. Most obviously and importantly, all include disabled persons in efforts to promote products, whether hamburgers, blue jeans, TV shows, magazines, cameras, or cars. They seek out handicapped Americans as a market and audience; they reject the fear that nondisabled consumers will be distressed or offended. Further, in order to sell their products, these commercials present a new image of disabled persons. They are not portrayed as helpless and dependent, but rather as attractive, active, and "with it," involved and competitive, experiencing "normal" relationships, and in the auto commercial, smart about what they buy. Ironically, these commercials offer perhaps the most positive media images of people with disabilities to date. Positive images in commercials and other programs reflect the growing sociopolitical perception of disabled people as a minority group and the increasing impact of the disability civil rights movement. Whether these new depictions will become an important trend depends partly on the response from the disability community itself. Advertisers and broadcasters pay close attention to the reactions of various audiences. They are more likely to expand inclusion of disabled performers in commercials and other programming if they receive positive reinforcement from the disability community. By the same token, they will avoid stereotyping and discrimination only if they know that such practices will evoke a negative reaction from handicapped viewers. It is *organized* constituencies, of whatever size, that have brought about changes in broadcasting and advertising.

NOTES

1. Michael Wood, *America In the Movies* (New York: Basic Books, 1975), pp. 16-18.

2. Erving Goffman, *Stigma: Notes on the Management of Spoiled Identity* (Englewood Cliffs: Prentice-Hall, 1963), p. 3; Beatrice Wright, *Physical Disability: A Psychological Approach* (New York: Harper and Row, 1960), p. 8.

3. Paul K. Longmore, "A Note on the Language and the Social Identity of Disabled People," *American Behavioral Scientist,* vol. 28, no. 3 (January/February 1985):419-23.

4. Paul K. Longmore, "'Mask': A Revealing Portrayal of the Disabled," *The Los Angeles Sunday Calendar*, May 5, 1985, pp. 22-23.

5

Framed: Print Journalism's Treatment of Disability Issues

Douglas Biklen

"It had all the elements of a good story. An eight-day-old baby girl, a lawyer who said he was fighting for her right to live, and a young couple who refused to let doctors perform surgery on their infant daughter."[1] So begins Kathleen Kerr's account of how, as a general assignment reporter for Long Island *Newsday,* she came to report on the Baby Jane Doe case. Baby Jane Doe is an infant who was born with several disabling conditions, including hydrocephalus and spina bifida. The story appealed to Kerr and other reporters around the country for several reasons. First, there was the drama of what appeared initially as a confrontation between doctors and parents. Second, there was the obvious concern that if the anonymous baby went for long without surgery, she might very well die. Third, a right-to-life attorney by the name of Lawrence Washburn had heard of the situation and had filed suit for a court hearing on the case. Washburn believed that if the child could benefit from surgery, she should have it, no matter what the parents wanted.

As the case unfolded, it became even more of a "good story." Within days it reached national proportions. Kathleen Kerr and other reporters made the connection between this case and several other recent news stories. A year earlier a child in Bloomington, Indiana, had been born with Down's syndrome and blockage of the esophagus. This Baby Doe was also the focus of a court battle. As in the Long Island case, the parents refused surgery. Baby Doe died of starvation in a matter of days, before the case could be resolved in court. Several families had volunteered to adopt the Indiana Doe infant, but their requests could never be pursued.

In the months that followed, the Reagan administration issued regulations establishing a hotline reporting mechanism and "Baby Doe squads" to investigate any case where someone believed an infant had been denied medical care. The American Academy of Pediatrics sued to stop the regulations—essentially they feared that the posted signs would spawn distrust by patients toward their doctors—and a federal court struck down the regulations on the grounds that they had been issued without proper opportunity for public comment.

But the government's interest in such cases did not stop there. Despite its difficulty in promulgating "Baby Jane Doe" regulations, the Reagan administration filed suit to gain access to Baby Jane Doe's hospital records to determine whether the State University Hospital at Stony Brook had discriminated against her. It was only natural that the Baby Jane Doe case would be seen in the context of the Indiana case and the controversy sparked by the federal government's proposed regulations. (See Chapter 10, "The Awful Privacy of Baby Doe," for the political content of these struggles.)

Hospital officials in Long Island told the parents that Baby Jane Doe, like Indiana's infant Doe, could probably not survive without surgery. Newspaper reports posed the choice this way: "without surgery, doctors say, she will die within two years; with it, she could survive into her 20's but would be severely retarded and bedridden."[2]

The Baby Jane Doe case became a major story for a number of newspapers—*Newsday,* the *New York Times,* and the *Washington Post* to name a few. Aside from the obvious drama over whether or not Baby Jane Doe would survive and the similarity of this case to its Indiana predecessor, there were other important issues at stake. In the words of *New York Times* reporter David Margolick, the case "goes beyond the issue of proper treatment . . . Involved as well are questions of parental autonomy, the obligations of the state, the legal rights of handicapped infants, and the value of even the most debilitating form of human life."[3]

At virtually the same time the Doe case was unfolding on Long Island another case emerged in the national press. Elizabeth Bouvia, a woman with severe cerebral palsy who requires assistance in order to live, sought to have a hospital give her pain-killing drugs to aid her suicide through starvation. When a California hospital refused her request and subjected her to forced feeding, she filed suit against the hospital. "I'm not eating because I wish to die," she said. "People are saying I've given up hope. That's not it. I'm just being realistic. I had high ideals. I thought I could succeed. But little by little I realized that supporting myself and living an independent life is an impossibility. Now I know what it will take. I'm more realistic."[4] While Elizabeth Bouvia's circumstances differ from Baby Jane Doe's—Elizabeth can consider her own options, she can speak on her own behalf, she has experienced life and relationships—her "story" raises many of the same ethical, legal, and moral issues.

If we examine how the print media treated the cases of Baby Jane Doe and Elizabeth Bouvia, it is obvious that they were communicating more than the facts about these two people or the ethical, legal, and moral issues that swirled around them. In a number of ways, the manner in which these cases were reported reveals much about the place of people with disabilities in American culture.

When we think about the media, we often think of its power. Conventional wisdom tells us that the media are powerful. The media shape what we think, who we vote for, and how we dress or what we buy. The titles of popular books about the media speak of their influence: *The Powers That Be* and *Remote Control.*[5] In fact, the media may be somewhat less powerful than we have previously imagined in shaping our individual actions and thoughts (for example, our vote, our prejudices, our position on an issue). When researchers have examined the relative power of the media to "shape" the public's thinking, they have come up with a reassuring finding, namely that the media's public has proven remarkably resistant to domination. The media's influence may be less effective in determining a particular decision or action as it is in shaping what we consider worthy of our attention, what we might call the public agenda. The media may not easily be able to make a prejudiced person unprejudiced, but it may help to keep us from even considering certain practices as matters of prejudice, articulating them instead in other terms, for example, as professional or social policy debates.

Besides specific, conscious content relevant to a story (for example, a person's age, the level of a person's disability, the ethical questions being raised) the media set a story's tone be it exciting, a drama, a tragedy, a contest, or entertainment. And usually, news writers have more or less "stock" ways of presenting a particular issue. Disability, for example, is typically cast in terms of tragedy, of charity and its attendant emotion, pity, or of struggle and accomplishment. When reporters approach any story, they bring with them one or a combination of such standard "frames" for presenting it to the readers.[6]

In the mid 1970s, Kenneth Jernigan, president of the National Federation of the Blind, wrote on the difficulty of moving the media beyond its stereotypic "frame" of people with disabilities. He recounted an incident in which a reporter at a political action convention chose to write from a traditional, debilitating "frame" rather than focus on the issues of discrimination, civil rights, and political organizing that were the meat of the conference:

> A reporter . . . came to one of our meetings and said, "I'd like to get pictures of blind persons bowling and of some of the members with their dogs." I tried to explain to him that such a story would be a distortion--that we were there to discuss refusal by employers to let us work, refusal by airlines to let us ride, refusal by hotels to let us stay, refusal by society to let us in, and refusal by social service agencies to let us out. He said he was glad I had told him and that it had been very helpful and enlightening. Then he added, "Now, could I see the dogs and the bowlers? I am in quite a rush."
>
> Deep down (at the gut level) they [the public and the media] regard us as inferior, incompetent, unable to lead an everyday life of joy and sorrow, and necessarily less fortunate than they. In the past we have tended to see ourselves as others have seen us. . . . But no more! That day is at an end. We have not (in the present day parlance) been perceived as a minority. Yet, that is exactly what we are--a minority, with all that the term implies.[7]

In a statement at the opening of the International Games for the Disabled, President Reagan "hailed the participants as champions of the heart."[8] That phrase, "champions of the heart," became the cornerstone of a *New York Times* account of the games' opening. The framework or dominant themes of the story were all too predictable: people with disabilities rising above sadness; overcoming physical limitations and inability; displaying courage and determination. The president provided the frame and the *New York Times* reported and featured it, offering no countervailing perspective:

> There's something that each of you understands that no one else can ever fully appreciate, something that has to do with courage, with willpower, and with the utter refusal to give up, that has enabled you to rise above your disabilities and compete.
>
> Sports has less to do with things like times and weights and distances than with something very simple—the human heart.
>
> And when it comes to that, the athletes in Los Angeles [at the Olympic Games] will have to tip their hats to you, because you're the champions of the world.[9]

President Reagan's comments were typical of disability sports coverage. When the *Washington Post* published an account of the Capital Wheelchair Races, the reporter commented in the second paragraph of the story, "Overshadowing the event itself was the spirit of the participants. If size of heart were the sole criteria [sic], all of the approximately 60 competitors, ranging in age from 8 to full-grown adults, would receive gold medals."[10] Similarly, for example, in covering the Special Olympics, reporters typically emphasize the "overcoming-great-odds" or "see-what-they-can-do" angle rather than more typical sports data. "It makes you feel lucky, just seeing them out here giving it a try. . . . It does one good," one reporter recounts being told by a self-congratulatory organizer. Then, speaking of the volunteers who helped stage the Olympics, there was the matter of charity: "You see the kids smiling a lot," the reporter was told, "It makes them feel good about themselves and helping other people raises their self esteem."[11]

When journalism transforms an issue or event into a story, the reported account is not the "real" event as perceived by the participants but is journalism's rendition or interpretation of the event. Journalism's account almost certainly cannot be a neutral or objective presentation. To understand this fact, we must examine the print media's inherent limitations and characteristics. Consider, for example, that newspapers are a commercial product. They employ limited numbers of reporters to cover nearly unlimited numbers and types of stories; reporters constitute one of the most expensive elements in producing news. Because reporters must cover a multitude of different issues, they cannot achieve expertise in all or even a few of them. Official sources (for example, government officials, professions, or experts) provide a ready, if managed, supply of background information. Reporters must meet urgent deadlines. They must quickly develop a framework for determining key elements to a story. They cannot delve into too much depth on a story—they have neither time nor space for that. They live by the principle "keep it simple." A reporter looks for "handles" that can make for a salient, recognizeable story.

Now let us return to the coverage of the Baby Jane Doe and Elizabeth Bouvia stories. How were these stories handled? What "frames" did journalism employ to present them? What were the dominant issues? What can we learn from these stories about the place of disabilities in American culture and social policy?

Baby Jane Doe and Elizabeth Bouvia attracted media attention for the controversies that surrounded them, but also because they provided a sort of modern-day version of the 1950s daytime television show "Queen for a Day" or the century-old *New York Times* 100 neediest cases. Contestants on "Queen for a Day" told their heart-rending stories of cancer, disability, lost jobs, death, and poverty, each hoping that the audience would determine her most worthy of becoming "queen" for the day and receiving a truckload of prizes. The audience would clap and yell for each contestant. An "applause meter" would measure the audience's preference. The Doe and Bouvia cases, like a prevailing stereotype of people with disability, presented the vision of despair, pain, sorrow, desperation, and defeat. Elizabeth Bouvia has been described as "the 26-year-old cerebral palsy victim who says she wants to starve to death to end a lifetime of severe disability,"[12] and as "paralyzed since birth as a result of cerebral palsy . . . [with] practically no use of her limbs or control of her bodily functions. She also suffers from severe arthritis."[13] A headline on the Elizabeth Bouvia story reads, "Paralytic Choosing Death Over Life of Pain."[14]

Descriptions of Baby Jane Doe were, if anything, even more bleak. The descriptions were spare if objective: "The infant, who is now 26 days old, suffers from spina bifida—a failure of the spinal cord to close properly—along with hydrocephalus or excess fluid of the brain."[15] It also became commonplace, as we noted earlier, for newspapers and other media to add that "doctors have said that without surgery she was likely to die within two years, and with surgery she could survive into her 20's but would be severely retarded and bedridden." An attending doctor did make such a prognosis, and it did not take long for that statement to become more or less accepted dogma for news accounts. On November 4, 1984, the *New York Times* editorial writers remarked:

> "He's not going to get better" is the gentle phrase people often use to describe someone who's *hopelessly ill.* It applies, tragically, to Baby Jane Doe, a deformed baby born on Long Island last month. Spina bifida is only one of her handicaps. Even if she underwent an operation to correct that and gained perhaps 20 years of life, *what a life it would be: severely retarded and bedridden.* Her parents, after considerable medical consultation, decided against the operation. Baby Jane, everyone agreed, is not going to get better (emphasis added).[16]

In one of the most extensive reports on the child's condition, Baby Jane Doe's father is quoted as saying:

> We were told she would have no control over her bladder or rectal functions. And we were also told that she probably had brain malfunction. We were told by our doctors that the part of the brain that controls much of our awareness was either missing or not entirely formed. The mother remarked, We are not talking about a spina bifida child, one who could perhaps walk someday with braces. They are showing these kids on television when they discuss our case. She will be an epileptic. Her condition for future life is to be bedridden, and she would not have use of her hands. Her legs are like dead fish. She doesn't feel them. *She would never know love.* And while she might feel sorrow and joy, her overall condition would be pain (emphasis added).[17]

The *Times* seems to accept uncritically Baby Jane Doe's parents' prognosis. Yet no one familiar with severe disabilities and with recent developments in educational and rehabilitation could share their certainty. Is it really possible to predict so early in a child's life that she will always feel pain? On what basis is it claimed that she will probably know sorrow and joy, but not love? Even the seemingly medical determination that "she will be bedridden for the rest of her life" appears overly pessimistic. One of the first families I met upon entering the field of social policy and disability was a family that included a child named Jeff who had the same disabilities as Baby Jane Doe at birth. He is severely disabled. He attended school, albeit his parents had to fight for it. And he developed far beyond what has been reported possible for Baby Jane Doe. He has feelings; he can express his feelings. He is very much a part of his family.[18]

Media analyst Steven Baer has called the reporting of the Baby Jane Doe case "the half-story."[19] In examining media coverage of the story, he discovered that doctors who observed Baby Jane Doe disagreed about whether or not she should be treated. Newspapers had incorrectly interpreted one doctor's remarks that Baby Jane Doe could live into her twenties as meaning that she could live only to 20 years, then repeated the error endlessly. And, as it turns out, the mainstream media (that is, the *New York Times* and the TV networks) failed to seek independent advice on how to analyze Baby Jane Doe's case. As Baer notes, few spoke with Dr. David G. McLone, professor of surgery at Northwestern University and a national expert on spina bifida who has treated over 1,000 such children and whose view of Baby Jane Doe, based on a reading of the trial transcripts, dramatically contradicts the media coverage. McLone predicted that with surgery she might achieve intelligence in the normal range and would probably be able to walk, with the aid of braces. (One of the few who did talk to Dr. McLone was Nat Hentoff, see Chapter 10.)

The vision we derive from the *Times'* barebones account is one of a family imprisoned by the presence of a severely disabled child. We learn nothing of the revolution in community-based, integrated (disabled and nondisabled children together) services emerging across the country as alternatives to noncare or to institutionalization. We learn nothing of respite care, homemaker service, independent living, integrated day care, special education, life sharing, and a host of other programs, which when available improve the life opportunities of people with severe disabilities.

To the extent that the *Times* hints at the existence or relevance of such services, it does so obliquely. The *Times* rightfully criticizes the Reagan administration for, on the one hand, saying it cares deeply for the equal rights of severely disabled students while, on the other hand, masterminding funding cuts in the very social programs that such children and their families will need to live decent, quality lives.

Elizabeth Bouvia articles virtually mimicked Doe accounts in their failure to address the matter of quality services. Scant mention is made in the dozens of articles that a principle difficulty in Elizabeth Bouvia's life was the unavailability of competent and reliable aides to assist her in daily living. Aides are typically paid minimum wage, have little if any training, and approach their work of assisting people with severe disabilities with uneven enthusiasm and care. Some, of course, accomplish their work effectively as true allies; more do not.

It is true that newspapers recounted many of the problems Elizabeth Bouvia faced in her life. The *Washington Post,* for example, on December 6, 1984, cited Elizabeth Bouvia's estranged husband's testimony that "his wife was placed in an institution when she was 10. She blamed herself for her parents' divorce when she was 5 years old and told him she felt like 'a spare suitcase, very unwanted and rejected' when they rarely visited her in the institutions where she spent her youth."[20] But we never learn, at least from the popular press, that finding aides, securing funding for quality support services, securing reliable wheelchairs, repairing wheelchairs, getting transportation, and the dozens of other essential support services are as a matter of course excruciatingly difficult to come by. Why did Elizabeth Bouvia declare, "I choose no longer to be dependent on others?"[21] Was it that she did not ask for help, or that help was so difficult in coming? Was it that she got tired of having to ask for help? Was it painful to have to ask continually every day? Was it depressing that assistance was not available naturally, as a matter of course, in the same way that giving a neighbor a lift to work, commenting on a colleague's draft article, teaching an office mate how to use the computer, or making dinner for friends are part of living the interdependent life? In only one news account do we learn of such difficulties. On December 9, 1983, Elizabeth Bouvia's estranged husband's court testimony was reported. He described how difficult it was for Mrs. Bouvia to keep home attendants who saw to her basic needs. After a turnover of several attendants, he testified she began doubting herself: "'What am I doing wrong?' she asked. A lot of times she would cry herself to sleep."[22]

Aside from that single instance, it was commentators, as distinguished from news reporters, who provided us a glimpse of these issues. Robert Bernstein wrote in an op ed published by the *New York Times:*

> We have officially abandoned the philosophy of Plato, in whose ideal society the "deformed" were to be "put away in some mysterious, unknown place, as they should be." We are also beyond the day when a Chicago ordinance made criminal the mere appearance in public of any person who was "in any way deformed so as to be an unsightly or disgusting object." But we are only a few years past the time when Harold Krentz, a blind lawyer who was the inspiration for the movie and play "Butterflies are Free," became perhaps the first Harvard Law School graduate ever to be turned down by more than 40 law firms. And we live in an age that often measures young women's appearance on a scale of 1 to 10, and young men's by their resemblance to the rollicking he-men of Miller-land. We've come a long way. But like some poor soul in a deodorant commercial, we apparently lack the "secure, confident feeling" that, in this instance, would enable us to quietly accept Elizabeth Bouvia into our midst.[23]

But acceptance in this case is so much more than an acceptance of diversity; if we read between the lines or, more accurately, read what did not appear in the popular press, we would know that acceptance would involve something affirmative, addressing needs related to independent living. As another commentator, this time a disabled author and activist, G. Janet Tulloch, found, the alternative to dying might mean life in an institution or life in relative isolation in the community. It is not a pleasant picture, but it puts disability in perspective, in a context created by the nondisabled world:

> Not everybody is created to live long years of physical impairment. Nursing homes are not staffed with personnel giving constant care with willingness and generosity. As a social worker, Bouvia would find this system particularly difficult. Unless she could afford a private nurse in her home she would be housed with the elderly and dying. Her companions would be few; she may even be ostracized for removing the mask of happy acceptance of severe tribulation.
> She has shattered the myth of Tiny Tim.[24]

Are these the alternatives? Nursing homes for the destitute disabled? Isolation and loneliness for the moneyed disabled?

It is no accident that the popular print media failed to investigate the day-to-day realities of severely disabled people stymied by a disability-ignorant and disability-denying society. The media's standard framework did not include such things. If the media were to cover that story it would do so in the context of noting the "high costs" of accommodating "the disabled." But more often, print journalism simply does not consider the disability rights movement's, or for that matter the individual disabled person's, perspective on independent living. The prevailing framework for covering disabilities, a combination of charity, pity, tragedy, and "overcoming disability" makes no place for this story.

By covering right-to-life and ethicist perspectives on the Doe and Bouvia cases, print journalism still came no closer to understanding or reporting what are to people with disabilities the real issues at stake. Both of these groups spoke of rights, but not of disability rights. As we have seen, to speak of "the right to live" does not really address society's failure to make that right appealing or enjoyable. The *New York Times* correctly saw through Surgeon General Dr. Everett Koop's remark that, "We're not fighting for this baby. We're fighting for the principle of this country that every life is individually and uniquely sacred. . . . If we do not intrude into the life of a child such as this, whose civil rights may be abrogated? The next person may be you."[25] To fight for the right to live is simply not enough--ironically, the *Times* never explained what services these might be, what they would look like, what the life opportunities can be for a person with a severe disability. Conservative columnist George Will, who also happens to be the parent of a child with a disability, implied in his account of the Doe case that the Reagan administration really did have a rights orientation:

> America is on the threshold of another great inclusion, that of handicapped, and especially mentally handicapped, persons. This is Ronald Reagan's doing, and he is getting neither help nor credit from the self-appointed custodians (liberal newspapers) of the nation's conscience regarding civil rights.[26]

But where is the evidence that Ronald Reagan's cause was civil rights, broadly defined? We know that Dr. Koop was concerned with the right to life. And we know that the Department of Justice was essentially of this mind as well. William Reynolds, an assistant U.S. attorney general, in an op ed published in the *New York Times,* noted the different life experience that families of children with severe disabilities face—"a difference in economic burden, in emotional strain, in responsibilities assumed and undertaken, and in just plain work."[27] But the civil rights issue was not defined by Reynolds as a right to quality living, rather it was a right against harm: "a child, no matter how young and how severely handicapped, has a claim of right to the protection of state laws prohibiting child abuse and neglect on an equal basis with any other child."[28]

The *Times* castigated Koop for this double-speak: of concern for people with disabilities coming from an administration that had systematically cut funding and had attempted to cut rights laws for people with disabilities. After all, the *Times* noted, this concern for Baby Doe was coming from "the same administration that came to office promising to get the Federal Government off people's backs."[29] But the *Times'* editorials still failed to recognize a broader vision of rights. The *Times* seemed more interested in protecting the medical profession's autonomy and possibly parental authority—although this seems not quite credible since the *Times* would protect nondisabled youngsters' rights to live or to receive other needed treatment when in conflict with parental wishes— than with articulating and defending the interests of people with disabilities. And, part of the problem was that the news media had a hard time viewing Baby Jane Doe as a discriminated-against person, much less part of a minority group that suffered massive systematic discrimination. In a nationally syndicated story, Carl Rowan articulated the difficulty that he and the press have in seeing Baby Jane Doe as the object of discrimination.

> This is interesting, because those who try to justify limited government intrusion into such matters are arguing that in swooping down to protect Baby Doe the federal government is only doing what President Eisenhower did when he sent in federal troops to end racial segregation in the public schools of Little Rock, or what President John F. Kennedy did when he used troops to get James Meredith into the University of Mississippi.
>
> The comparisons are illogical and unworthy of those bright and dedicated people who think Baby Jane Doe has gotten a bum deal.
>
> In Little Rock, Arkansas, and Oxford, Mississippi, our presidents faced situations where there was obvious discrimination against an entire race of people, with governors and other state and city officials not only admitting to violations of the law of the land, but boasting that they intended to continue to defy the law. Eisenhower and Kennedy had no choice but to uphold their oaths to enforce the law.
>
> In the case of Baby Jane Doe, the federal government did not move against obvious and defiant violations of the infant's civil rights. The baby's parents suffered night and day over the medical and other options before them. They got doctors, social counselors, religious advisers to agonize with them and help them to a decision. The courts found no civil rights violations.[30]

Would Carl Rowan have us believe that parents, doctors, and religious groups cannot discriminate? Would he have us believe that if a court proceeding fails to see discrimination or, as in the Doe case, evades the issue altogether by a narrow, perhaps even technical interpretation of the law, then there is no discrimination?

First, there was the question of how the *New York Times* and the *Washington Post* could have failed to connect the Baby Jane Doe case to the national experience with deinstitutionalization over the past two decades. Both papers had covered the horrors of institutions extensively. Both had detailed the development of community residences, supportive apartments, family support programs, and opportunities for schooling that were for the first time becoming available on a near universal basis to disabled students, including severely disabled students. And in the five years just prior to the unfolding of the Elizabeth Bouvia and the Baby Jane Doe cases, national rehabilitation policy and educational policy had placed nearly total emphasis on creating models of service for those most severely disabled. Public schools in many states had begun serving severely disabled students, including those with disabilities as severe as Baby Jane Doe's. The *Washington Post* had reported extensively on the development of national policies affecting severely disabled persons. Why then did neither paper connect these developments with the Doe and Bouvia cases?

Independent living had been a major policy thrust of the Rehabilitation Services Administration, modeled after the Center for Independent Living (CIL), a self-help organization in Berkeley, California. CIL has lobbied long and hard for adequate funding of basic support services such as personal aides, accessible mass transportation, accessible restaurants, housing, and public accommodations, income support, adequate funding of technological aides such as wheelchairs and communication systems, and so forth. But neither the Center for Independent Living nor other leading advocacy groups were queried in any but the most superficial terms about their perceptions of what it means to struggle for independence day-to-day and what this might tell us about Elizabeth Bouvia's case or Baby Jane Doe's future.

In both stories readers were led to believe that while the cases were surely symptomatic of larger issues, they were essentially individual dramas. Baby Jane Doe was one child about whom a handful of doctors and the child's parents were agonizing. Elizabeth Bouvia was one woman who was challenging the medical establishment by asking for assistance in suicide, which had never before been requested by a severely disabled, but certainly not terminally ill or dying person. But neither picture is quite true. Elizabeth Bouvia is certainly not unlike the elderly man in Frederick Wiseman's classic film *Titticut Follies* about institutional life, who decides to stop eating and thereby to kill himself.

And is her plight really any different than that of hundreds of elderly people who, when consigned to nursing homes, die within weeks of being "placed?"

In the case of newborn severely disabled infants, the decision to treat or not treat may be made more often than newspapers would lead us to believe, perhaps even in some cases virtually as a standard procedure rather than as highly individualized events. As evidenced in this article:

> Siamese twins are refused treatment and die, distinguished medical educators report that it is common practice to withhold lifesaving treatment to disabled infants, and there are scholars who devise schemes (even simple formulas) to determine whether an individual is human or not. At the University of Oklahoma Life Sciences Center, doctors report on an "early selection and treatment" program for newborns with Myelomeningocile. Of the 69 babies evaluated, 36 were recommended for aggressive treatment and all lived except for one who died in an auto accident. Of the 24 who were given only "supportive care" (food and water) all 24 died between 1 and 189 days of age. When parents rejected the advice to give their newborns only supportive care, several survived and are vigorous.[31]

How coldly and mechanistically the Oklahoma doctors invoked a formula: QL (Quality of Life)=NE (Natural Endowment) x H (Contribution from Home and Family, (that is, read social-economic status) + S (Contribution from Society) to determine who should live and who should die.[32]

Accounts of the Baby Jane Doe case, which began at precisely the same time (October 1983) as the Oklahoma doctors published their "procedures" in *Pediatrics,* simply did not reveal the extent to which handling of severely impaired newborn children may be subject to institutional procedures such as those developed at the Oklahoma Life Sciences Center. But of course to make such connections would involve viewing Baby Jane Doe as a member of a class of people, which, by prejudice, is placed in criminal danger, and not merely as a tragically deformed "case".

While the *Times* recognized the conflict between disability rights activists and right-to-life advocates such as the Baby Jane Doe intervener, Lawrence Washburn, coverage of this story did little to change the paper's framework for reporting the story. On February 19, 1984, Robert Pear wrote:

> Anti-abortion groups say they are concerned about the quality of the lives they save but some disability rights advocates say the concern was slow in coming. In a recent statement of principles, these advocates declared: "Once a decision to treat an infant has been made, government and private agencies must be

prepared to allocate adequate resources for appropriate services" to the child and family for as long as needed. By pushing for such allocations, disability rights groups say, they part from most anti-abortion organizations.[33]

Aside from this and two or three other paragraphs in a veritable sea of popular print media coverage of the Doe and Bouvia cases, reporting focused nearly exclusively on the narrower issues of whether Baby Jane Doe and Elizabeth Bouvia should be allowed to live or die and whose right is it to decide. A broader debate over rights to service and the responsiveness of society to people with disabilities never materialized as a story in the popular press. This point was not lost on disability rights advocates as their articles in movement publications attest.

Disability rights commentators begin from a perspective or frame of discrimination, not tragedy, charity, or "overcoming disability." For example, writing on the Doe and other such cases, Michelle Fine and Adrienne Asch (Women and Disability Awareness Project) shift our perspectives from the Baby Jane Does of the world to the society itself: "Further it is absolutely essential to understand that the pain and 'tragedy' of living with a disability in our culture, such as it is, derives primarily from the pain and humiliation of discrimination, oppression and anti-disability attitudes, not from the disability itself."[34] In a letter to the *Disability Rag,* Joyce Trout, like Fine and Asch, derives from this vision of social discrimination a need for basic rights. That, she says, is the big issue behind the more narrow right-to-die question advanced in Elizabeth Bouvia's stories:

> Our government is of the people, by the people, and for the people. For all the people. We as citizens are guaranteed freedom of choice under the First Amendment. However, it is denied to handicapped people—just another form of discrimination. We are alienated, manipulated and intimidated by a government that is supposed to protect all citizens. We don't have the right to choose a career, housing, transportation. We are patronized and spoken to in a condescending manner, without any concern for our emotional or physical needs.
>
> The "starving technique" Bouvia chose is only a manifestation of the deep rooted problems stemming from how disabled people are treated. We must continue to bring to the forefront our injustices and concerns. It is only through such national attention that society will deal with the real issue facing us.[35]

Despite the apparent support that disability rights groups found from the Right, namely from right-to-life advocates, they ended up feeling estranged and fundamentally at odds with both the Right and Left in the Doe case. *Disability Rag* editor, Mary Johnson, is as critical of the liberal press as she is of Baby Jane Doe right-to-life advocates in their failure to pose the question of Doe and Bouvia correctly. Of the right-to-life groups she complains:

> Washburn and others like him would save disabled infants; but would save them for a purpose very like that which Bouvia is convinced society has saved her for. Is that the legacy we wish for ourselves?
>
> This is not the Right to Life's issue; it is our issue.[36]

And to liberals and the rest of society, she asks:

> Why does society assume that deformed people must inherently be a "drain" on society—without ever once bothering to look at why we're a drain? Why doesn't society look at whether anything might be done about that?[37]

The central difficulty of the popular press, indeed of the society at large, was and is a failure of perspective. Again, and finally, we turn to the disability rights press for an analysis of "the central issue":

> Why isn't independence coming for us as it's coming for nondisabled society? Because society believes disabled people *ought* to be dependent. To be disabled is to be dependent *by nature*. To allow vast changes in the way disabled people live would shake the very foundations of this belief.
>
> This is why it's still so hard for most disabled people to get beyond dependence.[38]

NOTES

1. Kathleen Kerr, "Reporting the Case of Baby Jane Doe," *The Hastings Center Report*, vol. 14, no. 4 (1984), pp. 7-9.

2. David Margolick, "Battle for 'Baby Doe,'" *New York Times*, October 25, 1983, p. 81.

3. Ibid.

4. "Paralytic Choosing Death Over a Life of Pain," *New York Times*, October 30, 1983, p. 38.

5. Frank Mankiewicz and Joel Swerdlow, *Remote Control* (New York: Ballantine Books, 1978); David Halberstam, *The Powers That Be* (New York: Dell, 1979).

6. Todd Gitlin, *The Whole World is Watching* (Berkeley: University of California Press, 1980).

7. Kenneth Jernigan, "Blindness: Is the Public Against Us?" (Address at the banquet of the Annual Convention of the National Federation of the Blind, Chicago, July 3, 1975).

8. "Games for the Disabled Begin," *New York Times*, June 18, 1984, p. A1.

9. Francis X. Clines, "Reagan Hails Athletes in Games for Disabled," *New York Times*, June 18, 1984, p. B3.

10. Adam Goldstein, "Capital Wheelchair Races: 'Competing is the Real Fun,'" *Washington Post,* April 17, 1983, p. F16.

11. Scott Moore, "Pride and Self-esteem Special Olympics Products," *Washington Post,* May 6, 1984, p. H9.

12. Judith Cummings, "Husband Opposes Wife's Wish to Starve to Death," *New York Times,* December 9, 1983, p. A19.

13. Walter Goodman, "Quadriplegic's Efforts to Die Stir Deep Legal and Ethical Issues," *New York Times,* January 3, 1984, p. A16.

14. "Paralytic Choosing Death Over Life of Pain," *N.Y. Times.*

15. Marcia Chambers, "U.S. Has Hospital Data in L.I. 'Baby Doe' Case," *New York Times,* November 5, 1983, p. A30.

16. "Baby Janes's Big Brothers," *New York Times,* November 4, 1984, p. A26.

17. Marcia Chambers, "Parents of Baby Doe Criticize 'Intrusion' by U.S.," *New York Times,* November 6, 1983, p. A45.

18. Elizabeth Pieper, *Sticks and Stones* (Syracuse: Human Policy Press, 1975).

19. Steven Baer, "The Half-Told Story of Baby Jane Doe," *Columbia Journalism Review* (November/December 1984), pp. 35-38.

20. Jay Mathews, "Cerebral Palsy Victim Asks Help in Dying," *Washington Post,* December 6, 1984, p. A2.

21. Ellen Goodman, "Whose Life?" *Washington Post,* December 24, 1983, sec. 1, p. 15.

22. Cummings, "Husband Opposes Wife's Wish."

23. Robert A. Bernstein, "Accept the Disabled," *New York Times,* January 10, 1984, p. A23.

24. G. Janet Tullock, "A Case in Which Suicide Is Not Cowardly," *Washington Post,* January 29, 1984, sec. 1V, p. 5.

25. "Baby Jane's 'Defender,' " *New York Times,* November 11, 1983, p. A30.

26. George F. Will, "Unfashionable Civil Rights," *Washington Post,* November 13, 1984, p. C7.

27. William B. Reynolds, "Why the Government Is Pressing the 'Baby Doe' Case," *New York Times,* March 18, 1984, p. A25.

28. Ibid.

29. "Civil Rights: The Movement Moves," *New York Times,* November 4, 1983, p. 18.

30. Carl Rowan, "A Cry for Sanity in 'Baby Jane Doe' Cases," *Syracuse Herald American,* December 4, 1983, p. 24.

31. Burton Blatt and Douglas Biklen, "Ethics," in *Mental Retardation and Developmental Disabilities Review* ed. Joseph Wortis (New York: Plenum, 1985).

32. R. H. Gross, A. Cox, R. Tatyrek, M. Pollay, and W. A. Barnes, "Early Management and Decision Making for the Treatment of Myelomeningocile," *Pediatrics,* vol. 72, no. 4 (October 1983), pp. 450-58.

33. Robert Pear, "'Baby Doe' Advocates are an Unlikely Team," *New York Times,* February 19, 1984, sec. 1V, p. 20.

34. Michelle Fine and Adrienne Asch, "Amniocentesis, Treatment of Newborns with Disabilities and Women's Choices," *Carasa News* (Committee for Abortion Rights and Against Sterilization Abuse), vol. 8, no. 4 (June/July 1984), p. 3.

35. Joyce Trout, "Bouvia's Choice," (letter to the editor), *Disability Rag* (August 1984), p. 14.

36. Mary Johnson, "The Right Is the Wrong Group to Plead Our Rights," *Disability Rag* (February/March, 1984), p. 11.

37. Ibid., p. 12.

38. S. L. Rosen, "Dependency," *Disability Rag* (February/March 1984), p. 23.

6

Procedural Rights in the Wrong System: Special Education is Not Enough

Lisa J. Walker

INTRODUCTION

In November 1975, Congress passed and the president signed into law, Pub. L. No. 94-142, The Education for All Handicapped Children Act. Following three years of hearings, a decade of court cases, and prior congressional and state legislative actions, this legislation codified a baseline of rights, procedures, and guidelines for intergovernmental relationships that have defined public policy for children and youth with disabilities in educational services and, to some extent, in other social services areas as well. While it is not wholly unambiguous, Pub. L. No. 94-142 is the clearest expression by government of the rights and expectations of persons with disabilities in law.[1]

Ten years after passage of Pub. L. No. 94-142, there is substantial success, from the standpoint of implementation of national policy. The number of disabled children served by schools has increased by about 500,000 over the number served since 1976-77 (4.0 million in 1982-83),[2] and school officials believe they have identified and are serving all children in need of services.[3] Given the 10 percent decline in overall school enrollment since 1976-77, the number of students with handicapping conditions in schools has grown from 3 percent of enrollment to 11 percent in 1982-83.[4] Assessment and evaluation procedures appear to be in place (although timeliness and proximity continue to be problems), and thousands of students are evaluated or reevaluated, and placed or "decertified" each year. Compared to the early experience under the law, teachers generally agree that the Individualized Education

Program (IEP) is helpful in identifying learning needs and teaching options for each student. And, parents, in general, believe that schools are more responsive.

The federal mandate has had massive impact: in part because it paralleled state policy; in part because of its structuring of funding, governance, and rights requirements; and in part because its mission was timely.[5]

Pub. L. No. 94-142 was a lighthouse for disabled children and youth in our schools. It asked much of state and local officials, it promised much to parents and children, and it added much to our understanding and sensitivity about disability. Its careful analysis provides a picture of the status of disabled children and youth in our nation's schools. To what extent has the underlying purpose of the Education for All Handicapped Children Act—the integration of disabled children in our classrooms and the improvement in quality of their education—been accomplished? To what extent have the detailed requirements of this law structured the reform of education for children with disabilities and their treatment by educators and administrators? And, to what extent has the mainstream of public education embraced these goals and found ways to expand thinking about children as children regardless of their shapes, sizes, and coping abilities?

Court cases such as *Rowley, Tatro,* and *Smith* continue to raise questions in the public debate about the extent to which disabled students will be guaranteed access to an education that will serve them well in the mainstream in their adult life. To the extent that these questions are answered within the boundaries of special services in our schools, disabled students will continue to experience differences in options in education because the fundamental goal of integration cannot be reached by relying on the special services model. Unless new focus is provided nationally and at the state level on the broader issues of integration of program and resources, the debate about educational rights seems destined to be tied up in endless disputes over delivering special services with decreasing resources.

The Provisions of Pub. L. No. 94-142

The congressional reports filed with Pub. L. No. 94-142, floor statements during its debate, and the explicit statement of findings in the law convey a clarity of purpose: to correct the problems of exclusion and discrimination in the way children with disabilities were being treated. While speaking to the special needs of these children, nearly all of the provisions of the law were designed to remedy systemic effects—problems an excluded class of children experienced because the public school system (and other public agencies, for that matter) did not accept them as their charge.

Nine basic principles can be derived from the provisions of the law.

Establish the Right of Access to Public Education Programs

Prior to enactment of Pub. L. No. 94-142 and state mandatory statutes, disabled children had no guarantee that they would be accepted by public school agencies. Exclusionary clauses, refusal to provide services, charging parents for services in a system otherwise guaranteeing a free public education, and denial of entry to integrated programs were documented during the hearing process and in casework carried out by individual congressional offices. Congress concluded that the mandatory provisions of the federal law were justified under its responsibilities to guarantee equal protection of the laws under the Fourteenth Amendment to the Constitution.

Require Individualization of Services to Alter Automatic Assumptions about Disability

The special educational needs of disabled children, particularly those with more severe handicaps, were not being met in schools. Congress was clearly concerned that existing programs were based on categories of handicaps and not on individual needs, that services were not available in regular classrooms or in an integrated school environment, that parents and family members experienced difficulties in obtaining "appropriate" educational services for their children, and that minority and culturally different children were identified and placed in special education at rates substantially higher than their numbers in the general population would warrant.

Establish the Principle that Disabled Children Need not be Removed from Regular Classes

Congress was interested in the normalization of services for disabled children, in the belief that the presence of a disability did not necessarily require separation and removal from the regular classrooms, or the neighborhood school environment, or from regular academic classes. While children with severe intellectual or emotional impairments might require separate classes and highly specialized services, the emphasis on service delivery should be the needs of the child, not traditional or convenient patterns of services.

Broaden the Scope of Services Provided by Schools

Consistent with the principle of integration of disabled children in schools was the need to expand services available to support their academic program. The provision of related services necessary for a child to benefit from the integrated environment should be part of the school program, as are general health services, extracurricular activities, and other developmental and support services provided to nondisabled children. Pub. L. No. 94-142 reinforced a general move away from the medical model for disabled children, acknowledging that all children needed to be educated and that medical diagnoses were not always helpful in determining educational needs, although the law also stipulated that some related (medical) services were necessary to the educational mission.

Establish a Process for Determining the Scope of Services

Definitions of categories of services were delineated according to current service patterns, assuming that these would be a sufficient guide for service delivery for children in the least restrictive environment. Appropriate services meant what was sufficient to meet the student's diagnosed needs through the individualized program, with parents, teachers, and school systems being equal in the decision-making process. Safeguards through a negotiating and appeals process would allow parents the ability to challenge the school system's experts, to seek other experts and counsel, and to agree on a program of services, to appeal further, or to go to court. Congress was satisfied to describe the normalization principles it was concerned about, to provide examples of the services it intended to authorize, and to allow states and local agencies some discretion in an area of decision making that was likely to change.

Establish General Guidelines for Identification of Disability

However, Congress was not willing to leave definition and identification wholly to the good intentions of educators. In an area where there was some difference of opinion about the size of the population and the definitional characteristics of specific learning disabilities, Congress placed a 2 percent (of total school population) cap on the number of children eligible to be counted, pending a study by the Commission of Education. Further, the law placed an overall 12 percent cap on the proportion of the school population eligible to be identified and counted as disabled for the purposes of funding. Provisions establishing procedural protections in identification, assessment, and placement likewise guided the definition of disability.

Establish Principles for Primary State and Local Responsibility

Congress was assisting states and localities to provide education through federal financial assistance, although state and local educational agencies retained a primary role in providing an appropriate education for all disabled children. Congress acknowledged both that current resources were not sufficient, during the deep recession of 1974-75, and that it intended real action in return for financial assistance. Stringent programmatic conditions of eligibility had to be met prior to submission of a state plan and assistance was tied to children being served.

Clarify Lines of Authority for Educational Services

To resolve the overlapping lines of responsibility for services in each state in order to assure that educational services could be guaranteed to disabled children on the same basis as they were guaranteed to nondisabled children, Congress established a clear line of authority through the educational system in each state. The state educational agency and, through it, each local educational agency became responsible for assuring appropriate education and related services. While multiple agencies and funding sources might assist in service provision, the state remained the final responsible unit for assuring a free public education for all handicapped children regardless of where the child received services.

Move Beyond Staffing and Training of Personnel

While Pub. L. No. 94-142 addressed the issue of personnel training and required a comprehensive system of personnel development, it rejected the capacity-building models of the 1960s and the question of whether staff were sufficiently knowledgeable about or trained to educate disabled children. Inservice and preservice training would be necessary, but not insurmountable, barriers to the principal problem of establishing the rights of disabled children to a public education guaranteed to their nondisabled peers.

Congress did not focus at length on relationships between special education and general education in the public schools, the methodologies or curricular content of special education, or what would be sufficient to meet the learning needs of different disabled students. These were professional judgments, to be left to educators, within the parameters of procedural safeguards, including access to the courts. This would assure that the needs of children were individually examined and that conflicts in professional and parental judgments would be resolved.

Concerns about children with severe disabilities focused on their separation from the mainstream—that is, out-of-school and out-of-district placements, in separate schools, centers, hospitals, and institutions. The law reflects a strong presumption that public authorities would follow the prescriptive goals for all children with disabilities, that is normalization and services in the mainstream, once responsibility within the public education sector was established. Federal policy assumed that disabled children were children—some with different and specialized needs—but all able to participate in the public school without confronting problems of professional turf, stigma, and differential resource allocation. Having established detailed governance relationships and procedural protections to guide each step of the educational process, federal policy left definitional issues of who is eligible, what they are eligible for, and in what setting largely up to state and local judgment, checked by the strengthened hands of parents and advocates who could invoke due process procedures and appeals, if necessary.

WHERE ARE WE TODAY?

In comparison to the patchwork of services available previously, students have more options in curriculum, and school officials increasingly provide services within local school districts for severely and multiply disabled students who were previously served in private or other out-of-school or out-of-district placements.[6] However, fiscal constraints appear to be slowing the enlargement of options for students.

Given the overlapping lines of incomplete responsibility that existed in 1976-77, school districts and states have taken on enormous responsibility in identifying and providing services to students previously served by multiple agencies. Growth in state and local revenues for special education document these increases in responsibility. Estimated at $8.4 billion in 1979-80, these funds had been increasing by 10 to 20 percent for the previous three years, a rate much greater than the annual growth for general education funds.[7] States document that they are currently serving children and youth previously served in institutions, nursing homes, camps, foster homes, juvenile justice programs, and numerous private schools and other facilities.

There are, however, serious problems lurking behind these numbers. Some may be temporary problems that will be solved in time; others go to the heart of the mission of Pub. L. No. 94-142 and public education itself.

GROWTH IN NUMBERS OF DISABLED CHILDREN

While growth in students identified as disabled and served in education programs has increased since 1976-77 by some 500,000, this change has not been uniform across disability categories. By far the greatest change has occurred in the learning disabled category, which increased by 119 percent from 1976-77 to 1982-83 for an additional 1 million students so identified. There appears to be little consensus on definition of learning disabilities. A study by the Education Testing Service of 17 definitions has shown that 35 percent of the total school population can be classified as learning disabled,[8] and Ysseldyke has found that there is no difference in programs for low-achieving youngsters and learning disabled students.[9]

With the exception of students identified as seriously emotionally disturbed, which also shows substantial growth, all other categories (mentally retarded, orthopedically impaired, hearing impaired, speech impaired, and visually handicapped) show declines.[10] Despite analysis in the 1984 Annual Report to Congress indicating a slow-down in the learning disabilities category and with 19 states showing an absolute decrease in students identified as disabled, compared to the overall decrease in school enrollment, there is little change in the high rate of growth of the learning disabilities category and no substantial decrease in the disabled population generally.[11] While states cite reasons for the increases among the learning disabled (better diagnostic techniques, more knowledge) and seriously emotionally disturbed (better school programs), both categories are subject to social manipulation and should provide warning signals to policy makers.

ACCESS TO SERVICES AND EQUAL OPPORTUNITY

Similarly, increases in the quality and availability of services have not been uniform across districts, states, or groups of disabled students. Access to special education continues to be dependent upon availability of resources, procedures for evaluation and referral, and state definitions of disability and allowable services. While much progress has been made in improving options for students with disabilities at the elementary level, virtually every evaluation study documents that services to secondary students are minimal and that there is a great drop-off in population after the sixth grade. While some of this may be the result of remediation, it is likely that both the lack of and characteristics of secondary services explain part of the variation.[12]

Furthermore, as in other areas of school services, financial resources available to schools and districts greatly affect the types and quality of services available. Implementation studies have documented pressure on school personnel to identify in IEPs only services currently available, and placement options are often limited to a single type of placement by disabling condition (although this singular option may vary even within schools in a district).

In addition to poverty status as a predictor of poorer quality services, students of minority background are less likely to have access to high quality services, are more likely to be identified in certain categories (mentally retarded, emotionally disturbed), and are more likely to be placed in more restrictive environments.[13] Students whose lives are complicated by other factors (migration, military connection, involvement with the juvenile justice or foster care system) are less likely to have access to high quality services.[14] Students at risk by class, race, cultural difference, and poverty are more at risk in special education, more likely to have failed in general education, and less likely to return to general classrooms once referred to special education.[15]

INTEGRATION OF DISABLED CHILDREN

Despite increasing experience in educating students with handicapping conditions, inservice training for general and education personnel, and greater knowledge about effective methods of serving mildly and moderately disabled students in integrated classrooms and more severely disabled students in general school buildings, the percentage of disabled students served in the general school environment has remained constant since enactment of Pub. L. No. 94-142 at 92 percent of the disabled population. The 67 percent of disabled students served in general classes, and 25 percent in separate classes are precisely the figures for these placements in 1976-77. With the disproportionate growth in the learning disabled population and a decrease in most other categories, the constancy of this figure suggests there has been little change in placement procedures as a result of the enactment of Pub. L. No. 94-142.

Furthermore, there have been disturbing trends within other categories: placement in separate classes and separate schools has increased for orthopedically impaired students and for mentally retarded youngsters, numbers which can only be partially explained by the decrease in enrollment in separate nonschool environment.[16] The fact that school officials explain the increase in separate, more restrictive placements for orthopedically disabled students with a rationale that it is more effective and economical to centralize these services raises serious questions about the implementation of the normalization principle. These data, combined with reports from advocacy organizations about struggles over placement because of a lack of commitment to general classroom placements, reports from evaluation studies about the slow-down of development of multiple options for placement for children by category,[17] the fact that placement of students after evaluation often is determined by available space and (dis)incentives within funding categories,[18] and research on referral practices indicates that placement and integration of disabled students in the school environment leaves much yet to be achieved.

IDENTIFICATION, REFERRAL, AND EVALUATION

The path to special education placement and the assessment of learning problems is hardly an exact science unfettered by other biases and compromising factors. Findings prior to and in the early days of implementation of Pub. L. No. 94-142 that referral is often based on race, sex, physical appearance, and socioeconomic status[19] have been repeated as recently as the National Board of Inquiry report on *Barriers to Excellence*[20] and confirmed in extensive research by Ysseldyke and colleagues.[21]

A recent study of school districts in ten states by the Research Triangle Institute broadens these findings, reporting that for students eventually classified as learning disabled, mentally retarded, and emotionally disturbed referral occurs when student behavior and academic progress varies negatively from the school norm and that this is often a function of socioeconomic status and varies within districts and across districts.[22] Furthermore, this study finds that minority students are disproportionately referred when their socioeconomic level is considerably lower than the norm of the community. The number of students referred is greater if there is no requirement for prereferral documentation of strategies tried within the classroom and where there are loose eligibility criteria. The population referred depends on whether there are other compensatory or remedial programs available, IQ cutoffs in the eligibility definition, local or standardized norms used, or the category of socially maladjusted is eliminated from the definition of emotionally disturbed.

Once a student has been referred for special education evaluation, the task is often assumed to be to find an internal or physical cause for difficulty in the classroom, rather than examining the classroom teaching and organization strategies.[23] And, Ysseldyke has found that the assessment is hindered by inadequate instruments, staff who lack competency in critical evaluation skills, and results that are often ignored in decision making.[24]

The fact that most referrals result in placement poses again the question asked during consideration of Pub. L. No. 94-142 and raised by advocacy groups since then: Does special education serve as a convenient institutional mechanism to sort unwanted students from the mainstream of education?

EFFECTIVENESS AND QUALITY OF SPECIAL EDUCATION PROGRAMMING

Finally, the research on quality and effectiveness of educational services provided to mildly and moderately disabled students in special education poses serious questions. While there are specialized types of instructional or curricular areas such as braille, self-care skills, sign language, mobility training, lip reading, creative thinking and social interactive skills, and supportive related services, it is not clear that these methods require highly specialized comprehensive programs, should be separate from the mainstream, or need to be only available to disabled students.[25] Second, some studies on the effectiveness of a primary methodology employed in special education, differential diagnosis-prescriptive teaching, have concluded that academic performance may not be improved by such programs.[26]

The quality of education has been found to suffer substantially when children are removed from the regular classroom because special education programming bears little relationship to the real cause of the student's performance problem and are accompanied by inconsistent instructional efforts, inferior programming, and diversion from academic learning, as well as lowered teacher expectations and damage to school and peer relationships.[27]

These findings underscore the need to pay more attention to what we know about effective mainstreaming models, classroom organization, teacher training, and student support techniques. Research on mainstreaming shows that regular teachers with access to special training can demonstrate effective achievement gains, and that the general classroom supplemented by resource room assistance works for emotionally disturbed students.[28] The effectiveness of integrated instructional designs, including the Adaptive Learning Environment Model, which combines a highly structured learning component with an open-ended exploratory component using students' own planning and management skills in general classrooms, presents a powerful model for effective instruction.[29] Furthermore, evaluation of the integration of severely disabled students in general school environments shows that the amount of integration and interaction with nondisabled students is positively related to the educational progress of severely handicapped students.[30]

Thus, there is continuing documentation that the placements of students in the least restrictive environment is an effective, if underutilized, principle of Pub. L. No. 94-142. That general classroom placement has remained stable at 67 percent, when removal from the general classroom has been shown to have harmful effects, affirms the need to pay greater attention to the forces that inhibit maintaining students in the general classroom.

Several factors come into play in placement decisions. Students may need additional assistance that cannot be found in the general classroom or school environment because of resource constraints, inflexibility of structure, inadequate teacher training and knowledge of options, lack of remedial and other support services, and lack of will, energy, and administrative support. Disincentives exist in categorical special education funding formulas, which provide financial rewards for more rather than less restrictive placements. Cultural, racial, class, and socioeconomic biases may foster judgments about students' capabilities in the general classroom. Structural factors that artificially separate "special programs" from the mainstream of academic education remove responsibility for "problems" or disabled students from general education administrators. And in these settings, teachers may be able to use referral to special education as a way to avoid difficult students.

SOCIETAL ASSUMPTIONS ABOUT DISABILITY

Pub. L. No. 94-142 was a product of its time. Developing out of *PARC* and *Mills,* cases dealing with exclusion from education and training services on the basis of disability, the law passed when the rights of a disabled person to participate in the community were just beginning to be voiced. It came when institutionalization was being questioned, but the history of services and the knowledge of disability, as public policy matters, were limited. It came at the beginning of the civil rights movement of disabled adults before many articulate disabled veterans and disabled young adults had been integrated into society, able and willing to fight for their rights. It came as a new generation of parents with disabled children confronted the school system for the first time and were not willing to take "no" as an answer for their children.

The language of the law also reflects the knowledge and assumptions of that time. Its intent was the establishment of public policy to protect disabled children and youth from exclusion from and discrimination in the public school setting. Disabled students were to be dealt with as individuals—their needs were to be assessed individually—but also as a group who were presumed to need special and individualized services different from what were presumed to be needed for students without disabilities. This services model and the mechanisms for identifying the students who could be best served by this model were assumed to be, if not a science, an art which sensitive professionals, in consultation with parents, would deliver once the discriminatory barriers to services were removed.

While underscoring that it intended to remove the medical treatment model as the basis on which public policy should be set, Pub. L. No. 94-142 established the right of students with handicapping conditions to be treated equally and on an individual basis in determining their school needs. But without adjusting the organization of services within schools, changing attitudes toward disability, altering the substantial state and local funding streams that make it difficult to treat disabled students as part of the mainstream, nor collapsing the categorical definitions that define the population as being different, Pub. L. No. 94-142 may have served to reinforce a hybrid structure—one with elaborate protections to assure the rights of disabled students, but carried out by a separate delivery system of special education services, which remains in many instances outside the normal scope of school business.

Furthermore, in recent years, with the constraint in funding for other remedial and support services, the separateness of this system may have placed other students—at risk by learning differences, race, class, and culture—in jeopardy of being removed from the mainstream by the draw of individualized help. Again it is the age-old question of how to provide services to a group and maintain their rights to be treated equally.

Neither the continued separateness of disabled students in special education nor the use of special education as an alternative for students who are at risk in the classroom for other reasons than disability was intended by Congress.

If the law has been massively successful in assigning responsibility for students and setting up mechanisms to assure that schools carry out those responsibilities, it has been less successful in removing barriers between general and special education. Pub. L. No. 94-142 and other public policies of the time did not anticipate the need to take special steps to eliminate turf, professional, attitudinal, and knowledge barriers within public education. It did not anticipate that the artifice of delivery systems in schools might drive the maintenance of separate services and keep students from the mainstream, that the resource base for special education and other remedial services would be constrained by economic forces, or that special education might continue to be dead-end programs in many school districts. Nor could it anticipate how deeply ingrained were our assumptions about the differences between students with learning problems and those without, and the substantial power of high (or, unfortunately, low) expectations in learning.

Much more is known now than in the early 1970s about school organization, effective school practices, assessment practices, and teaching and learning. The problem today is to find ways to deliver the highest quality services to all students without removing them from the general classroom or, in the instance of the severely intellectually impaired or severely emotionally disturbed, without removing them from the general educational environment. Administrative convenience, more cost-effective centralization of services, or incentives for receiving badly needed extra funds or personnel resources are not adequate reasons for removing students to an environment where research findings indicate the quality of education is second-class or worse, and where the path back to the mainstream is nearly impossible. The primary problem appears to lie in our assumptions about students and the consequences for the organization of schools: that there are distinct groups of youngsters, disabled and nondisabled, and thus need for distinct sets of services, special and general, which require divisions of funding, service delivery, and organizational patterns.

The destructive practices and their resulting effects on students, based on these assumptions, are documented in more than a sufficient way to warrant change in school policies and practices.

WHAT IS TO BE DONE?

Statistics on the growth of the learning disabled category and the stagnancy in the availability of learning options and placements in less restrictive placements point to the fact that there are two substantial issues at hand: first, that students at risk for reasons other than disabilities have few options within our schools and second, that students with disabilities need to be provided with quality educational services. The current emphasis on school reform in general and improving the quality of education only suggests that these problems will get worse if new strategies are not found.

State reforms have been directed at early gates for achievement, increased academic standards, and increased standardization in testing, but little attention (or funding) has been directed to students who fail to master these hurdles. More rigid tracking of youngsters and referral for remediation or special services may make the problems greater. The increase in referral and identification of learning disabilities and the limiting of options for disabled students have occurred as economic constraints in state budgets became greater, funding for remediation under Chapter 1 leveled off, and Pub. L. No. 94-142 funds failed to meet the projected expenditure.

The question remains whether ways can be found to provide individualized supporting services to all students in our schools that do not require their separation from the mainstream. To do this, we need to overcome the barriers created by funding schemes, by patterns of service and administrative support, and by qualitative differences in instruction.

AVAILABILITY AND FLEXIBILITY OF RESOURCES

Funding formulas that create incentives for more restrictive and separate class placement or that support particular configurations of services based on special education teacher allocations maintain an inflexible program structure and fail to allow models that encourage students to remain in general classrooms with resource room or individualized help. One need only examine the variation in statistics between general classroom placements at the state level and the state funding formulas to know that states that provide financial incentives for separate placements, or which traditionally have had dual systems of services, place students disproportionately in more restrictive placements. States such as New York, Illinois, Florida, Maryland, the District of Columbia, Pennsylvania, New

Hampshire, and New Jersey have much higher rates of separate classroom placements for certain disability groups for these reasons.

While the removal of disincentives to general classroom placement by establishing resource-neutral allocation formulas is one step in the right direction, inflexible administrative and fiscal accounting requirements encourage a mindset that inhibits the more flexible use of resources to suit individual student's needs. Clearly, accountability for resources and assuring that funds are spent for the purposes they were intended are important issues; however, the separateness of funding streams maintains organizational patterns that may be dysfunctional to the integration of disabled children in schools. Close examination of states that have established less categorical and unified formulas for funding education and more flexible accounting requirements would show ways to achieve programmatic and accountability goals.

To the extent that funding for remedial and individualized attention for all students is constrained, more are likely to be identified as disabled who need not be. Artificial boundaries in funding between students with learning differences and those without create programmatic boundaries in schools. Currently, schools operate with several such boundaries: academic programs (soon to be further differentiated by "excellence" programs and regular academic tracks), vocational and general tracks, remedial programs, and special education. Given the lack of bona fide differences in students or in the effectiveness of programs that serve them, financial support questions need to be resolved so that educational benefits are not sacrificed. While financial accountability mechanisms may have made sense in a simpler day, it may be that a greater reliance on program monitoring and the resulting educational achievement by a student (through review of the IEP or other measurement) would serve students and schools better than the infinite categorization of financial supports. At the very minimum, financial and program models need to be examined so as to separate instructional support and placement from rigid financial accounting, or to allow the flexible transfer of funding across program boundaries.

PROGRAM AND SCHOOL ORGANIZATION

Given the boundaries that continue to exist between special education, support programs for students with learning problems and what is currently defined as general education, and the failures of programs based upon these boundaries, research and experimental models need to be examined that have the goal of programmatic and administrative integration for education and support services in the mainstream for students with special needs. Rather than trying to establish definitional rigor in certain areas of disability, concentrating instead on the development of nonobtrusive and nonstigmatizing ways of meeting learning needs that allow provision of support and individualized attention will be more fruitful in the long run. The current focus on raising standards in public education, with the concomitant need to expand remedial services, makes timely attention to this issue important. The infusion of targeted funding in these areas by special education, along with the focus on academic achievement of disabled and nondisabled students in the mainstream, could provide new energy and emphasis on mainstream service delivery.

Programmatically, these strategies need to be tied to findings about school and program effectiveness. Studies of mainstreaming models indicate the importance of characteristics similar to those found in studies of general education, which build school, community, student, and parental acceptance. All of these studies are clear about the importance of key leadership support (superintendent, school board, and principal), as well as conscious strategies to eliminate the separateness of teaching and administrative personnel between special education and general education, including the involvement of personnel responsible for special services on the school leadership team.

To bolster model development for school services integration, it would be extremely helpful if state and national agencies responsible for special education service delivery would focus on providing support and setting useable standards for interpretation of mainstreaming requirements so that program development could proceed with workable and enforceable concepts.

PROGRAM EFFECTIVENESS

If, as the research indicates, there is not substantial difference in the problems children exhibit and the teaching methodologies that work among children identified as low-achieving, those in need of remedial or compensatory help, the educably mentally retarded, and those served as learning disabled, attention needs to be given to the documentation of real differences in these areas, if any. Absent such findings, alternative support patterns need to be found that will keep these students in regular classrooms and reduce the harm often done to them by lowered teacher expectations, damaged peer relations, and the potential of inferior educational services outside the general classroom. Two specific requirements that would have substantial impact in halting unnecessary referrals to special education are the incorporation of a specific step in the assessment process that requires the demonstration of prereferral strategies used and the involvement of multidisciplinary teams in the referral process. These two procedures would hold the general classroom teacher responsible for difficult students, at least interrupting an automatic referral process into special education or into more restrictive placements. Obviously, such steps would need to be bolstered by training and support to the general classroom teacher.

Finally, the quality and effectiveness of instructional programs in special education need to be studied for the same reasons that the quality of general education has been examined by state legislatures in the last several years: to know how well we are preparing students for their adult lives, and to be able to document the impact costly programs have. Questions have been raised about the effectiveness of particular teaching methodologies and the costs and benefits of alternative forms of service delivery. Commenting on the instruction in self-contained classrooms in New York City, a recent report puts it this way: "Without such improvement (in the quality and content of instruction in self-contained classrooms), children placed in self-contained special education programs will have little hope of ever returning to regular education."[31] Evaluations and documentation of the effectiveness of various aspects of special education would assist policy makers as they face continuing pressures on program dollars in the future.

Students with handicapping conditions sometimes need specialized and individualized services, but so do many other students. Until these services are mainstreamed, schools have no way of overcoming the barriers to integration. The group we loosely refer to as disabled covers a broad spectrum of students, some who have substantial impairments and need specialized help, and some who are greatly disadvantaged by being identified as disabled. More special help is needed for some and far, far less for others. Unfortunately, public policy has been painted with far too broad a brush to treat either group fairly at this point.

It is time to refocus that policy so that students are not disadvantaged by labeling or diminished in the quality of their learning. The degree of individualization accomplished by Pub. L. No. 94-142 (and similar public policy) has, in many instances, not changed our primary assumptions about disability. Like race and other suspect classifications, disability automatically changes our expectations about ability. Unlike race, some disabilities—but only some—require specialized assistance. It is time to rethink the nature and need for this specialized assistance and put it in its proper context as an ancillary service necessary to a primary goal—academic and vocational instruction for independence and adult life.

NOTES

1. Enacted in 1975, Pub. L. No. 94-142's provisions became effective at the beginning of school year 1977-78, with requirements that all children with handicapping conditions be identified and enrolled in school services by September 1, 1978. In August 1984, New Mexico submitted a state plan, thus becoming the fiftieth state to participate under Pub. L. No. 94-142.

2. *Sixth Annual Report to Congress on the Implementation of Public Law 94-142: The Education for All Handicapped Children Act* (U.S. Department of Education, 1984), p. 3.

3. Report of the Comptroller General to the Chairman, House Subcommittee on Special Education, General Accounting Office, *Disparities Still Exist in Who Gets Special Education* (September 1981), p. 41.

4. *The Condition of Education,* Statistical Report, National Center for Education Statistics, ed. Valena White Plisko (U.S. Department of Education, 1984), p. 5.

5. Other education statutes affecting disabled students, while adapted to the requirements of Pub. L. No. 94-142 in recent years, follow the format of discretionary federal financial assistances; set asides within existing general programs (Head Start, Vocational Education, Chapter 1—state agency programs); discretionary target programs (other provisions of the Education of the Handicapped Act, Rehabilitation Act); and language requiring a degree of individualization (Head Start, Vocational Education, Chapter 1). Implementing regulations of section 504 of the Rehabilitation Act of 1973 stand as the only other expressions of governmental policy that extend and expand the rights protections of Pub. L. No. 94-142 by prohibiting discrimination on the basis of disability and requiring that no disabled child, youth, or adult be denied options or services extended to nondisabled participants in educational programs supported by or benefitting from federal financial assistance.

6. Report of the Comptroller General, GAO, p. 37.

7. Mary T. Moore, Lisa J. Walker, and Richard P. Nolland, *Finetuning Special Education Finance: A Guide for State Policymakers* (Education Policy Research Institute of the Education Testing Service, July 1982), p. 60.

8. Bennett and Rogosta, *A Research Context for Studying Admission Tests and the Handicapped Population* (Princeton: Education Testing Service, 1984), p. 14.

9. J. Ysseldyke et al., "Similarities and Differences Between Low Achievers and Students Classified as LD," *Journal of Special Education* (Spring 1982):73.

10. *Sixth Annual Report to Congress,* pp. 5-8.

11. Michael Gerber, "Is Congress Getting the Full Story?" *Exceptional Children,* vol. 51, no. 3 (1984):209-24.

12. Recent initiatives of Assistant Secretary Will at the U.S. Department of Education targeting funds on transitional and secondary services focus on this problem and may counter these findings.

13. Report of the Comptroller General, GAO; *A Study to Evaluate Procedures Undertaken to Prevent Erroneous Classification of Handicapped Children,* Applied Management Sciences, 1983, as cited in *Annual Report to Congress,* 1983.

14. Report of the Comptroller General, GAO, pp. 41-56.

15. *Barriers to Excellence: Our Children at Risk.* Report of the Board of Inquiry of the National Coalition of Advocates for Students (January 1985), p. 29.

16. *Annual Report to Congress,* 1984, pp. 37-38; Table 3C3, pp. 182-93; analysis of annual report data, 1976-77 to 1981-82.

17. *Longitudinal Study of the Impact of P.L. 94-142*, SRI International, 1982.

18. Ibid. A particularly graphic example citing disincentives in New York State funding patterns is provided by Alan Gartner in testimony presented to the New York City Commission on Special Education, November 27, 1984.

19. Patricia Craig et al., *Status of Handicapped Students*, vol. 2 (SRI International, 1978), pp. 77-119.

20. *Barriers to Excellence*, p. 14.

21. J. Ysseldyke, B. Algozzine, R. Regan, and M. Potter, "Technical Adequacy of Tests Used by Professionals in Simulated Decisionmaking," *Psychology in the Schools* 17 (1980):202-9; J. Ysseldyke, B. Algozzine, L. Richey, and H. Graden, "Declaring Students Eligible for Learning Disability Services: Why Bother with the Data?" *Learning Disability Quarterly* 5 (1982):37-44; J. Ysseldyke, and B. Algozzine, "LD or not LD: That's Not the Question!" *Journal of Learning Disabilities* 16 (1983):29-31; J. Ysseldyke, S. Christenson, B. Pianta, B. Algozzine, "An Analysis of Teacher Reasons and Desired Outcomes for Students Referred for Psychoeducational Assessment," *Journal of Psychoeducational Assessment* 1 (1983): 73-83; J. Ysseldyke et al., "Generalizations from Five Years of Research on Assessment and Decisionmaking," *Exceptional Children Quarterly* 4 (1982):75-94.

22. Hocutt, Cox, Pelosi, *A Policy Oriented Study of Special Education's Service Delivery System, Phase I: Preliminary Study*, vol. 1 of *An Exploration of Issues Regarding the Identification and Placement of L.D., MR. and ED Students*, Research Triangle Institute Report Number RTI/2706-06/013s (October 1984).

23. Ysseldyke, "Generalizations from Five Years of Research," p. 88.

24. Ysseldyke, "Why Bother With the Data?"

25. W. Stainback and S. Stainback, "A Rationale for Merger of Special and Regular Education," *Exceptional Children*, vol. 51, no. 2 (1984):103-4.

26. Judith A. Arter, and Joseph R. Jenkins, "Differential Diagnosis—Prescriptive Teaching: A Critical Appraisal," *Review of Education Research* 49 (1979):517-35; G. Glass, "Effectiveness of Special Education," *Policy Studies Review*, vol. 2, Special no. 1 (January 1983):65-78.

27. J. Lloyd, "How Shall We Individualize Instruction—Or Should We?" *Remedial and Special Education* 5 (1982):7-15; Lois McDermott, *The Effectiveness of Special Education: Selected Literature and Unpublished Documentation with Recommendations for the Future* (State of Minnesota: Department of Education, 1983), p. 11.

28. Donald R. Moore et al., *Child Advocacy and the Schools: Past Impact and Potential for the 1980's* (Chicago: Designs for Change, 1983), as cited in *Barriers to Excellence*, p. 29.

29. See Margaret C. Wang and Jack W. Birch, "Comparison of Full-Time Mainstreaming Program and a Resource Room Approach," *Exceptional Children*, vol. 51, no. 1 (1984):33-40; "Effective Special Education in Regular Classes," *Exceptional Children* (February 1984):391-98.

30. Richard Brinker and Margaret Thorpe, *Evaluation of Integration of Severely Handicapped Students in Regular Education and Community Settings: Executive Summary* (Princeton: Education Testing Service, Division of Education Policy Research and Services, August 1983), pp. 32-33.

31. Richard Beattie et al., *Special Education: A Call for Quality, A Final Report to Mayor Koch* (New York: Commission on Special Education, 1985), p. vii.

7

The Employment Dilemma for Disabled Persons

Cheryl Rogers

Over half of all the nearly 22 million disabled adults in the United States—12.3 million persons—are not in the labor force. This means they are not working and they are not looking for work. At the same time, we spend large sums of money on the disabled. One estimate shows that public and private disability transfer payments (that is, cash payments made to compensate individuals for their disability) made to persons aged 18-64 reached $70.6 billion (2.4 percent of GNP) in 1981. In addition, an estimated $114 billion was spent on health care costs for disabled persons in 1981, bringing the total costs of direct transfer payments and health care to $184.6 billion (6.28 percent of GNP).

No one is satisfied with the results of the expenditure of these large sums of money. Disabled persons say they are neither enough nor do they meet their needs for integration into the mainstream of society. Employers feel cheated because they believe some of their employees are abusing the system. And public officials express frustration at their inability to move a large portion of the disabled population into the work force despite the massive public expenditures on their behalf. While there are dozens of programs that provide benefits and/or services to disabled individuals at a cost of billions of dollars to private industry and the government, too many disabled persons remain outside the labor force and economically dependent on cash benefits.

There is no coherent set of policies or programs serving the disabled, but rather a patchwork of disparate programs that provide multiple benefits to some beneficiaries and offer no protection to others. Current public and private programs spend a great deal of effort attempting to distinguish the "disabled" from the "nondisabled," yet relatively little attention is give to (re)employment strategies for either group. Although some fairly sophisticated medical rehabilitation techniques have been developed to aid certain groups of disabled individuals, insufficient attention has been given to the problem of placing or retaining the individuals in the work force once their medical needs are met. In addition to the human tragedy of unproductive and isolated lives, vital economic productivity is being lost.

Moreover, current programs operate as a work disincentive: persons with an impairment who work are not awarded any benefits while only those who do not work or work for very low wages are offered cash compensation. The dilemma for policy makers, as in any social insurance or means-tested program, is how to balance this incentive issue with adequate benefits for those who cannot work.

The typical sequence now is for individuals to suffer an injury or progressive illness, become unemployed or fail to find employment, exhaust all resources, find it impossible to provide for themselves or their families, and then, facing an uncertain and threatening future, turn to disability compensation as the last remaining hope for a measure of economic security and personal dignity. It is not at all surprising, therefore, that the great majority of those who successfully run the gauntlet of the disability claims process are steadfastly reluctant to reenter the hostile arena in which they have had more than ample experience with rejection and failure. Having achieved at least a modest degree of economic security, having made some adjustment to their new circumstances of life, and having proved—as they must—that they are totally unable to work, small wonder many beneficiaries turn away the offer of rehabilitation and view with suspicion assurances that they will not lose all benefits immediately, if they should decide to enter the work force and are fortunate enough to find employment.

The field of disability has never been an area that has attracted the sustained attention of policy makers. Indeed, most legislators, human service officials, business people, and insurance executives are frustrated by their inability to deal with problems of disability. There is no common definition of who needs support, let alone what form this support should take. Myths surrounding disability persist today, leaving many people—including top decision makers—with false and stereotyped notions of what disabled persons can and cannot do for themselves. Once a person becomes disabled, business people often view the person's incapacity as if it meant the individual were unable to work at all. Policy makers latched on to the concept of "able-bodied" declaring that all able-bodied persons are required to work as if there were a clear, precise, and permanent way to determine who is "able-bodied." Policy makers and administrators are further confused, because, on the one hand, they hear that disabled people want independence and equal access, while at the same time, they receive requests for preferential treatment from different, and often competing, disability interest groups. It should be no surprise that disability policies are fragmented and pose perverse incentives. In part, of course, this is a function of genuinely different interests among the disabled, as well as a feeling among others that as long as the present nonsystem exists it is both appropriate and necessary to get from it what one can.

While some of the problems here are a function of any social-insurance or means-tested program, the predicament in which policy makers here find themselves stems from the lack of a useful and coherent definition of disability. It is widely recognized that neither a medical model of disease nor a sociological model of deviancy is entirely useful in describing disability. However, no adequate substitute model has been developed. Without a new and different conception of disability, there is not a rational model that holds constant over time. Is a person with only three fingers on one hand "disabled"? Is a person with an IQ of 80 "disabled"? And although we are a long way from dealing adequately with the most severe and visible disabilities, vocational reha-bilitation personnel are now talking of serving those with "hidden" disabilities.

Most often, disability is defined in terms of deviation from the norm: if one cannot walk up stairs as "normal" people do, if one cannot see an eyechart as most people do, if one cannot understand intellectual con-cepts as the average person does, then one is considered disabled. Of course, each of these definitions finds the disability in the individual, not in the context of the environment.

Policy makers need to develop clear bases to distinguish the disabled from the nondisabled for purposes of determining eligibility for various public benefits. Generally this has meant a binomial distinction, one that categorizes individuals as either "in" or "out"—either disabled or nondis-abled—with no gray area in between. If one's eyesight is 20/200, one is considered legally blind; but if one's eyesight is 20/190, one has "nor-mal" vision and is not considered disabled. The cut-off is arbitrary and may bear little relation to an individual's functioning.

Guided by misleading information and pejorative stereotypes, it is no wonder that people holding high offices are confused and immobilized as to what should be done. Without a more precise conceptualization, policy makers will remain vulnerable to conflicting demands from differ-ent groups—from within the communities of the disabled, employers, insurance providers, taxpayer groups, and the citizenry at large—and compassionate notions of equity and distributive justice will continue to elude them.

Much of this confusion in disability policy stems from conflicting attitudes that nondisabled members of society hold about disabled members. On the one hand, many people regard the disabled with pity and are inclined to offer charity to the blind beggar or crippled flute payer on the sidewalk. As a sort of "tyranny of goodwill," this approach is based on the belief that disabled people can't (and thus shouldn't) be expected to work. According to this line of thought, the disabled person's misfortunes usually occurred through no fault of their own, so why be punitive and force them to suffer any more? Instead, the argument goes, we should provide cash and other forms of assistance to help the disabled live out of the rest of their lives. Those who subscribe to this school of thought, although often with the best of intentions, are really "buying off" the disabled; that is, they want to give the disabled persons a cash payment and, by doing so, avoid any further interaction or worry about those persons and their problems. If disabled people are not expected to work, we as a society can avoid the many headaches and public expenditures associated with, for instance, retrofitting buses so they can get to work or providing a special speech unit on a computer for a blind employee. It is much easier to make a monthly cash payment and forget about the disabled person.

Another and directly conflicting school of thought adopts the view that disabled persons can and should work. Disabled persons are seen as potentially productive members of society, according to this view. Held most strongly by disabled persons themselves, this school of thought was expressed most vocally beginning in the 1970s with the independent living movement. Disabled persons demanded that they be allowed to participate fully in the life of the community, including employment as a way to enhance self-esteem, be productive, and increase their economic self-sufficiency. The opening declaration of the 1965 Rehabilitation Act Amendments conveys this principle well:

> The Secretary is authorized to make grants as provided in . . . this title for the purpose of assisting states in rehabilitating handicapped individuals so that they may prepare for and engage in gainful employment to the extent of their capabilities, thereby increasing not only their social and economic well-being but also the productive capacity of the nation.[1]

These two opposing sets of attitudes—one contending that the disabled are to be pitied and not expected to work and the other demanding full integration into society, including the opportunity to work

—have coexisted uneasily for at least 20 years. In fact, people subscribe to both viewpoints at the same time. As a result, our public policies are bifurcated: paying lipservice to the goal of enhancing employment among the disabled while at the same time not really expecting the disabled to work.

The two major public compensation programs, Social Security Disability Insurance (SSDI) and Supplemental Security Income (SSI), use "ability to work" as the test of who is and who is not disabled. The definition of disability for both of these programs is as follows:

> An individual must have a medically determinable physical or mental impairment which, when modified by demographic factors, renders him/her unable to engage in any "substantial gainful activity" (SGA) defined as work which ". . . exists in the immediate area in which one lives, or exists in the national economy, regardless of whether a specific job vacancy exists or whether one would be hired if one applied for work."[2]

In both of these programs, full-time work at regular wages is considered evidence of ability to "engage in substantial gainful activity" and thus makes one ineligible for benefits after the individual has demonstrated such work ability for a period of nine months. The message from the federal government to disabled persons is: If you can't work (and meet the other eligibility requirements), we'll provide you with cash benefits; if you can work, whether or not a job is available, you're on your own.

Although there are a few policies that attempt to encourage work among the disabled, most disability policies in the public and the private sectors do not actively promote work. In establishing SSDI in 1954, Congress declared that it is "the policy of the Congress that disabled individuals applying for a determination of disability . . . shall be promptly referred" to the state vocational rehabilitation agency so that "the maximum number of such individuals may be rehabilitated into productive activity."[3] Further, Congress enacted a work incentive that allows SSDI and SSI applicants to exclude the first $65 of monthly earnings plus half of the remainder in calculating their benefits.[4]

Yet despite these intentions, current disability programs do not sufficiently promote work. While some disabled persons return to their former lives after medical rehabilitations, too many others are relegated to the back rooms of boarding houses, with little attention paid to their employment potential. Current programs—both public and private—offer help only after the disabling condition prevents or seriously hinders work effort.

The very process by which disabled applicants become eligible for benefits leads to learned states of helplessness. For example, disabled claimant's must prove total and long-term disability to become eligible for SSDI and/or SSI. As a result, a disabled "mindset" sets in and the applicants may inevitably come to view themselves as totally dependent and unable to work. This situation is even worse for those disabled who do not qualify for cash benefits under existing programs: After identifying those disabled individuals who appear to be capable of work and therefore ineligible for disability benefits, we do nothing further. The message once again is: If you can work, don't expect any help; if you cannot, the government and/or the private sector will take care of you as long as you remain invalid.

This explicit policy has impeded labor force participation among the disabled. Fifty-six percent of the 21.9 million disabled working-age adults are not in the labor force; that is, they are not even looking for work. Only 34 percent of all disabled adults are employed full-time, compared with 50 percent of the entire working-age population. For women, the statistics are even worse. Almost 70 percent of all disabled women—8.1 million—remain outside the labor force; only 11 percent are employed full-time.

Among those who receive disability compensation, subsequent work-force participation is also low. The number of disabled individuals who receive SSDI and eventually return to work is miniscule. Between 1967 and 1976 the number of successful terminations from SSDI due to return to work or medical recovery fell from 33 per 1,000 beneficiaries to 15 per 1,000. Of these, only 20 percent—3 per 1,000—have been able to return to work. The remainder work in sheltered workshops or stay at home. And only about 75 percent of those who return to a job—fewer than 1 per 1,000—are able to stay employed for more than a few years. The other 25 percent eventually return to the SSDI rolls because they are no longer able to continue working.[5] It is important to remember that SSDI provides benefits to only the most severely disabled persons. However, a survey of workers' compensation claimants found that 81 percent of persons with permanent and total disability, 46 percent of those with major permanent partial disability, and 27 percent of those with minor permanent partial disability were not working two to three years after their claims were settled.[6]

The federal government has not assumed an effective leadership role in moving or returning disabled persons to the labor force. It has chosen not to enact national legislation imposing employment quotas, as have other industrialized countries.[7] Nor has it taken steps similar to other Western European countries such as establishing networks of sheltered workshops or cooperatives to ensure reemployment of disabled persons. Instead, there is a loose and ineffective array of incentives and affirmative action programs for federal government contractors, but these cover, at best, only about one-third of the labor force. Current administration policy is aimed at weakening these programs both in their coverage and implementation. Another federal initiative, the Targeted Jobs Tax Credit, which provides a tax credit of 50 percent of an individual's first year wages and 25 percent of the second year wages to companies that hire disabled (and other disadvantaged) workers, has not had a substantial impact on employment practices.

The private sector has likewise fallen short in its efforts to employ or reemploy disabled persons. Insurance companies generally have adopted a passive role in paying claims without taking steps to see that disabled workers are returned to productive employment. Many insurance companies view disability only as a piece of paper that comes across a claims examiner's desk and the response is often to pay the claim without making the effort to see if the claimant could be reemployed. Employers also find themselves in a reactive position rather than a proactive one that seeks to get disabled persons back to work. Systematic efforts by employers to check on disabled persons and encourage them to come back to work seem to be the exception rather than the rule. Moreover, it is not uncommon for companies to use disability benefits as a "dumping ground," that is, employers decide they would rather get rid of an employee because of unsatisfactory performance by giving the employee disability benefits than to have the employee return to work.

Even collective bargaining agreements, which one would expect to provide for the rehiring of disabled workers, have been negligent. A study by the Bureau of Labor Statistics in 1976 revealed that only about one-fourth of the collective bargaining agreements representing nearly 8 million workers had clauses stipulating that an employee who becomes disabled and cannot perform his regular work shall be retained in a job situation suitable to his capacity.[8] Even these clauses, however, are frequently tempered by additional conditions, such as the employee must have been employed for a specified minimum length of time, or that suitable work exists, or that both union and management must approve of the arrangement. Furthermore, only 6 percent of sample agreements made provision for the protection of disabled workers from layoffs or discharge. As one source sums it up:

> The measures taken by labor, private employers and the states have not yet eliminated the reemployment problems of the disabled population, and the national efforts, when examined within the context of international measures to ensure job opportunities for handicapped individuals, appear inadequate.[9]

Neither the public nor private sectors have been successful in returning disabled persons to the work force through vocational rehabilitation. Previous efforts at rehabilitation by both public and private agencies have over promised what they can do, leading to false expectations with too few positive results. Public agencies have largely focused on the rehabilitation process, developing job potential through counselling with too little attention paid to the task of matching a person's capacities to particular jobs and the outcome of job placement. Moreover, public agencies often "cream" applicants—that is, accept only those applicants with the best potential for successful outcomes.

Private rehabilitation agencies, a rapidly growing field and one in which businesses are very interested, do not have data to prove that they are successful in returning disabled workers to a job. Employers are thereby forced to take the word of these agencies without being able to document their outcomes.

Overall, current rehabilitation programs do not reach a substantial number of disabled persons. For example, the total number of persons nationwide served by public vocational rehabilitation agencies in 1979 was only 94,936. Private sector rehabilitation reaches an even smaller number of persons. Few corporations are involved in vocational rehabilitation; those that are generally refer disabled persons to a private medical rehabilitation firm, and they may or may not follow up with the employee.

The length of time it takes to receive vocational rehabilitation services also hinders rehabilitation efforts, often allowing disabled clients to deteriorate in their functioning before services are offered. In 1978, the median length of time that elapsed between application for SSDI or SSI and receipt of vocational rehabilitation services was 7.5 months.

In summary, existing programs fail actively to move disabled persons into the labor force. This suggests that policy makers still think of the disabled as incapable of work, as objects for pity or compassion. Or else policy makers merely prefer to provide cash benefits and not worry about finding a suitable job for and retraining the disabled individual.

How can we overcome the long-standing and deeply held attitudes that disabled persons should not be expected to work? The best way is through public policy, through a set of legislative initiatives that force action. If public attitudes are to be remolded, we should use action strategies to force such change instead of tackling attitudes in a vacuum. It matters less what preconceived notions people have about the disabled if there is an action agenda that forces the breakdown of long-standing prejudices. This is also the only way to force changes in the delivery system; public policy that mandates a certain action may be the best stimulus for creating an operational system to meet that goal. In this case, the goal is to develop a national employment policy for the disabled.[10]

The emphasis of the new policy should be on training, early rehabilitation and job placement for those with some work capacity. For those with very limited work capacity, there should be modification of work tasks and environment and supported work arrangements before offering lifetime cash benefits. In short, we need to restructure existing policies and vocational rehabilitation programs fundamentally so that one's abilities are enhanced and greater effort is made to avert a lifetime of total dependency. The rehabilitation or reemployment process should be oriented toward economic self-sufficiency and should come first as part of the determination of eligibility for disability benefits. Instead of presuming that disabled persons cannot work, policies should start with the assumption that they can and do want to work.

By offering prospects of a job at the outset of the disability, rather than only cash benefits, disabled applicants will be less likely to adopt the mindset of total and permanent disability. Emphasis on a person's functional capacity, measured in terms of performance instead of reliance on the individual's incapacity defined by medical labels, should likewise help direct disabled persons into the labor force. Altering the nature of the rehabilitation process from one traditionally focused on social work and counselling to one that uses employment specialists to achieve job placement with the active cooperation of employers would more likely result in disabled persons being placed in jobs.

While current disability programs reflect the view that disabled persons are not really expected to work, a new employment system should be based on the assumption that disabled persons can and should work. A great deal of attention has been focused on the question of why more and more people are becoming disabled but hardly any attention has been turned to what has happened in the social, economic, and political structure that forces people with various degrees of impairment out of the work force. Current solutions have tended to modify incentives for the individuals rather than to examine more deeply what can be done to modify the environment to provide greater opportunities. This is because it is much easier to ascribe the problem of the disabled to the individual and to the impairment rather than to the societal setting. Thus, programs classify the individual by medical criteria—treat the individual, rehabilitate the individual, improve the individual's motivation—without altering significantly the total social and economic milieu. Continuing along this line will only defer the high social and economic costs of disability.

A political agenda is necessary to achieve any new employment policy for disabled people. Such an agenda must encompass both the public and private sectors, and it must be related to the agendas of other disadvantaged groups. Disability compensation and rehabilitation are not the sole province of government agencies; private insurance companies and private rehabilitation agencies play a major role as well. In fact, one of the foremost goals of disabled persons is to actively participate in the labor force, a goal in which private businesses are the key players. Disabled persons do not want just a public welfare program; they want the same opportunity to work in the private marketplace as other non-disabled people have. This requires an agenda that forges public and private sector interests.

Perhaps the single most important feature of a political agenda is that it be related to those of other disadvantaged groups. Disabled persons are not the only ones demanding jobs and equal treatment; discrimination touches many others in our society as well. Minorities, some of whom may be disabled, seek government action to ensure equal opportunities through civil rights laws; poor people seek jobs, public benefits, and an adequate federal minimum wage through antipoverty programs; women demand equal pay through the women's movement; and elderly people, many of whom are disabled, demand that they not be discarded merely because they reach age 65. If disabled persons are to attain their goals, they must join these other parallel movements. It may turn out to be more significant that someone is poor and black than that the same person cannot walk. In either case, it should be the responsibility of the federal government to establish the necessary procedures to ensure equal treatment and opportunity for all those in need. If the joblessness of disabled persons is not viewed as part of a much broader societal problem, if workable coalitions are not formed with other groups, the goal of equal opportunity will remain at the level of political rhetoric only.

NOTES

1. 79 Stat. 1282, 29 U.S.C. Section 31 (Supp. I 1965).
2. Title II, Social Security Act, Section 223, (d) (1) (A) and (d) (2) (A).
3. 42 U.S.C. 422, Section 222.
4. 42 U.S.C. 1382a, Section 1612 (b) (4) (A) and (b) (4) (B).
5. Aaron Krute, "Reintegration of the Severely Disabled into the Work Force: The U.S. Experience," in *Social Security and Disability: Issues in Policy Research,* The International Social Security Administration, Geneva, Studies and Research No. 17, 1981.

6. Ronald Conley and John Noble, *Workers' Compensation Reform: Challenge for the 80's,* vol. 1, Research Report of the Interdepartmental Workers' Compensation Task Force, June 1979, p. 21.

7. Austria, Belgium, France, Great Britain, Germany, Luxembourg, and the Netherlands have national legislation which legally obligates private and public employers to hire a quota of disabled persons in their organizations. See "Reemployment Programs for Disabled Workers," in *Research Report of the Interdepartmental Workers' Compensation Task Force,* vol. 5, June 1979, p. 66.

8. Ibid., p. 73.

9. Ibid., pp. 73-74.

10. A start toward this is to be found in the report *Toward Independence* by the National Council on the Handicapped (Washington, D.C.: U.S. Government Printing Office, 1986).

8

The Application of Technology In The Classroom and Workplace: Unvoiced Premises and Ethical Issues

Al Cavalier

Today's advanced technology represents the most powerful set of tools yet devised for human implementation. Within the last decade, the rehabilitation and special education communities have begun to realize the significance of these advances for the persons they serve. By all accounts, this increased realization and resultant application will escalate at a rapid rate in the coming years with the use of technology mediated through the professional service provider.

At the same time, the responsibilities that the use of such technology carries must be confronted. The widespread application of technology in developmental disabilities requires consideration of far-reaching human consequences and, ultimately, perceptions of the value of human life.

This chapter has three purposes. The first is to describe a sampling of the applications of technology designed to improve the lives of persons with disabilities. The second purpose is to highlight some issues that can easily be, and have been, overlooked in the rush to put technology to work for people such as the role of the professional vis-à-vis the consumer and the manufacturer. The third purpose is to call for a concerted and collaborative action by the involved professional disciplines and consumers in specifying standards for the application of technology and in mapping out procedures to be employed for the responsible resolution of ethical issues based on these standards.

In comparison to most treatments of the application of technology to persons with disabilities, the tone of this chapter is likely to be viewed as negative. It would more appropriately be regarded as cautiously optimistic: cautious, because service providers generally do what they do because they are deeply committed to improving lives, and the potential for technology to assist in this process is tremendous if employed responsibly. The challenge is to not just give the appearance of improvement, but to have substantive benefits verified by those for whom the efforts were undertaken—the consumer.

CURRENT DEVELOPMENTS IN TECHNOLOGY APPLICATIONS

Among the developments intended to improve mobility are a technological aid to reestablish independence in walking and an intelligent wheelchair with head-operated controls. In Functional Electrical Stimulation, a large computer is responsible for sending successive bursts of electricity to over 30 electrodes attached to the major muscle groups in a paralyzed person's legs. Each burst is orchestrated to trigger appropriate movement in the right muscles at the proper time, and sensors are attached to the legs to provide feedback that allows the computer to make correction automatically. The current goal is to miniaturize the system so that it can be implanted, much like a cardiac pacemaker, to offer true independence in walking for persons with paraplegia.[1]

The Smart Wheelchair, as it is labeled, is a motorized wheelchair under development that allows control of speed and direction by the position of the user's head. Ultrasonic sensors determine whether the user's head is positioned in front of, left of, right of, or behind the center head position, and the wheelchair moves in a corresponding direction. Forward-facing sensors detect the presence of obstacles in the chair's path so that the chair will automatically slow or stop to avoid collisions. Side sensors detect walls to the right and left of the chair and permit it automatically to travel parallel to a wall without user intervention. Such a wheelchair offers persons with quadriplegia the opportunity for independent and fatigue-free mobility.[2]

The ability most commonly cited as uniquely human is our vast potential for communication. As such, several applications of technology have been designed to augment both the reception and expression of language. Persons with hearing impairments who rely on lip reading for decoding of spoken messages often encounter difficulty because similar lip movements may signify different words. A technological aid that would eliminate many of these ambiguities is under development by researchers at Gallaudet College in conjunction with NASA scientists at the Research Triangle Institute and the Goddard Space Flight Center. The aid, labeled the Speech Autocuer, consists of a specially-adapted pair of eyeglasses equipped with a miniature microphone and projector; it can be used electronically to "hear" words as they are being spoken and project lexigraphic cues that clarify the lip movements into the immediate visual field of the deaf person.[3] Through use of the Autocuer, the amount of understanding by the lip-reading person can improve dramatically.

Ineraid, an assistive device currently under development, is a Walkman-sized unit that receives sounds from a microphone in the ear, translates the sounds into electrical impulses, and transmits these impulses to the brain by way of electrodes implanted in the inner ear.[4] This aid offers the potential to restore hearing to persons who are deaf.

A number of different electronic speech synthesizers are available to nonspeaking persons. Some of these are embedded in communication devices (such as the Phonic Mirror Vois 130 and Prentke-Romich Express III), while others are available as peripherals for microcomputers. The self-contained communication devices typically present a gridlike configuration of vocabulary choices from which the message-sender selects. They may also offer the full range of English sounds so that the message-sender can construct any word that is not in the system's core vocabulary. By activating choices in sequence, a user can "speak" practically any phrase or sentence. Many of these devices are programmable, allowing the user to create vocabulary or store long strings of connected speech.[5]

A communication device called the Eyetyper is currently available for use by nonspeaking persons with severe physical limitations. The system consists of an upright display module divided into nine cells on which are displayed pictures or words. A sensor uses an infrared video camera to sense which of the nine display areas a person is looking at, and an output module translates the selection into a voice appropriate to the age and sex of the user. With this system, a person can "speak" to another person with no greater effort than subtle eye movements.[6]

Persons with visual impairments are also benefitting from technological advances. An orientation and navigational aid called the Russell Pathsounder is in use with persons who are blind, or deaf and blind. This portable device sends out inaudible beams of ultrasound that bounce back to the device upon striking an object in the environment such as a wall or a post. The reflected beams are then translated into tones corresponding to the distance between the device and the environmental barrier; it produces a low tone if the object is three to six feet away and a high tone if it is within three feet. The aid also provides two types of tactile feedback for users who are deaf and blind.[7] Such an aid provides basic information about the environment, permitting more independent and confident movement.

Another technology application for persons with visual impairments is the Kurzweil Reading Machine. This computerized device can "read" practically any printed or typed material such as books, newspapers and magazines, flipping pages as it reads. It scans the material, which can be in any format, font style, and type size, and converts the printed words into speech.[8] Through such technology, a blind person is no longer dependent on braille translations for reading material and practically the whole world of printed information is available.

Many technological aids have been designed to assist the user in accomplishing activities of daily living. Persons who are severely physically-impaired such as those with quadriplegia can use computerized voice recognition systems, such as The Shadow/VET and the Introvoice, in conjunction with environmental control systems to perform a variety of functions in their daily living. Through uttering intelligible or at least consistent sounds, a person with such a system can open a door for a visitor, answer and dial a telephone, operate a television set, turn a radio on and off, control the temperature in the room, write letters, etc.[9]

To permit persons with high-level spinal cord injury some independence in self-feeding, robotic arms have been developed that automatically dip a spoon into one of three bowls or plates of food and then position it near the user's mouth. By voice command or the nudge of a chin switch, the user can activate the next spoonful and select the bowl or plate of choice.[10]

Another device under development will assist persons with mental retardation to learn independent toileting skills and will return toileting control to persons who are incontinent for medical reasons. This is a portable and noninvasive Walkman-sized device that uses ultrasound to continuously monitor the volume of urine in a person's bladder. When a threshold volume is reached, the aid unobtrusively signals the user.[11]

Lastly, there is a microcomputer-controlled interactive videodisc system designed to teach such skills as time telling, coin identification, reading, and mathematics to students with mental retardation. The system presents a student with a vivid display on a video screen and an audio instruction, and the student responds to questions by directly touching the image of the answer on the screen. The system in turn detects the location of the student's response and searches for and displays a particular audio-visual segment from the videodisc if the response was correct or provides appropriate remedial instruction if the response was incorrect. The feedback includes vivid and dynamic animation and motion picture sequences. The system allows a teacher to specify the requirements for advancing to each succeeding level of instruction in terms of the number of correct responses, and automatically records student performance data for later review.[12]

UNDERLYING PREMISES AND ETHICAL ISSUES

Human service provision can be regarded as an act of communication. The type of service being provided and the style of its provision reveal a great amount about the manner in which the provider views the client. In many cases, the content of these messages is not always fully appreciated by the service provider, particularly when the area of service provision is a new one and the territory is relatively unfamiliar. Unvoiced premises and underlying views often serve as the basis upon which service decisions are made, and their unintended communications often run counter to the ostensible goals of these service efforts. Consequently, it is necessary for the service community to give serious consideration to the ramifications of such premises and communications. Three attitudes illustrate the potentially dangerous implications of technological applications.

In one case, the focus is on the technology, rather than on the child or adult with disabilities. Instead of having the goal of enhancing a person's ability more fully to participate in life, the service provider's goal becomes the identification of a new technology application; the person with the disability becomes only the means by which the value of the application is substantiated. Focusing primarily on the technology relegates users to a secondary role, and often fosters the belief that users need to adjust or readily adapt themselves to the requirements or demands that the devices place on them for successful operation. In such cases, a portion of the user's individuality is traded to "fit the system" rather than adapting the system to meet the particular individual's need.

Related to this is the case in which the needs of the service provider or researcher take a primary role, rather than those of the consumer. The public acclaim for novel applications of technology and new inventions, for which the researcher or service provider may claim responsibility, is sometimes the driving force. The potential danger inherent here is an increasing obliviousness to the needs of the clients and to the most direct path for meeting those needs. For example, a high-technology approach may be chosen when a low-technology approach, while less flashy or attention-getting, is more appropriate. Similarly, in the last three years there has been a proliferation of conferences focusing exclusively on research and application of computers and other technological aids for persons with disabilities. That major conferences are conducted by highly respected professional organizations and universities carries the implicit message that there is real substance to the particular service approaches in question, often long before any reliable evidence is in hand.

To many persons, such an investment of resources in an area legitimizes the exaggerated claims that typically characterize the advertising campaigns of the vendors who market the aids. This in turn is often the basis for increased purchases because of serious peer pressure among service providers, school districts, and clinics to "be users of the most powerful approaches" and supervisory pressure to "keep up with the competition," often long before the necessary parameters of successful application are known, for example, appropriate client characteristics for the application, most beneficial modes of operation, specific user guidelines, extent of the results to be expected, etc.

In the third case, the focus is on the client, but concentrates exclusively on the disability rather than on the person's abilities. When providing technological assistance, there is a strong tendency to see the person totally in terms of disabilities—to see needs, limitations, and incapacities and miss the person's strengths, abilities, and distinctive attributes. By mechanizing a person to provide some of the actions that machines can accomplish, service providers are extremely susceptible to ignoring the behaviors, thoughts, and emotions that separate humans from machines. In society, machines are increasingly taking over jobs once done by humans. In many segments of the population, these machines are producing extreme discomfort that is unrelated to the loss of a job; it has to do with basic beliefs about what people do and, more importantly, what human beings are. As McMurray points out in Chapter 9, "Easing Everyday Living: Technology for the Physically Disabled," the question must be raised as to the end result of such technological assistance—the mechanization of the person and loss of individualization or the enhancement of function and greater participation in life.

For service providers and researchers who employ technological aids there is a serious danger of viewing the client as "a broken person" whose defective parts require service or repair. To the degree that the "fix" is more visually apparent, this perception may be more pronounced. Associated with this premise is the increased possibility of viewing the person as no more than the sum of his or her parts, the assumption being that those requiring few or no fixes are more operationally sound or have greater functional integrity. If, in fact, the way in which people are perceived determines the manner in which they are treated,[13] these assumptions initiate a cycle of increasing dehumanization.

Related to the "broken person" concept is the assumption that all persons with disabilities want to be fixed and that the nature of the fix is not nearly as important as the end result. Consequently, persons who have disabilities are frequently not questioned about their desire for an assistive device and are not included among the persons who design the features of their aid and its external configuration.[14] The person with disabilities is viewed as a passive and grateful recipient of services, with no voice or only token participation in the "expert" decisions regarding those services. This is true not only at the individual level but also in terms of society's allocation of resources to developing technological devices as opposed to other uses of resources for the benefit of persons with disabilities.

An implicit premise that can be conveyed when service providers attempt to secure an aid for a client is that the provision of the aid is the responsibility of public charity, and, as a consequence, there is an underlying message that the person is a burden of charity.[15] This attitude brings with it a rash of assumptions concerning the aid and the user, the first being that "anything is better than nothing," and, therefore, that the client is in no position to make demands, and the service approach does not have to exceed minimal expectations. Also, as a charity recipient, the client is expected to be extremely grateful for whatever favors are bestowed. Relegating a person's right to a normalized lifestyle to the hit-or-miss game of charitable chance is unethical and unjust. The high probability of inadequate and inappropriate services is wasteful of human potential. The negative connotations of being "a charity recipient" can also be devastating to a person's feelings of self-worth and the perception held of the person by others.

With the need to be ever mindful of the disabling images that a well-intentioned intervention attempt may create, it is very possible that the less typical the intervention—that is, the assistive device—the more different the person will be perceived in terms of human feelings, preferences, expectations, and dislikes. Service providers may bolster the perception of a person as "disabled" or "not normal" by heightening the visibility of the disability through the use of an obtrusive assistive device, although they may claim that the heightened visibility is more than compensated for by the increased independence that the device affords.

In designing and applying technological aids to reduce disabled person's dependency on others, professionals often implicitly assume that the person's dependency on the aid to accomplish what other persons previously performed for the client is preferable to the dependency on the other persons. (This dehumanization of the world of the disabled person is the thrust of McMurray's argument in Chapter 9, "Easing Everyday Living: Technology for the Physically Disabled.") It also presupposes that improved independent functioning is more desirable than the possibility of performing the skill unaided in the future through the slower and more arduous process of teaching the person the necessary skills. While the immediate benefits of aid-use may be welcome, the long-range ramifications for the user could be total dependence on an assistive device prone to malfunction and breakdown.

Federal law Pub.L. No. 95-602 mandates that persons with developmental disabilities should be served in the "least restrictive environment" (LRE), which is defined as an environment that is "least restrictive of the individual's rights, yet provides the individual with a setting in which he or she can function effectively."[16] This is typically interpreted as referring to a setting that is the most "normal" in which the person can reasonably function. The concept of LRE, however, is not easily interpreted in terms of the use of technological aids. "Normalization" is the concept around which the LRE guidelines are based, but what is the appropriate target of the normalization attempt? In one view, it would be the environment, if one held that being in a "normal" environment results in normalized perception and acceptance and that in a more "natural" or unmodified environment less restrictions are imposed on an individual's personal liberty. Consequently, the fewer the environmental adaptations, or technological aids, the better. On the other hand, the target would be the success of the person's functioning, if one held that competency or proficiency, regardless of how it is attained, results in normalized perceptions and acceptance. Proponents of such a view typically ascribe to the belief that one of the hallmarks of basic humanity is the sophisticated use of tools to adapt the environment to one's own advantage. Therefore, it is appropriate to adapt the environment to reduce restrictions on effective functioning, and any technological aids that assist a client in acting in an optimal way would be embraced.

The scenarios presented above illustrate examples of the kinds of unvoiced premises upon which decisions to use technological aids are often based and the implicit images and messages that these decisions communicate about persons with disabilities. Given that such service decisions and the ethical issues involved can have serious and far-reaching effects on a person's rehabilitation, professionals need to develop a framework for their responsible resolution.

A CALL FOR ACTION

Service approaches employing advanced technology provide an increased number of powerful options for professionals when choosing instructional and rehabilitative procedures, but they also place more complex demands on them for responsible and accountable action. The technological explosion in the homes, classrooms, and workplaces of persons with disabilities has taken place for the most part without any attention to the associated ethical issues and concerns, much less providing any guidelines for their resolution. As a result, there is a real and serious danger that professionals and lay persons will be largely unprepared to deal knowledgeably, responsibly, and effectively with the issues that advanced technology has spawned and that are embedded in their professional decision making.

Technical competence does not insure wisdom. Intelligent and informed decision making is vitally necessary as technology applications and marketplace demands come face to face with concepts such as normalization, mainstreaming, the least restrictive environment, and reasonable risk, as well as client independence and autonomy. As technological advances are rapidly and powerfully transforming the world, special education and rehabilitation professionals are responsible for seeing that such advances are used to benefit not only the strong majority but also the vulnerable minority in the most appropriate ways. This necessitates that professionals maintain a heightened awareness for responsible decision making.

Some professional organizations have addressed the general issue of ethics in the professional conduct of their disciplines by creating written ethical standards of practice; among these are the American Psychological Association's Ethical Standards of Psychologists and Standards for Providers of Psychological Services,[17] and the Council for Exceptional Children's Code of Ethics and Standards for Professional Practice.[18] Identifying the potential areas of professional conflict, clarifying the ethical issues involved, and developing standards of practice are important steps for professionals to take in safeguarding the rights and interests of their clients, insuring the delivery of appropriate services, and advancing their disciplines.

As stated in the introduction to the CEC documents, "the code of ethics and standards for practice provide guidelines for professional etiquette, for effective interpersonal behavior, for resolution of ethical issues, and for making professional judgments concerning what constitutes competent practice." This statement notwithstanding, there is very little attention devoted to applied ethics in university training programs for prospective service providers in the fields of special education and rehabilitation. This is in sharp contrast to the practice in other service-related professions; within the last decade almost every medical school in the country has initiated the study of medical ethics, and almost 90 percent of the law schools require courses in professional responsibility.[19]

Five components merit consideration in the pursuit of ethical applications of technology in the homes, classrooms, and work places of persons with disabilities. First, it is essential that all of the contributory issues be identified. Raising consciousness about the potential areas of conflict and clarifying the pivotal points begin the process of insuring an informed and responsible community.

The second component concerns the delineation of the process(es) to be employed in resolving an ethical issue and in deciding on an appropriate course of action. Determination of an effective process is the most important component in a responsive decision-making framework. Essential to the realization of this component is agreement among all involved parties on the appropriateness of the process. This agreement insures that, while the final decisions may not be totally agreed upon by all concerned parties, the parties involved in the decision making observe a uniform set of procedures that are acknowledged to result in ethically responsible action. The actual formulation of the process might appropriately be accomplished through collaboration of the leading professional organizations in the country (for example, the American Psychological Association, the National Association of Social Workers, the American Association on Mental Deficiency, the Council for Exceptional Children, the Association for Persons with Severe Handicaps, and the American Speech-Language-Hearing Association) and the leading disability organizations (both the large traditional groups, for example, United Cerebral Palsy, the Association for Retarded Citizens of the United States, and the Association for Children and Adults With Autism, and the newer advocacy groups, for example, Disabled in Action, Disability Rights Education and Defense Fund).

The third component is the selection of the appropriate persons to participate in the decision-making process when a potential conflict or ethical issue has been raised in the consideration of rehabilitative procedures for a particular client. The selection of the participants in the decision-making process will, in part, be determined by the process that is consensually delineated. The nature of the specific issue being addressed and the consequent decision-making procedures to be employed should specify key individuals and disciplines that need to be included to have confidence in the appropriateness of the decisions. These participants, in turn, carry the responsibility for keeping abreast of the latest developments in their field and related fields and for acting in the primary interests of the client for whom the technology service approach is being considered.

The fourth component is the formulation of professional standards according to which the key decisions can be made. This component is the foundation of the decision-making framework. Standards provide the criteria to be employed in the established process for resolving the ethical issues raised in a particular case. They are the criteria by which not only the intermediate and final decisions are judged—but also the professional disciplines of those making the decision. Standards do not provide absolute answers, but rather are critical tools for arriving at responsible answers. They are not immutable, but reflect the highest values of the society at a given point in time. These critical standards can be arrived at by the same types of organizations that are involved in the formulation of the consensual decision-making process and procedures.

The final component to be addressed is, in essence, the end result of the others: the actual decision reached on the ethical issue in question and the resultant course of action. The resolution of an ethical issue in service approaches involving technological aids with persons with disabilities will probably rarely, if ever, be agreed upon by all parties interested in the client. However, this is less important than coming to the resolution by following systematic guidelines employing professional standards that insure ethically responsible action, that reduce the chance of client manipulation by the professional. Without prejudging the outcome of such a process, clearly client benefit must be the primary value, a determination in which the client's informed consent must be central.

CONCLUSION

It is clear that the current uses of technology in the service of humanity are only a small beginning. With continuing research on technological aids and their application, society can realize unprecedented benefits for persons with disabilities in terms of increased personal independence, improved learning, increased productivity, and enhanced personal satisfaction. If a framework such as that proposed above becomes an integral part of service delivery, the tremendous promise of advanced technology in the education and rehabilitation of persons with disabilities will be realized, and their fundamental human dignity will be honored and preserved. In the final analysis, the delivery of appropriate service to persons with disabilities and the overall ethical fabric of our society may be more intimately related to the questions posed by technology than anyone has yet to realize.[20]

NOTES

1. A. Kralj, T. Bajd, R. Turk, J. Krajnk, and H. Benko, "Gait Restoration in Paraplegic Patients: A Feasibility Demonstration Using Multichannel Surface Electrode FEES," *Journal of Rehabilitation Research and Development*, vol, 20, no. 1, (1983) pp. 3-20. E. B. Marsolais and R. Kobetic, "Functional Walking of Paralyzed Patients by Means of Electrical Stimulation," in *Proceedings of the Fifth Annual Conference on Rehabilitation Engineering*, ed. J. P. O'Leary and J. R. O'Reagan (Bethesda, Md.: The Rehabilitation Engineering Society of North America, 1982).

2. D. L. Jaffe, "Smart Wheelchair," in *Proceedings of the Fourth Annual Conference on Rehabilitation Engineering*, ed. J. Timble, J. Boubler and C. Heckathorne (Bethesda, Md.: The Rehabilitation Engineering Society of North America, 1981).

3. T. E. Bell, *Technologies for the Handicapped and the Aged* (Washington, D.C.: NASA, 1979).

4. "Bionic Ear Restores Hearing," *Science Digest* (June 1984).

5. M. Capozzi and B. Mineo, "Nonspeech Language and Communication Systems," in *Language Disorders in Children: Recent Advances*, ed. A. L. Holland (San Diego: College-Hill Press, 1984).

6. M. B. Friedman, G. Kiliany, and M. Dzonura. "Eyetracker Communication System," in *Proceedings of the Fifth Annual Conference on Rehabilitation Engineering*, ed. J. P. O'Leary and J. R. O'Reagan (Bethesda, Md.: The Rehabilitation Engineering Society of North America, 1982).

7. C. M. Mellor, *Aids for the 80's: What They Are and What They Do* (New York: American Foundation for the Blind, 1981).

8. R. C. Kurzweil, "Kurzweil Reading Machine for the Blind," in *Proceedings of the Johns Hopkins First National Search for Applications of Personal Computing to Aid the Handicapped*, ed. P. L. Hazan (New York: The IEEE Computer Society Press, 1981).

9. A. Cavalier, "Bioengineering for Mentally Retarded Persons: Increasing Independence Through New Technologies," *The Forum* (Arlington, Tx.: NCEARC, 1984); T. S. Serota, "A Voiced Controlled Personal Computer System with Word Processing Capabilities for the Severely Physically Handicapped," in *Discovery 83: Computers for the Disabled*, ed. J. E. Roehl (Menomonie, Wi.: Stout Rehabilitation Institute, 1984).

10. W. Schneider and W. Seamone, "A Microprocessor Controlled Robotic Arm Allows Self Feeding for a Quadriplegic," in *Proceedings of the IEEE Computer Society Workshop on the Application of Personal Computing to Aid the Handicapped*, ed. P. L. Hazan (New York: IEEE, 1980).

11. Cavalier, "Bioengineering for Mentally Retarded Persons."

12. R. Thorkildsen and A. Hofmeister, "Interactive Video Authoring of Instruction for the Mentally Handicapped," *Exceptional Education Quarterly,* vol. 4, no. 4 (1984) pp. 57-73.

13. D. F. Allen and V. S. Allen, *Ethical Issues in Mental Retardation* (Nashville: Abingdon, 1979).

14. D. Kaplan, "The Consumer and Basic Engineering Research: Problems in Co-invention," and I. K. Zola, "Involving the Consumer in the Rehabilitation Process: Easier Said Than Done," in *Technology for Independent Living Proceedings of the 1980 Workshops on Science and Technology for the Handicapped,* ed. V. W. Stern and M. R. Redden (Washington, D.C.: American Association for the Advancement of Science, 1982).

15. W. Wolfensberger, "The Origin and Nature of our Institutional Models," in *Changing Patterns in Residential Services for the Mentally Retarded,* ed. R. Kugel and W. Wolfensberger (Washington, D.C.: President's Committee on Mental Retardation, 1969).

16. M. P. Burgdorf, "Legal Rights of Developmentally Disabled Persons," in *Program Issues in Developmental Disabilities: A Resource Manual for Surveyors and Reviewers,* ed. J. F. Gardner, L. Long, R. Nichols, and D. M. Iagulli (Baltimore: Paul H. Brookes, 1980).

17. *Ethical Standards of Psychologists* (Washington, D.C.: American Psychological Association, 1977); *Standards for Providers of Psychological Services* (Washington D.C.: American Psychological Association, 1977).

18. The Council for Exceptional Children, "Code of Ethics and Standards for Professional Practice," *Exceptional Children,* vol. 50, no. 3 (1983) pp. 205-9.

19. D. Callahan and S. Bok, *Ethics Teaching in Higher Education* (New York: Plenum Press, 1980).

20. Allen & Allen, *Ethical Issues in Mental Retardation.*

9

Easing Everyday Living: Technology for the Physically Disabled

Georgia L. McMurray

Everyday human behavior reaffirms the commonality of the human experience. Each day, countless numbers of people around the world get up, dress, and eat a meal, almost without thought. As they go off to work, they hardly think about the discrete physical manipulations they carried out less than an hour before, the exertion of muscular strength, the finger dexterity. They routinely use the street, the bus, the car, all adaptations to the natural environment, to carry them from their home. But for some people, these everyday activities are not routine, nor is such transportation easily available or accessible. For this group of people to function, the modification of the environment or the use of technology to compensate for reduced physical capabilities is crucial. (See Chapter 8, "The Application of Technology in the Classroom and Work Place: Unvoiced Premises and Ethical Issues.")

Over 32 million persons were considered disabled in the United States in 1981, based upon estimates of the National Center for Health Statistics, the latest data available.[1] To most, disability usually conjures up images of a person with physical limitations. However, the term can cover a wide variety of physical, emotional, or mental limitations that prohibit a person from carrying out tasks in a full and competent manner by the norms of a given society. We are all familiar with the adage, "In the kingdom of the blind, the one-eyed man is king," which reflects the relative nature of disability, as well as, perhaps more subtly, the political power that accrues to individuals who have greater physical dexterity.

Within the broad categories of physical, emotional, or mental disability, there are a number of differences; for instance, a person who is physically disabled may be visually impaired, hearing impaired, or have an orthopedic limitation, or that person might have a chronic illness or disease such as a cardiac condition, kidney ailment, or cancer. Similarly, someone who is orthopedically handicapped may have the loss of an arm or a leg, or may be a quadriplegic. Some persons may have more than one disability, and so may be considered multiply disabled. The technology needed to compensate for these various limitations will differ in complexity and cost.

Demographic dimensions of disability also exist. Disabled persons differ by sex, race, age, ethnicity, language, and socioeconomic level. Family or economic resources can make a major difference in the capability of the disabled person to adjust to a social or work environment. For example, a disabled child born into a family of wealth who can afford to purchase the service of around-the-clock personal care, arrange for individualized home tutoring, and assure the availability of a chauffeur-driven car, as well as the best of medical care, will live and function far differently than the disabled person living in a walk-up tenement building, whose income is derived from public assistance. Similarly, a disabled person whose family can provide personal care is usually better off than someone who must rely on paid services, which are often impersonal and unreliable.

The lack of access to affordable and reliable transportation is considered by many to be one of the major inhibiting factors to the full participation of physically disabled people in the everyday world. The society is not constructed to accommodate the wide variety of physical differences that exist. Buildings, work sites, and homes are built for "normal" people, but normal is usually narrowly defined. Because of this, many people, both those traditionally considered disabled and others are shut out from jobs, from decent living arrangements, and from seeking fun and pleasure.

Only recently has there been much interest in addressing the need of disabled people for assistance in dealing with everyday living. Much of this momentum sprang from the struggles over the past two decades of disabled people (and their allies) to address the right of disabled people to full citizenship, that is, to assure the right to education, housing, employment, transportation, and other social benefits and programs that are commonly available. The pressure for the establishment of civil rights for the disabled is a continuous theme that now extends to every aspect of American life.

Basic to the civil rights of disabled people, as to any other aggrieved group, is the right to self-determination. Deciding what one's life will be and having access to the resources to achieve that objective is a fundamental tenet of human rights. For disabled people, this means the right to participate fully in the society at large: to have accommodations made so that they may work, travel and play as any other. Indeed, the thrust of the Rehabilitation Act of 1973 was to establish the full participation of disabled people in the mainstream of society (see Chapter 1, "Disability Rights: From Caste to Class in the Context of Civil Rights.")

Though directed at activities supported through public dollars, this legislation has had an impact far beyond that. With the increased visibility of disabled people, as they move out of the home and institutions into the public plazas and the labor market, private and commercial enterprises have begun to show interest in meeting the not inconsiderable market demand that is being generated by their presence.

In spite of this, major and often insurmountable barriers continue to exist in meeting basic survival, communication, mobility, and self-improvement needs of large numbers of disabled people. Activists among them insist, however, that the intellectual and economic resources do exist, certainly in the United States, to eliminate natural and artificial barriers to full and independent living.

This chapter describes current trends in the use of technology to assist disabled people with disabilities in everyday living—in personal care and self-improvement, in housing, and in transportation. Rather than provide an inventory of the technology, it will discuss how technological trends reflect the images disabled people hold of themselves, the attitudes held by government officials and the general public toward the disabled, and the controversies that arise from these conflicting views.

DEFINING TECHNOLOGY

Technology to aid persons with disabilities has many manifestations from the development of audio or visual equipment to specialized installations in transportation systems. In the field of health care, technology has taken on a special meaning, referring to medical breakthroughs in prosthetics, organ transplantations, and the discovery of vaccines to eradicate diseases such as poliomyelitis and smallpox. In an article prepared for the 1977 White House Conference on Handicapped Individuals, Dr. W. A. Ayers calls technology "the systematic application of scientific or other organized knowledge to practical tasks."[2] To him, the most important consequence in technology is breaking a task into its component parts, after which organized knowledge can be applied. This chapter, which deals particularly with the physically disabled, will expand upon his categorization to include engineering advances as well as programmatic innovations.

Technology can be defined by what it is not. For example, Dr. Ayers has a category—*nontechnology*—often called supportive therapy, where the operative tasks are usually caring for and standing by, for example, home attendant care. To compensate for certain physical malfunctions, some technology goes only "half-way." Examples of this type are organ transplants, appliances, or environmental modifications. In general, the technology available for physically disabled persons falls within the range of half-way measures. Then there is *"decisive technology,"* which encompasses changes based on discovery of the cause for a disease. Preventive methods would fall in this category, for example, the use of vaccines or behavior modifications such as campaigning against drunken driving or the use of alcohol or tobacco.

PERSONAL CARE

Until recently, family members, usually the female in the home—mother, daughter, or sister—provided personal care for a disabled relative who was unable to dress, bathe, or eat without assistance. These caregivers were responsible for cooking the meals, cleaning the house, doing the laundry, and most importantly, nurturing the children. Thus, caring for the disabled family member was a natural extension of these tasks. This was and continues to be woman's work—unpaid labor in the home. Society expects that the family will care for its dependent members such as children, the elderly, and the disabled.

In past years, chronic disability was unusual. Persons suffering a debilitating disease did not live long and so did not become a "burden" on the family. This was particularly true of children who were born with severe physical disabilities. Some families kept their disabled members closeted, particularly those with emotional or mental disabilities, out of a sense of family shame. But those closeted at home did have their personal care needs tended to by the family, although in some families, the attitude toward disabled members was less than benign. Children and adults who required full-time care and whose behavior was such as to create a stigma for the family were usually placed in institutions. These persons were literally "locked up" until death, often completely abandoned by their own family.

Today the role of the family in providing for the personal care of disabled persons has changed radically. First of all, rehabilitation medicine has assisted disabled persons to become more self-reliant. Technological advancements in the use of plastics, metals, and other materials have spurred the development of aids that can compensate for the loss of dexterity in dressing and eating, for example, oversized eating utensils and Velcro inserts on clothing rather than zippers. The use of handgrips, shower benches, and lifts has made bathing much easier for the disabled and has diminished the need for outside assistance.

Second, the way families function now has radically changed, placing stress on family relationships and demands upon public resources for outside support in complementing or substituting for the family responsibility. Families are less available today to provide care, particularly female family members who have now moved into the labor force and are no longer able to provide full-time care at home. This irreversible trend, a central ingredient in the struggle for women's rights, has made more public the needs of those disabled people who are unable to care for themselves. It is perhaps ironic that the movement for the deinstitutionalization of the chronically physically and mentally disabled, which cast vast numbers of disabled persons, particularly the mentally disabled, adrift,[3] occurred at a time when women were flocking in large numbers to paid jobs.

The demand for government intervention to deal with these cataclysmic changes has markedly increased over the past ten years, particularly for home health and personal care service for the disabled. Much of the pressure has been for financing such services through Medicaid and Medicare. In 1982, for example, $597 million of the total national Medicaid budget was expended for home health care, approximately 77 percent of which was provided in New York State, because of the rapid growth of the home attendant program in New York City during the 1970s. Much of these program resources are used for frail elderly people; few are available for disabled young people. Additionally, Title XX (Social Services block grant) funds are used for home health care. Nationally, in 1982, approximately $400 million (15 percent of Title XX funds) were spent for these purposes, again mostly to the frail elderly. Medicare and services under the Older Americans Act are also used to support home health care and private insurance pays for a sizable portion, too.

The use of home health care services to provide for personal care is basically a nontechnological approach to the needs of the disabled. Such services rely on the skills and commitment of dedicated staff, and the use of rehabilitative aids plays only a small role in the provision of such care.

Recently there has been experimentation in the use of robots as substitutes for human provision of service to the disabled in the home. Such engineering feats can only be viewed as half-way efforts. It is highly unlikely that robots will be routinely available as substitutes for human labor or provided at reasonable cost. Most disabled people will not be able to afford to purchase or rent such a machine on their own. Government subsidy or third-party insurance carriers may be alternative sources for financing; however, the large expenditures of public dollars to purchase high-tech equipment for a relatively small group of people may have serious public consequences for financing health care and rehabilitation services generally.

More fundamentally, however, the disabled and their advocates should consider whether such uses of technology would be truly beneficial. First of all, do we wish to promote a population of people whose primary source of care is through a machine that does not nurture the psychological, emotional, or spiritual aspects of life? The absence of personal care should not be used as a justification for the use of a machine. Machines as substitutes for human care are contrary to social values that seek to increase direct contact of disabled people with others as a way to break down stereotypical attitudes about disability. Do we wish to reinforce an individualistic, atomistic society where disabled people are even less dependent on family and friends? Is independence to be achieved at any cost? The promotion of machines as technological advances for the disabled will move us in that direction. Rehabilitation specialists, counselors, and others comment frequently about the resistance that many disabled people have to using aids because they bring attention to their limitations. And then there is the question of cosmetics. Many rehabilitation aids might more readily be used if they were more aesthetic in design or style, for example, wheelchairs are bulky in size, constructed of metal which has a hard, cold look. The look of soft colors and fabrics might be preferable. Many of the rehabilitation aids now available look like hospital equipment, connoting an image of illness that disabled people are struggling to avoid.

U.S. business and industry have been quite adept at sensing the demographics of a consumer public. As the income of disabled persons rises, consumer demand for rehabilitative aids to assist in personal care will increase. Undoubtedly, the marketplace will respond by creating devices that are both utilitarian and aesthetic and, which, ideally, can be used within the context of a loving and caring community of family and friends.

HOUSING

Finding a suitable dwelling place can be an exhausting and exasperating experience for disabled people who do not have a physically accessible home or where assistance in personal care, if needed, is not nearby. Suitable housing, then, depends upon having a home free of architectural barriers such as steps, elevators that require visual acuity to operate, or other humanmade structural elements. In addition, suitability means having access to personal care and housekeeping services, depending on the nature of the disability.

Housing for disabled people falls into two categories—independent and institutional—each of which may be available through public, not-for-profit, or commercial arrangements. They may include private rental, home ownership, or cooperative living arrangements; sometimes they may be supported through government subsidy, or the disabled person may pay for the full cost of housing without help.

As indicated earlier, by and large, in the past disabled people lived at home with their families or, when their families could not care for them, in institutions. The latter was particularly true for those who were poor or severely disabled. The warehousing of disabled people, especially those mentally ill or retarded, has had a long history in this nation. In fact, it has only been recently, through the deinstitutionalization movement, that warehousing has become socially unacceptable.

Like most people in the United States, disabled people are almost totally dependent on the private housing market to secure a place to live. Also, like other persons who have little or no income, disabled people find it very difficult to secure decent, affordable housing.[4] This problem exists in rural, suburban, and urban communities throughout the United States and with increasing frequency, as evidenced by the growing numbers of homeless people, many disabled who are living on the streets of major cities and towns.[5]

In recent years, some disabled people have formed self-help groups or independent living centers, to provide mutual support, housing assistance, information about benefits, job referrals, and other services needed to maintain themselves free and independent from families or institutions. The Center for Independent Living in Berkeley, California, the first of its kind, has become a model for the nation. In these centers, the disabled people serve as the board, the staff, and the consumers, becoming effective advocates in their local communities.

With the movement for independent living, the desire of the disabled to have their own place has become a dominant theme, but most housing construction has not taken account of physical disability. Not only do steps and elevators present risk to life and limb, most doorways are not wheelchair-accessible, that is, they are less than 30 inches wide. Suitable placement of electrical sockets and protective covering around them to prevent a sightless person from being burned is necessary. The height of lighting fixtures and kitchen and bathroom appliances and fixtures is critical for wheelchair-bound persons, as well as the provision of ramps rather than stairs. What is most interesting about the litany of these physical barriers to suitable housing is that the removal of these barriers is relatively simple and inexpensive. Indeed, many of these adaptations would benefit fully able-bodied persons as well.

Newly constructed housing, particularly that financed through federal subsidy, is, by and large, barrier free since the passage of section 504 in 1973; but the rehabilitation and construction of housing through government subsidy has almost ground to a halt due to recent federal budget cutbacks. Disabled people must compete in the private market for rental housing that is also being sought by others with greater economic means.

Even in the days when government subsidized housing was available, disabled people were poorly served. Take, for instance, section 202 housing which was ostensibly enacted to meet the housing needs of the elderly and the handicapped in the 1960s. The experience of that program is representative of the more than 130 federal programs that used to be available for both the elderly and the handicapped, the two groups which are invariably linked in legislation addressing special needs. According to a 1979 report issued by the federal Department of Housing and Urban Development, although the section 202 program was amended in 1964 to include "handicapped persons and families," very few of these persons actually lived in projects supported through the legislation.[6] Moreover, sponsors had not been required to maintain specific data on the number of handicapped or disabled people served. Beyond the bias in favor of the elderly, particularly the white middle-class elderly, reflected in the development of the section 202 projects, a specific prejudice against disabled people was noticed by HUD when the study was conducted. For example, some project managers stated that they did not accept handicapped persons because such people created a "depressing atmosphere" for other tenants. The majority of managers did not want medical personnel located in the building for fear that an atmosphere of despair and weakness would be generated. Some stated that the handicapped would not fit in "with our kind of tenant"; and, further, that the project had not been built to accommodate handicapped persons (no handrails or no barrier-free design had been mandated). Interestingly enough, some reported that the elderly tenants would perceive nonelderly persons as intruders.

Section 202 was enacted to provide independent living for elderly and handicapped individuals whose income is above the public housing income limits but below the level to afford standard private sector housing. Yet in this instance, neither the government nor the project managers felt it necessary to ensure that disabled persons received any equity in the program.

Other government programs have affected advances in housing for disabled persons by providing alternatives to rental housing that include community-based facilities, half-way houses and long-term care facilities, but these are primarily institutions whose physical structures have been altered to assure a barrier-free environment. One major advantage of institutional arrangements is that personal care services, housekeeping, meals, and other amenities are assured, all of which represent a nontechnological approach to meeting living needs of the disabled. To a large extent the persons who live there are served well, but these represent a minuscule portion of those disabled persons with special housing needs.

What is often overlooked is that the housing needs of disabled people, except those who require significant help with personal care, are similar to the general population. For example, at a recent meeting on women's issues, much discussion took place about the need for housing design that considered changing family lifestyles—ramps to ease the pushing of baby carriages and shopping carts, elevators, and communal kitchens. Pressure should be placed on architects, housing developers, and others involved in the housing market to respond to an increased consumer demand from a variety of quarters that is based on an awareness of how real people live.

A major issue for disabled people, though, is whether special housing for disabled people should be pursued or whether the thrust should be for a general liberalization of the housing market so that the disabled, like others, would have a free choice of a place to live. Certainly, as the income of disabled persons increases through expanded employment, such a demand may not be far off. Already, real estate developers in Southern California are soliciting buyers for homes specifically designed for those who use wheelchairs. Advertised in 1981 for $127,000 and up, these homes provide for easy entry and modifications in the bathroom. Obviously, however, their cost is beyond the means of most disabled persons.

Government assistance, both for mandating requirements in various federal housing programs for barrier-free design and for providing subsidy to low-income disabled people and pressing for their inclusion in federal housing programs, is a must. However, in the absence of any major government subsidy program in the near future for all persons in need of housing support, the national production of new rental housing is projected to fall short of overall demand, largely due to continuing high interest rates and the ongoing gap between rent levels required to make development feasible and what tenants can be expected to afford.[7]

Despite this, advocacy groups must insist that a range of housing options be made increasingly available for disabled persons. Most of all, this means accessible private housing. Not all disabled people will be able to live independently; some may prefer or require residence within the family home, if only to assure that personal care is routinely available. Many of these persons may need full-service institutions when they are older and parents or other family members are no longer available.

RECREATION AND CULTURAL ACTIVITIES

Play and leisure are as necessary as work, perhaps even more so, for disabled people, who also need to have positive self-images and an affirmation that they too can express themselves through active participation in artistic or athletic endeavors. And some disabled people may wish to have a place for quiet reflection outside the home or participate in artistic and cultural events. In either case, limited opportunities for recreation and culture have only recently become available.

Radio, television, and videocassette recorders, are technological inventions which bring art, culture, and entertainment to the home. But not everyone wants to stay in the house. While some progress has been made by advocacy groups in alerting public attention to the need to have facilities barrier free, theaters, movie houses, museums, and restaurants need to be made accessible to wheelchairs, not only for front entrances but also for the use of bathroom facilities, seating arrangements, and the like. Part of the difficulty in dealing adequately with the problems of accessibility is that most public buildings were constructed prior to the pressure for barrier-free facilities. With low market demand from disabled consumers, public managers and private proprietors can effectively resist renovations that would facilitate the use of recreation and cultural activities by disabled people.

But there are some beginnings. For example, the main branch of the New York City Public Library now advertises its Project Access, which offers special materials and equipment to link "people with visual, hearing, and mobility problems to the full range of library resources," including a Kurzweill Reading Machine (a computer capable of converting the printed word into synthetic speech), and telecommunication devices for the deaf.[8] All of the library's collections are fully accessible to wheelchairs. In Nevada City, California, an Independence Trail has been created for wheelchair hikers to enjoy the out-of-doors. And then there is "Sparky," a mobility vehicle with four-wheel stability and two-speed transmission, which is capable of climbing steep hills.[9]

Although wheelchairs are still primarily designed for inside use only, some are being redesigned for use as special basketball and racing chairs. Customized devices now can help wheelchair users enjoy activities once denied them: fishing, camping, rafting, canoeing, and skiing. A downhill ski-sled for disabled people, the ARROYA, has been developed that "allows the ski-sled user to interact naturally with skiers using other types of equipment, that is, skis, boots, poles."[10] This interaction between ambulatory and nonambulatory persons is in contrast to sports that are segregated events.

In the attempt to demonstrate that disabled people can compete effectively in activities that have heretofore been closed to them such as athletic events for the disabled, the segregation of the disabled from mainstream society may be inadvertently reinforced. The establishment of the International Olympics for the Disabled may keep disabled people from competing in the well-known Olympic spectacular, even though they may have the capability to do so.

Disabled people need the opportunity in and outside the home, to interact with others, disabled and able-bodied, in the pursuit of pleasure. Again, the issue is not whether the activity should be for disabled persons only, or whether disabled should be fully integrated into those activities that are available to the general public. Rather, the question is one of individual choice.

The image of physical prowess is fundamental to human and animal society, therefore, the need for disabled people to demonstrate physical competence is understandable. However, many disabled people have talents and strengths which lie elsewhere. Not everyone can race fast, either in wheelchairs or on foot. We must be careful that in promoting the specific talent or skill of a few, we do not cause the less talented to shy away. Disabled youth who may believe themselves inferior because of physical limitations may have that image reinforced if they see other disabled people making herculean efforts in physical competition which they cannot—or wish not—to make.

TRANSPORTATION

Before the 1960s, most disabled people with mobility problems stayed at home, not out of choice but out of necessity. Transportation to work or recreation was seldom available, except by private car or taxi, both of which could be costly. With the breaking down of the legal barriers in the 1970s to full participation in public life, the right to fully accessible transportation has become a major rallying cry for the disabled community and their advocates. Indeed, fueled by the activism of returning disabled Vietnam veterans, no other issue is as much associated with advocacy for disabled rights in the public eye.

The Urban Mass Transportation Act of 1964, amended in 1970, explicitly established government responsibility for making mass transit service accessible to disabled people. The amendment authorized the development of paratransit services and the elimination of barriers in mass transit systems as well. Despite pressures over the decade, federal and local authorities have been ambivalent about pursuing these objectives, which reflect conflicting views about the transit needs of the disabled and the extent to which government should be held accountable for meeting these needs. In 1981, the federal government issued new regulations establishing a local option provision, thereby delegating substantial responsibility to local transit authorities for assuring the requirements of the federal law. This move, though championing participation of disabled consumers in devising plans for making transit systems accessible, in fact, signaled the withdrawal of the federal government as a major protector of rights for the disabled.

The controversy about making mass transit accessible has been fractious and sometimes bitter. To press local authorities to carry out the intent of the federal law, disabled rights advocates have had to seek court action. New York City is a particular example of how bitter the struggle can be. Most people in New York City depend upon the public transit system for their economic—and often social—survival. Disabled advocates demand equal access to the same public utility, pointing out the potential ridership that exists among the disabled. For example, the New York Office for the Handicapped estimates that 137,000 persons have a public transit disability. Less than 10 percent of these believe that they are adequately served by existing services.[11] In 1982, the Eastern Paralyzed Veterans Association obtained a preliminary injunction against the Metropolitan Transportation Authority (MTA) in New York to prevent substantial renovations at subway stations because they excluded plans for handicapped accessibility. In a countermove, the MTA sought to weaken state laws to obtain a total exemption from requirements to make transit stations accessible. According to the MTA, the issue was cost, and a large volume of data was compiled to document that newly constructed or substantially renovated stations would require far more public dollars than budgeted. The Veterans Association, in seeking a resolution to the stalemate, is insisting upon a multimodal transportation system that would include access to at least 50 percent of the buses, renovations of key subway stations, and possibly a supplemental paratransit feeder. Governor Cuomo has given his support to this, while Mayor Koch has been opposed.[12] Opponents to assuring fully accessible mass transit usually base their arguments on cost. Certainly, much bureaucratic time has been spent on "documenting" how costly the major renovations or new construction of subway stations would be. However, as Moakley and Weisman pointed out in a 1981 article in *Paralegia News,* cost figures developed by transportation authorities may be inflated because of assumptions made about such items as the time frame in which the conversion should occur, the additional equipment that will be required to make up for lost seating capacity, and lift operation delay during rush hour service.[13]

Arguments about costs for making transit changes accessible may hide more basic reservations. For example, as with housing project managers, managers of transit systems might prefer that disabled people be served through separate facilities through benign concerns expressed for their safety and protection. Some who resist change state that disabled people might be injured during the rush hours or that they might be more vulnerable to criminal attack; others cite the physical hazards of the transit system—subway platforms, for instance—but offer few solutions as to how such hazards might be corrected.

But to some, the issue is less cost or benign concern and more one of attitudes: attitudes of the public bureaucracy and, to some extent, the public itself. Proponents of fully accessible mass transit assert the basic civil right of disabled persons to such public service. The key issue here is integration; indeed, references are often made to the *Brown* v. *Topeka* decision outlawing school desegregation in 1954, with the dictum that "Separate facilities are inherently unequal."

Arguments have been raised by advocates that disabled people pay taxes like other citizens, and thus have a right to benefit from public services already supported by tax dollars. To them, equality is not the only issue; equity must be addressed as well. Such arguments are coherent with political ideologies that promote the notion that government policies should be redistributive.

Because of the demand for accessible transportation over the past two decades, however, some progress has been made. Two major trends reflect the conflict over whether or not disabled persons would be better served through transit services that are separate from a mass system. The issue of integration versus segregation underlies such conflict.

Some communities have opted for developing paratransit systems as a way of assuring protective accessible transportation for disabled persons. These systems usually involve vans or minibuses that pick up and discharge passengers, often on a designated route or at their homes. Most of these systems require that appointments be made and the cost for service is usually much higher than the relatively inexpensive mass transit; thus, these paratransit systems may sometimes be subsidized through government funds.

In Reading, Pennsylvania, for example, such a service exists for handicapped and elderly citizens, utilizing a combination of 34 vans, omnibuses, busettes, and station wagons equipped with a variety of mechanical and motorized devices for boarding, seating, and alighting. All of the vehicles are radio-equipped and linked to the dispatchers and office staff. The system operates door to door on a demand/response basis. Most of the riders receive the service through a local social services contract. Many drivers work part-time as ambulance drivers or as licensed practical nurses; most are Red Cross certified.[14]

Westport, Connecticut, has also established a paratransit service. It did so out of an expressed community interest to seek a waiver from federal Department of Transportation requirements that all buses used in fixed route service be wheelchair accessible after a certain date. The promotion of such a system was initiated by the Mobility Advisory Group of the Westport Transit District, who cited the local terrain as a major barrier to the mobility-impaired in getting to a lift-operated bus on a fixed route. The purpose of this paratransit system is to foster the integration of the mass transportation system with the paratransit service. The cost of the "maxitaxi" is the same as the regular bus. The Mobility Advisory Group does not perceive this specialized service as separate or specialized for the handicapped.[15]

The development of specialized equipment for use in a mass transit system first occurred in the 1960s as a result of an Urban Mass Transportation Administration demonstration grant. This equipment, the Transbus, was ostensibly designed as an incentive for increasing the use of public transit by auto-bound commuters. This bus had a wider front door and an electric ramp that extended at each stop to board all passengers, including the disabled, who were somewhat involved in developing its design specifications. Although some prototype models were, in fact, developed at a total project cost of $27 million, the Transbus was never fully adopted by local transit authorities. Moakley suggests two reasons for this: the shift of grants to private and public agencies in the 1970s to establish paratransit services and the dilution of federal regulations in 1976 to require only local authorities receiving federal funds to make special efforts to improve mass transit service for the disabled.[16] As a result, the Transbus project was dropped.

Today, however, local transit authorities have a wide array of options that can be used to make mass transit accessible, from renovation and construction of facilities to the use of specialized equipment such as lift-operated buses. For example, the Eastern Paralyzed Veterans Association, in its critique of the New York Metropolitan Transportation Authority's resistance to making transit facilities accessible, points out that the agency has not considered the availability of new transit station elevator technology that could increase the utilization of public transportation. They cited the screw column elevator, which has a minimum of site preparation, thick insulation, and low maintenance cost. In a similar vein, a study of the Washington, D.C. Metro subway system indicated that many of the 7,000 elevator users counted were nondisabled persons who preferred the convenience of an elevator, either because of a mild mobility problem or age.[17]

Commercial airlines have been amenable to providing special assistance to some handicapped passengers, including wheelchairs for those unable to walk long distances from the terminal. Railway lines are now providing similar help as well. And bus companies permit a travel companion to ride free of charge if the disabled persons needs such help and has a medical statement to that effect.

Some barriers are easier and less costly to remove than others. Removing high steps, narrow aisles, and unnecessary doors are easily within the realm of current technology. But, according to Kinley, the barriers most critical to disabled passengers appear to be movement-oriented ones relating to vehicle acceleration and deceleration.[18] One improvement that could be considered, without necessitating changing propulsion systems or roadbed design, would be putting additional doors on vehicles so that seating could occur more rapidly. Handgrips and warning signals within easy reach would be most helpful. All of these recommendations are simple and would not require the major outlay of funds anticipated for the installation of specially designed lift-operated buses or elevators.

CONCLUSION

The use of technology in personal care, housing, transportation, recreation, and culture has been fostered by a desire for independent living. But many difficulties remain in accomplishing this objective because of attitudinal barriers, either in the society or by the disabled community itself.

Several issues must remain in the forefront. It should be understood that the disabled community is not monolithic; the range and degree of disability among various groups are undocumented, which leave major gaps in knowledge as to the kind of technology needed to adapt the environment or enable the disabled person to function with less reliance on others. Also, information about the incidence and prevalence of particular disabilities is required for projection of needs. Such information bears directly on the issue of consumer demand. Concurrently, much of the demand for making mass transit accessible has come from wheelchair-bound persons; less has been heard from persons with other disabilities whose mobility needs may be just as inhibiting but of a different order.

Major improvements in wheelchairs have resulted recently from demands of younger, mostly male, disabled persons who may be athletic minded or who have a strong need to project muscular strength, while the extent of the market demand for such technological innovations is unknown. More unsettling, however, is whether this image of the disabled person, while overcoming one stereotype, may at the same time be a disservice to countless others whose needs for accessible services are going unnoticed. Consumer demand has another facet as well. Because of the low income of most disabled people, commercial interests have little incentive in developing technological innovations to address housing, personal care, and the mobility needs of a vast number of disabled people. It is disabled people at a higher income level who thus can create a market demand.

More fundamentally, this society may need to address whether disabled people, as any other aggrieved group, should be expected to rely solely on their own resources to arrange for their basic living needs. To some degree, this question has been partly addressed through the availability of Social Security Disability benefits, Supplemental Security Income, vocational rehabilitation services, and various other government subsidies. However, the available help from government—federal, state, and local—is minuscule when compared to the actual income, employment, education, and rehabilitative needs of most disabled people. Moreover, the costs of assuring barrier-free design in housing and transportation and recreation-cultural facilities can become astronomical. The issue then is: Are we as a society prepared to pay the price? To what degree should the needs of the disabled be given greater priority over the needs of poor children, the elderly, the historically discriminated against minorities, for example? There is no easy answer to the question, particularly when the political process operates to accommodate these special interests in a system based primarily on economic power.

The disabled community has demanded its right to independent living, to integrated rather than segregated facilities, to equal opportunities. To deal with the multivariate needs of the disabled, this society should provide a choice and an opportunity based upon the recognition of the commonality of human experience. In this way, the special needs of disabled persons may not be special at all, but ones which the nondisabled people share as well.

In addressing individuals' needs to approximate normal lifestyles, we must shy away from a propensity to gadgetry, to which this society is so prone. The use of esoteric technology to compensate for the loss of a particular physical function may be self-defeating, because if machine functions predominate, we may in fact negate the human being. This is contrary to what we are seeking: a human response to another human being, recognizing that person's right to exist with a choice as to how that existence can be made comparable to the lives of others.

NOTES

1. *Statistical Abstract of the United States,* (Washington, D.C.: U.S. Bureau of the Census, 1984; 1983).

2. W. R. Ayers, "Application of Technology to Handicapping Conditions and for Handicapped Individuals, Part A," vol. 1 (Washington, D.C.: White House conference on Handicapped Individuals, May 1977).

3. Susan Cina and Francis G. Caro, *Supporting Families Who Care for Severely Disabled Children at Home: A Public Policy Perspective* (New York City: Community Service Society, 1984).

4. According to the Interim Report of the President's Commission on Housing, October 1981, "Less than a sixth of all households (15.6 percent) pay excess housing costs [more than 30 percent of their income], but among low income renters nearly two out of every three households (63 percent) bear excessive rent burdens."

5. Dan Salerno, Kim Hopper, and Ellen Baxter, *Hardship in the Heartland: Homelessness in Eight U.S. Cities* (New York: Community Service Society, 1984).

6. U.S. Department of Housing and Urban Development, *Housing for the Elderly and Handicapped: The Experience of the Section 202 Program from 1959 to 1977* (Washington, D.C.: U.S. Government Printing Office, 1979).

7. Anthony Downs, *Rental Housing in the 1980s* (Washington, D.C.: The Brookings Institution, 1983).

8. Informational brochure on Project Access, distributed by the New York Public Library.

9. Bulletins on Science and Technology for the Handicapped, vol. 4, no. 3 (Summer 1984).

10. Bulletins on Science and Technology for the Handicapped, vol. 2, no. 2 (July 1981).

11. 1983 Memorandum from the New York City Mayor's Office of the Handicapped.

12. *Paraplegia News,* vol. 38, no. 1 (January 1984).

13. Terry Moakley and Jim Weisman, "Cost: Is the Price of Accessible Mass Transit Too High?" in *Paraplegia News,* vol. 35, no. 10 (October 1981).

14. "Memorandum on Specialized Transportation for the Handicapped and Elderly: An Update for 1980," describing the specialized transportation service of the Berks Area Reading Transportation Authority in Pennsylvania.

15. Taken from the Resolution passed by the Mobility Advisory Group of the Westport Transit District in Connecticut on February 28, 1980.

16. Terry Moakley, "History: A Personal Look Backward at the Mass Transit Issue," *Paraplegia News,* vol. 35, no. 10 (October 1981).

17. Terry Moakley, "Case Studies of Accessible Mass Transportation" *Paraplegia News,* vol. 38, no. 1 (January 1984).

18. Holly J. Kinley, "Latent Travel Demand of the Aging and Handicapped and Barriers to Travel," unpublished manuscript.

10

The Awful Privacy of Baby Doe

Nat Hentoff

Eighteen months had passed since the Indiana baby, born with Downs syndrome and a defective digestive system, had been allowed to die of starvation and dehydration. But Linda McCabe, a registered nurse in the special-care nursery of Bloomington Hospital, was still mourning both the infant and her inability to save him.

"At least I wasn't part of the killing," she told me when I asked her to talk about it. "The other nurses in special care and I told the hospital administration we would not help starve that child. So the baby was moved to another part of the hospital, and the parents had to hire private nurses."

Linda McCabe, remembering the evening the orders came to give the baby nothing by mouth and no intravenous feeding, became angry all over again. "Who did they think they were—asking me to do something like that? By the fourth day it got so bad, thinking about that baby just lying there, crying, that some of us nurses started checking in law books to see if we could find some legal arguments to stop the killing of that baby. But as it turned out he only had two more days to live."

I had found Linda McCabe through a Bloomington pediatrician, James Schaffer, who when the baby was born had strongly recommended routine surgery to correct the infant's deformed esophagus, so that he could eat normally. The parents rejected Dr. Schaffer's advice. They did not want a retarded child.

This chapter first appeared in the Atlantic Monthly (January 1985), pp. 54-63. Reprinted by permission of author.

It is impossible to tell so soon after birth whether a child with Down's syndrome will be mildly, moderately, or severely retarded. The coroner wrote later: "The potential for mental function and social integration of this child, as of all infants with Down's syndrome, is unknown."

Nonetheless, the parents had agreed with their obstetrician, Dr. Walter Owens, that a child with Down's syndrome cannot attain what Dr. Owens called "a minimally adequate quality of life." On the baby's last day Dr. Schaffer and two colleagues, despite the wishes of the parents, went, bearing intravenous equipment, to feed the baby. They were too late. The process of dying could not be reversed.

The baby died on April 15, 1982. Two days later *The Evansville* [Indiana] *Courier* printed a letter from Sherry McDonald: "The night before little Infant Doe died, I called the Indiana Supreme Court and told them I wanted the baby saved. Then my 16-year-old called and said, 'I am a Down's syndrome child and I want the baby boy saved.'"

I had come to Dr. Schaffer and Linda McCabe while trying to learn more about this form of infanticide—the decision by parents and physicians to deny lifesaving medical treatment (and sometimes nourishment) to handicapped babies. I had started looking into the subject because of conversations I'd had, in New York and elsewhere, with nurses and pediatric surgeons who felt that unless more public attention were paid to quiet killings, they would continue and perhaps increase, as if these newborns were still unborn, and therefore subject to the summary judgment of abortion.

One specialist in the treatment of newborns has terminated so many brief lives that, as he told B. D. Colen, the science editor for *Newsday,* he has a recurring dream: "I've died and I'm going to Heaven, and as I go through the gates, I see what looks like this field of gently waving grass. When I look closely, it's babies, slowly undulating back and forth—the babies I've shut off."

A good many of those lives could not have been saved, because the infants were born dying. Even doctors and nurses who are critical of the ways in which irreversible decisions are made in neonatal intensive-care units would not want heroic measures to be taken in these and certain other cases: babies born with only a brainstem, for instance, or with Lesch-Nyhan syndrome, an incurable hereditary disorder that leads to mental retardation, uncontrollable spasms, and self-mutilation.

At issue are lives that could be saved, the lives of infants with such handicaps as Down's syndrome, cerebral palsy, and spina bifida. Spina bifida involves a lesion in the spinal column that can be repaired through surgery, the sooner after birth the better. Without surgery there is considerable likelihood of infection, which can lead to permanent brain damage. Nearly all children with spina bifida also have an accumulation of spinal fluid within the brain. Unless a shunt is inserted to drain the fluid, the pressure on the brain can and often does lead to mental retardation.

As a result of these medical procedures, however, along with knowledgeable follow-up treatment, children with spina bifida can grow up to be bright, productive adults, who may need braces in order to walk. Yet death is the prescription some doctors give for newborns with spina bifida. The prediction is that the child will never walk, will be severely retarded, and will suffer progressively worse bladder and bowel problems. In one highly publicized case, that of Baby Jane Doe on Long Island, the physician chosen by the parents added that the child would be in constant pain throughout her dismal life.

The leading medical expert on spina bifida is Dr. David McLone, the chief of neurosurgery at Children's Memorial Hospital, in Chicago. McLone has successfully operated on hundreds of infants with spina bifida, and he and his staff follow the children for several years and perform indicated surgery and other therapy. He asserts that physicians who do not know enough about spina bifida leave infants with that handicap untreated in hospitals throughout the country. In an interview on CBS-TV's "Sunday Morning" last August, McLone said, "Physicians are making decisions not to treat certain numbers of these children on the basis of criteria that are invalid. They are assuming that by examining a newborn child they can predict the quality of life or how independent or how productive that child is going to be, how much stress that child is going to be on the family, how much of a burden on society. They make all of these judgments based on that initial exam, and almost every one of the criteria that they use to make that judgment is invalid."

Invalid or not, as a result of those judgments many infants with spina bifida and other handicaps are allowed to die. It is as if we were already living in that ideal special-care nursery envisioned (in the context of a discussion of quality-of-life issues) by Francis Crick, the 1962 Nobel laureate in medicine and physiology: "No newborn infant should be declared human until it has passed certain tests regarding its genetic endowment and . . . if it fails these tests, it forfeits the right to live."

No one knows exactly how many Baby Does forfeit their right to live each year. No death certificate is going to declare infanticide as the cause of an infant's departure. With regard to babies with Down's syndrome, Dr. Norman Frost, a professor of pediatrics at the University of Wisconsin, noted in the December 1982 issue of *Archives of Internal Medicine:* "It is common in the United States to withhold routine surgery and medical care from infants with Down's syndrome for the explicit purpose of hastening death." With regard to infants otherwise handicapped, the President's Commission for the Study of Ethical Problems in Medicine declared in its March 1983 report, "Deciding to Forego Life-Sustaining Treatment": "Decisions to forego therapy are part of everyday life in the neonatal intensive care unit; *with rare exceptions, these choices have been made by parents and physicians without review by courts or any other body"* (emphasis added).

In consideration of the shock and grief of parents, such decisions must be private, the American Civil Liberties Union tacitly agrees. In Baby Doe cases, after the whistle has been blown by a nurse or a right-to-life organization, not once has an ACLU affiliate spoken for the infant's right to due process and equal protection under the law. Indeed, when the ACLU has become involved, it has fought resolutely for the parents' right to privacy. Baby Doe's own awful privacy, as he or she lies dying, is also thereby protected.

Along with my fellow civil libertarians, most liberals strongly support parents, and only parents, in these situations. It is hard to imagine anyone more powerless than a handicapped baby who has just been given the black spot but to my knowledge no organization of liberals or civil-rights group has ever said a word about the rights of Baby Does. Nor has any feminist group, even though the civil rights and liberties being violated in these infanticides are not only those of males.

I have discovered, moreover, that most members of these groups do not take kindly to questions on the subject. Some liberals and feminists, for instance, have told me sharply that if I were to look more closely at the kinds of people trying to save those Baby Does, I would understand such rescue efforts are a way to make women subservient again to those who would tell them what they can and cannot do with their own bodies.

It is true that the most prominent defenders of the Baby Does are such conservative hobgoblins as Ronald Reagan, the right-to-life squadrons, and the Reverend Jerry Falwell. Having picked up bad companions so early in life, the Baby Does indeed bear out the adage that people are judged by the company they keep.

After mighty internal struggles, a few liberals have decided that handicapped infants might, after all, have some constitutional rights independent of their parents' wishes for them. One such heretic, a professor of education with a history of passionate involvement in civil-liberties and civil-rights matters, told me, "For a long time I shut off on this one. If anyone asked, I gave the standard liberal line: 'At a time of such tragedy for the parents, only they have the right to decide. All we can do for them is protect the privacy of their decision.' But then, as part of some research I was doing, I began to talk to handicapped people about Baby

Does. I found out how many of them had come close to being killed in the nursery because some doctor thought their 'quality of life' wouldn't be worth a damn. But their parents had rejected that advice, and here were these severely handicapped adults—tough, resilient, leading lives that, however you define that term, were not without 'quality.'"

Many of the disabled have spoken for Baby Does, in *The Disability Rag* and others of their own publications, and in letters to magazines and newspapers. Indeed, one of the more compelling polemics in the "quality of life" debate was written, a decade ago, by a severely handicapped woman, Sondra Diamond. Her "Letter From a Vegetable," published in *Newsweek,* requires a prologue, because it was one link in a chain of circumstances that began with an article in the October 25, 1973, issue of *The New England Journal of Medicine.*

That article, "Moral and Ethical Dilemmas in the Special-Care Nursery," was the first in an American medical publication in which physicians admitted having withheld treatment from babies until they died. The killings had taken place in the special-care nursery of Yale-New Haven Hospital. (I say "killings" because, as Joseph Fletcher, a theologian who does not object to certain kinds of infanticide, has pointed out, "It is naive and superficial to suppose that because we don't 'do anything positively' to hasten a patient's death we have thereby avoided complicity in his death. Not doing anything is doing something.")

Drs. Raymond S. Duff and A. G. M. Campbell, the physicians who wrote the article, had withheld treatment from 43 babies over a two-and-a-half-year period. Their report was in no way an act of contrition. They wanted to demonstrate that in certain cases one "management option" in the special-care nursery is death. Those for whom this option was chosen were infants "considered to have little or no hope of achieving meaningful 'humanhood.'" These decisions were made in consultation with the parents, who, Drs. Duff and Campbell pointed out, believed they would be relieved of enormous long-term emotional and financial stress if they chose that particular management option.

Among the infants thus doomed was a baby with Down's syndrome who had a routinely operable intestinal obstruction—a case very much like that of the Bloomington baby. Drs. Duff and Campbell explained in the article that "his parents thought that surgery was wrong for their baby and themselves. He died seven days after birth." He died because he was retarded, although no one had any way of knowing how retarded he would be. (In 1984 the poster of the National Organization on Disability was a photograph of Matthew Starr, of Baltimore, reading the Torah during his bar mitzvah. Matthew has Down's syndrome, but that service was not simplified for him. He also wrote and read the traditional speech given by a boy entering the adult Jewish religious community.)

At the end of their article Duff and Campbell, having discussed the ethical and legal implications of decisions (including ones in which they participated) to let infants die, wrote; "If working out these dilemmas in ways such as those we suggest is in violation of the law, we believe the law should be changed."

An authoritative guide in these particular legal matters is John A. Robertson, a professor of law at the University of Texas and the author of *The Rights of the Critically Ill.* Robertson asserts that an infant born with severe mental and physical disabilities has the same right to be treated as anyone else, new or old. That right, Robertson says, "does not depend on his IQ, physical abilities, or social potential." The only exceptions are "a few very extreme cases in which . . . the burdens of treatment outweigh the benefits," as when the treatment inflicts severe pain and only delays death briefly. Otherwise, even though certain handicapped infants "appear from the perspective of 'normal' people to face a meaningless or greatly limited life," that is no justification "for denying them essential medical treatments."

Accordingly, Robertson says, parents who refuse treatment for infants with such handicaps as Down's syndrome and spina bifida "with the intent and result that they die" can be prosecuted for murder or manslaughter, not to mention child abuse and neglect. Physicians in these cases can also be prosecuted, for homicide, child neglect, and violation of child-abuse reporting laws (the parents should have been reported).

Yet Drs. Duff and Campbell, and the parents who agreed to the denial of treatment for their children, were not charged with any crime. Actually, Robertson says, "while parents of retarded children have been convicted for directly killing them, there has been only one prosecution of parents and doctors for nontreatment of defective newborns." In that case the charges were dismissed, because no one would testify at a preliminary hearing that the parents and doctors had ordered that the Baby Does—Siamese twins joined at the waist—be starved to death.

That prosecutions have been so rare is traceable to a widespread belief that decisions about the welfare of newborn infants should be made only by the parents and physicians. A more proximate factor is the infrequency with which these infant deaths become known outside the nursery. On occasion the refusal of treatment to a handicapped infant does become news—as with the Bloomington baby and, in 1983, with Baby Jane Doe on Long Island. But in neither of these cases were the parents prosecuted.

Very occasionally a court's attention is drawn to a Baby Doe who seems about to die. The hospital, unsure of its legal ground, may initiate the court action lest it be sued later for complicity in the killing of the infant. Or an outsider, learning of the imminent death from a nurse or someone else in the hospital, may try to bring a court action to save the child. No consistent pattern of court decisions has emerged, although treatment has been ordered more often than not in the relatively few cases that have come before a judge.

In one such case an infant was born with only one eye, no ear canals, a deformed esophagus, and almost certain brain damage. He soon developed convulsive seizures of unknown cause. The parents wanted him starved to death, and their doctor agreed. But Justice David Roberts, of the superior court in Cumberland County, Maine, ruled in February 1974, that "at the moment of live birth, there does exist a human being entitled to the fullest protection of the law. The most basic right enjoyed by every human being is the right to life itself."

The doctor in the case had predicted that should the infant live, he would not have a life worth living. Said Justice Roberts: "The doctor's qualitative evaluation of the value of life to be preserved is not legally within the scope of his expertise." The baby died soon after the ruling, but Justice Roberts told me ten years later that he had no regrets about his decision, because the infant had been entitled to his chance to live.

But Justice Roberts would not have known about this Baby Doe if the hospital and, initially, the parents' doctor had not asked for a hearing because they wanted to treat the child (the doctor later changed his mind). No court intervened, however, in any of the 43 infant deaths described by Drs. Duff and Campbell in their *New England Journal* article. No court knew about any of the cases. Indeed, no one except doctors reading that medical journal might have learned about the killings if *Newsweek* had not picked up the story.

In its coverage of death as a management option at Yale-New Haven Hospital, *Newsweek* used the term *vegetables* to describe some severely handicapped newborns who eventually died. Sondra Diamond wrote a letter to the magazine, and here is some of what she said:

> I'll wager my entire root system and as much fertilizer as it would take to fill Yale University that you have never received a letter from a vegetable before this one, but, much as I resent the term, I must confess that I fit the description of a "vegetable" as defined in the article . . . .
>
> Due to severe brain damage incurred at birth, I am unable to dress myself, toilet myself, or write; my secretary is typing this letter. Many thousands of dollars had to be spent on my rehabilitation and education in order for me to reach my present professional status as a Counseling Psychologist. My par-

ents were also told, 35 years ago, that there was "little or no hope of achieving meaningful "humanhood" for their daughter [afflicted with cerebral palsy].

Have I reached "humanhood"? Compared with Doctors Duff and Campbell, I believe I have surpassed it!

Instead of changing the law to make it legal to weed out us "vegetables," let us change the laws so that we may receive quality medical care, education, and freedom to live as full and productive lives as our potentials allow.

Four years later, in 1977, Sondra Diamond wrote an afterward in *Human Life Review*. She told of being taken to the hospital with third-degree burns over 60 percent of her body when she was in her early twenties. "The doctors felt that there was no point in treating me because I was disabled anyway, and could not lead a normal life," she reported. "They wanted to let me die. My parents, after a great deal of arguing, convinced the doctors that I was a junior in college and had been leading a normal life. However, they had to bring in pictures of me swimming and playing the piano."

The doctors were still reluctant to treat her, but Sondra Diamond's parents insisted. Once she was again living what she considered a normal life, Diamond observed: "To take the time and effort to expend medical expertise on a person who is physically disabled seems futile to many members of the medical profession. Their handiwork will come to naught, they think." Even so, she said, "I would not give up one moment of life in which I could have another cup of coffee, another cigarette, or another interaction with someone I love."

Some physicians' prophecies about imperfect babies are shown to be startlingly wrong when the child has a chance to live long enough to confound the prediction. A particularly vivid illustration of auguries turned upside down appeared as part of "Death in the Nursery," a 1983 series on the Boston television station WNEV-TV. The segment focused on two classmates in a West Haven, Connecticut, elementary school, Jimmy Arria and Kimberly Mekdeci. The boy, born prematurely, had weighed only four and a half pounds at birth, contracted pneumonia a day later, and suffered seizures. The girl was born with spina bifida.

A pediatrician suggested to the parents of both infants that they choose death as the preferred management option. Kimberly Mekdeci's father remembers that doctor saying that his daughter would probably grow up to be a vegetable. The quality of Jimmy Arria's life, the doctor predicted, would be very poor.

Jimmy Arria is a good student; Kim is also bright. According to the parents of both children, the physician who counseled death back in the nursery was Dr. Raymond Duff.

Not all physicians approve of withholding treatment for the parents' and the baby's own good. *The New England Journal of Medicine,* shortly after the Duff-Campbell report had appeared, published a letter from Dr. Joan L. Venes and Dr. Peter R. Huttenlocher, of the Yale University School of Medicine:

> As consultants to the newborn special-care unit, we wish to disassociate ourselves from the opinions expressed by [Duff and Campbell]. The "growing tendency to seek early death as a management option" that the authors referred to has been repeatedly called to the attention of those involved and has caused us deep concern. It is troubling to us to hear young pediatric interns ask first, "should we treat?" rather than "how do we treat?"
>
> We are fearful that this feeling of nihilism may not remain restricted to the newborn special-care unit. To suggest that the financial and psychological stresses imposed upon a family with the birth of a handicapped child constitute sufficient justification for such a therapy of nihilism is untenable and allows us to escape what perhaps after all are the real issues—i.e., the obligation of an affluent society to provide financial support and the opportunity for a gainful life to its less fortunate citizens.

After months of talking to parents, doctors, judges, and a number of the severely handicapped, I thought I had a reasonably clear sense of the scope of deliberate death in the nursery. But then I discovered a new frontier: a death row for infants in Oklahoma.

As Drs. Duff and Campbell had done, the physicians themselves told of the deaths they had caused, and once again they spoke not in confession but in pride. The article, "Early Management and Decision Making for the Treatment of Myelomeningocele," appeared in the October 1983 issue of *Pediatrics.* Among the authors were Drs. Richard H. Gross, Alan Cox, and Michael Pollay.

Over a five-year period an experiment had been conducted at the University of Oklahoma Health Sciences Center. The subjects of the experiment were newborn infants with spina bifida. Each was evaluated by a team of physicians, nurses, physical and occupational therapists, a social worker, and a psychologist. The team decided, in each case, whether to recommend "active vigorous treatment" or to inform the parents that they did not consider them obligated to have the baby treated; the family could choose "supportive care only." Each infant in the first group was given all medically indicated treatment, including an operation to close the spinal lesion and the implanting of a shunt to drain spinal fluid from the brain. The unfortunate infants relegated to supportive care received no active medical treatment: no surgery, no antibiotics to treat infection, and no routinely administered sedation during the dying process that began inexorably with only supportive care.

Of the 24 infants who did not get active, vigorous treatment, none survived. The mean age at death was 37 days. As the babies' physicians wrote in *Pediatrics*, "The 'untreated survivor' has not been a significant problem in our experience."

All but one of the infants who received active, vigorous treatment survived. The exception was killed in an auto accident.

To determine which infants were to be given death tickets, the medical team relied in substantial part on a "quality of life" formula: $QL = NE \times (H+S)$.

QL is the quality of life the child is likely to have if he is allowed to live. NE is the child's natural endowment (physical and intellectual). H is the contribution the child can expect from his home and family. S is the probable contribution to that handicapped child from society.

Since under this formula the patient's natural endowment is not the sole determinant of the medical treatment he gets, his chances of being permitted to stay alive can be greatly reduced if his parents are on the lower rungs of poverty. If, moreover, he is poor and has been born during the Reagan administration—which prefers missiles to funding for the handicapped—the baby has been hit with a double whammy.

The creator of this powerful formula, which has influenced physicians around the country, is Dr. Anthony Shaw, the director of the Department of Pediatric Surgery at the City of Hope National Medical Center, in Duarte, California, and a clinical professor of surgery at the UCLA School of Medicine. He is also the chairman of the Ethics Committee of the American Pediatric Surgical Association. When I charged Dr. Shaw, during a television debate, with having created a means test for deciding which infants shall continue to live, he said he had intended no such thing. I asked him how else one could read his formula, and he said that its purpose was to help the parents. And, of course, the baby.

The last two elements of the formula, plainly, have nothing to do with medical judgments. Yet Martin Gerry, a civil-rights lawyer who was the director of the Office for Civil Rights of the Department of Health, Education and Welfare from 1975 to 1977, and who investigated the Oklahoma experiment, found that the parents of the infants involved "were told by representatives of the [medical] team that the proposed treatment/non-treatment alternative represented a medical judgment made by the team. The quality-of-life formula used was neither discussed with nor revealed to the parents."

An appalled reader of the article in *Pediatrics* was Dr. John M. Freeman, of the Birth Defects Treatment Center at Johns Hopkins Hospital, in Baltimore. Writing to *Pediatrics*, Freeman observed that while the Oklahoma medical team did prove that it "can get the infants to die quickly," such skill hardly qualifies as "the best available alternative" for the management of babies with spina bifida. Dr. Freeman added that the 24 infants who died "might also have done well and might have . . . walked with assistive devices, gone to regular school, been of normal intelligence, and achieved bowel and bladder control."

Should anyone be charged with criminal responsibility for their deaths? "The facts, just as written by the doctors themselves in the article, clearly demonstrate violation of both state and federal law," Martin Gerry says. "I think there are clearly violations of state child-abuse laws; there are violations of state criminal laws. I think what you have here is a conspiracy to commit murder." So far, however, no prosecutors have been interested in going after indictments. The Reagan administration says it is unsure that it has sufficient legal basis—given the laws in force at the time of the Oklahoma experiment—for moving against doctors who withheld treatment.

Two years ago, however, after the death by starvation of the baby with Down's syndrome in Bloomington, Indiana, President Reagan angrily ordered the secretary of the Department of Health and Human Services to apply section 504 of the Rehabilitation Act of 1973 to handicapped infants. Section 504 says that under any program receiving federal assistance a handicapped person cannot be discriminated against because he or she is handicapped. Accordingly, handicapped infants must—like all other infants in the nursery—be fed and given appropriate medical treatment.

Regulations came down from Washington to enforce the application of 504 to handicapped babies. A hotline was set up so that anyone hearing that treatment or food was being denied a Baby Doe could report the details to federal investigators. And the Justice Department claimed that because of section 504 it had the authority to review a Baby Doe's medical records in order to determine whether the baby was being discriminated against.

So it was that the Justice Department demanded the records of Baby Jane Doe, the Long Island child born with spina bifida whose parents, acting on the advice of their doctors, had refused operations to close the spine and to insert a shunt in order to drain the fluid pressing on her brain. (Months later a shunt was implanted.)

The privacy of Baby Jane Doe was protected against the federal government by the attorney general of the State of New York, the New York Civil Liberties Union, the American Hospital Association, the American Academy of Pediatrics, and other medical groups. Supporting the administration's position were the American Coalition of Citizens with Disabilities, the Association for Retarded Citizens, the Association for the Severely Handicapped, the Disability Rights Education and Defense Fund, Disabled in Action of Metropolitan New York, and the Disability Rights Union. They said they were on the side of Baby Jane Doe.

The federal government lost all the way, up to and including the United States Court of Appeals for the Second Circuit, where, on February 23, 1984, a panel decided two to one that if Congress meant section 504 of the 1973 Rehabilitation Act to apply to Baby Does, it ought to say so loud and clear. Until then the privacy of the parents and of the infant must not be violated.

In a strong dissent, overlooked by much of the press, Judge Ralph Winter wrote that the question wasn't even arguable. He drew an analogy to race. "A judgment not to perform certain surgery because a person is black is not a *bona fide* medical judgment. So too, a decision not to correct a life-threatening digestive problem because an infant has Down's syndrome is not a *bona fide* medical judgment." Both decisions are acts of discrimination. Buttressing the logic of this analysis, Winter added, was the fact that section 504 of the Rehabilitation Act of 1973 had been patterned after, and is almost identical to, the antidiscrimination language of section 601 of the Civil Rights Act of 1964.

No major newspapers that I know of published editorials lauding Judge Winter's dissent. Practically all of the nation's leading and lesser newspapers had claimed throughout the odyssey of Baby Jane Doe that the infant and her parents were being persecuted by a grossly intrusive and insensitive federal government.

Baby Jane Doe had been saved from Big Brother. "The federal government," said Richard Rifkin, a spokesman for the attorney general of the State of New York, "is now barred from conducting any investigation of medical decisions regarding defective newborns."

Liberals and civil libertarians cheered. This had been one of their few victories over Ronald Reagan.

Signs persisted, however, that Congress might come to the aid of Baby Does. On February 2, 1984, the House debated with much passion a bill to extend the Child Abuse Prevention and Treatment Act. The amendments to one section broadened the definition of child abuse to include the denial of medical treatment or nutrition to infants born with life-threatening conditions. The section also mandated that each state, to keep getting funds for child-abuse programs, would have to put in place a reporting system that could be alerted whenever a handicapped infant was being abused by denial of treatment or food.

Liberals led the debate against those provisions on the House floor, and conservatives, by and large, supported the measure. Particularly eloquent was Henry Hyde, an unabashed Tory, whose history of implacable opposition to abortion reinforced the view of many liberals, in and out of the House, that all of this compassion for Baby Does was actually propaganda to gain sympathy for the unborn.

"The fact is," Hyde said during the debate, "that . . . many children . . . are permitted to die because minimal routine medical care is withheld from them. And the parents who have the emotional trauma of being confronted with this horrendous decision, and seeing ahead a bleak prospect, may well not be, in that time and at that place, the best people to decide . . . I suggest that a question of life or death for a born person ought to belong to nobody, whether they are parents or not. The Constitution ought to protect that child . . . Because they are handicapped, they are not to be treated differently than if they were women or Hispanics or American Indians or black. [Their handicap] is a mental condition or a physical condition; but by God, they are human, and nobody has the right to kill them by passive starvation or anything else."

On the key vote concerning this section of the bill Congresswoman Geraldine Ferraro joined other renowned liberals in the House in voting against protections for handicapped babies, though most, to be sure, said they were supporting the right of parents to make life-or-death decisions about their infants and opposing government interference in that process. Among the others in opposition were such normally fierce defenders of the powerless as Peter Rodino, Henry Waxman, Don Edwards, Barney Frank, John Conyers, Thomas Downey, Charles Rangel, Robert Kastenmeier, Gerry Studds, George Crockett, and Barbara Mikulski.

The vote on expanding the definition of child abuse to include the neglect of handicapped infants was 231 to 182 in favor. Not until July, however, did the Senate pass a bill protecting the lives of Baby Does. An unusually ecumenical team of senators sponsored the bill: Orrin Hatch, Alan Cranston, Christopher Dodd, Jeremiah Denton, Don Nickles, and Nancy Kassebaum. Edward M. Kennedy was involved until nearly the end.

Handling the day-to-day maneuvering were members of the staffs of various senators. They were continually fearful that the fractious coalition of medical, right-to-life, and disability-rights organizations that had to agree on the language of the bill would fall apart. Yet at the end the AMA was the only medical group to walk out. Its representative had kept insisting on the need to allow physicians to make "quality of life" decisions as to whether an infant should live or die. Staying behind and signing the agreement were, among other medical organizations, the American Academy of Pediatrics, the American College of Obstetricians and Gynecologists, the American College of Physicians, and the American Nurses Association.

As finally passed, the Senate bill (which, with a few modifications, was accepted by the House in conference) redefines child abuse and neglect, for purposes of this federal statute, to include "the withholding of medically indicated treatment from disabled infants with life-threatening conditions." No heroic measures are required, however, if treatment would merely prolong dying and would be "virtually futile in terms of the survival of the infant," or if the baby "is chronically and irreversibly comatose."

Under this Child Abuse Prevention and Treatment Act each state, in order to get federal child abuse and neglect grants, is required to create a system for reporting to state child-protection agencies cases in which infants are being denied treatment. As a last resort these agencies have the authority to "initiate any legal remedies" needed to prevent such a child from being killed. In effect, this means that Baby Does have rights independent of the rights of their parents. If they are not born dying or irreversibly comatose, handicapped infants, as persons under the Constitution, are entitled by federal statute to due process and equal protection under the law.

Meanwhile, the American Medical Association is likely to test all this in court, having already indicated its preferred approach to the Baby Doe question. On June 29 [1984] delegates to the AMA's 133rd annual convention, in Chicago, voted to support the concept of "local option" for Baby Does. That is, they wish communities and hospitals to have the legal right to set their own life-or-death standards for handicapped infants. Baby Does to come are not out of danger. Parents as well as doctors will be trying to get the new law struck down.

One of the first things I did when the bill passed was to send the news to a woman in Mount Airy, Maryland, who has been much dismayed at the infanticides in the nurseries in her county. She told me of going to a hospital seminar on the subject a couple of years ago and listening to the head of a neonatal nursery staff complain that it was awfully hard on her nurses when a baby deprived of treatment took 15 days to die. Other infants, she felt the lecturer had implied, were more accommodating.

This woman in Mount Airy had written to me last summer: "As a social studies teacher of ancient civilizations, I conducted classroom discussions covering the topic 'Ideals of Sparta vs. Ideals of Athens.' It was always . . . a shock for my students to learn that the Spartans, who valued 'body' over 'mind,' could be as callous and cruel as to leave their deformed newborns on the rocky hillsides to die.

"In this matter, it would seem, we have not come very far. What shall be written of us in years hence? That we merely brought this barbaric practice indoors?"

UPDATE TO THE AWFUL PRIVACY OF BABY DOE

Since the above article appeared in *The Atlantic,* the Child Abuse Amendments of 1984 have gone into effect, along with accompanying rules and regulations. Although some bioethicists and less exalted commentators claim the act's protections for Baby Does are more symbolic then substantive, a reading of the actual text indicates that the deterrent value of this legislation should be considerable—provided that in every state, those who oppose infanticide keep steady watch on how the law is working.

My own experience with some of those in the informal life-saving network before there was a statute taught me how tenacious these folks are, and I doubt that they'll let up now that there are official procedures —including a provision for legal intervention if all else fails. They know that no law works by itself.

Of all that has been written about the Child Abuse Amendments of 1984, the clearest analysis I've seen is by James Bopp in the September 1985 *Issues in Law and Medicine* (Office of Publications, P.O. Box 1586, Terre Haute, Indiana 47808-1586). Bopp is not nonpartisan in these matters—is anyone?—but he is a very careful lawyer and, as I can attest from interviewing him on various stories, unfailingly accurate.

In his article, Bopp goes through the language of the statute, the rules and the regulations while also pointing out some of the attempts to subvert the legislation that have already begun. For instance, the American Academy of Pediatrics, which now appears to regret having been part of the coalition that negotiated the language of the bill itself, has now stated that "nowhere in the legislative history or in the extensive deliberations leading up to the enactment of [the act] is there any indication that Congress clearly intended to exclude consideration of the infant's quality of life."

As for the "extensive deliberations" leading to the passage of the act, every participant with whom I've talked—including staff assistants to the senators involved—emphasizes the intensity of the debate about "quality of life" considerations and the fact that the American Medical Association pulled out of the negotiations because "quality of life" considerations were indeed excluded. And then there is this statement in the Final Rules attached to the act itself by the Department of Health and Human Services: "A number of commentators argued that the interpretation should permit, as part of the evaluation of whether treatment would be inhumane, consideration of the infant's future 'quality of life.' The Department strongly believes such an interpretation would be inconsistent with the statute." .

And indeed, as James Bopp notes, Professors Nancy Rhoden and John Arras—two true believers in the need for "quality of life" considerations—get no comfort from the language of the act. Ruefully, they point out that ". . . even though the caregivers of a severely impaired child might view her subsequent life, should she somehow manage to survive, as 'inhumane' (that is, painful, isolated, limited), they are not licensed to forego treatment . . . unless the treatment itself [for example, surgery] under the circumstances, is deemed 'inhumane' . . ." That is speculation as to the child's "*subsequent* life" is not a basis for foregoing treatment now.

Considering how prevalent this presumptuous, let alone lethal, "quality of life" doctrine is among physicians, it is no small victory to have it ruled out by the statute and the rules covering the treatment of handicapped infants.

Nonetheless, such bioethicists as Rhoden and Arras are at work trying to undo the act. Bopp writes that the two professors "openly call for what amounts to a conspiracy between hospital-based 'Infant Bioethics Committees' and local child protection agencies to insure that there is no interference when such committees occasionally condone nontreatment in circumstances not contemplated by the act and its implementing regulations. They euphemistically suggest that the committees 'educate' local child protection personnel so that they come to appreciate *all* of the morally relevant factors involved and will, accordingly, defer to the decisions made by parents, doctors and committees, except in cases where the child's best interests are *clearly* being threatened."

It's hard to give up God-like power.

Obviously, since the life-saving provisions of this act go against the "principles" of many—far from all—physicians and conflict with the desperate decisions some parents might choose, the Baby Does to come are going to need protection from those who wish that this legislation had never come into being. One such protective organization already in place is the National Legal Center for the Medically Dependent and Disabled, which publishes *Issues in Law and Medicine.*

This group, along with various disability rights organizations, have joined in a lawsuit concerning the infanticides in Oklahoma that I described in *The Atlantic* article. One indication of a certain change in perspective in the attitudes of some toward handicapped infants is the presence as one of the plaintiffs in this suit of the American Civil Liberties Union. All through the previous litigation concerning alleged discrimination in the treatment of handicapped infants, the ACLU supported the privacy of the parents rather than the awful privacy of the Baby Does.

One last point, which I did not stress sufficiently in *The Atlantic* article, I quote here from an address by Dr. Mildred Stahlman, Professor of Pediatrics at Vanderbilt University School of Medicine, on the occasion of her ascension to the presidency of the American Pediatric Society in May 1985. She does not like the new law, preferring the old way of handling these matters in private; but in her speech she does say something thoroughly relevant:

> Nowhere does the law address the huge monetary costs incurred by hospitals, parents or society, which are necessary for acute and long-term children, some of whom will survive to be severely handicapped adults. Some of the same legislators who supported this law will almost certainly vote billions for the MX missile, but are proponents of restrictions in funds to the handicapped, restriction of programs involving the health of infants and mothers, and restrictions of research funds which might make many of these conditions obsolete.

The legislation that has begun to end infanticide in the nursery was, of course, preceded by much political activity: in the streets, as in the aftermath of the death of the Bloomington Baby, and in meeting after meeting between proponents of the new legislation and Senate staff members. For this law to be a beginning, and not an end, in fulfilling the post-survival needs of the handicapped will require a lot more sustained use of politics.

What has already happened has begun, in any case, to change the public image of the Baby Does. They are beginning to be seen as human beings, *individual* human beings, not as solely the damaged property of their parents. They are beginning to be seen as persons under the Constitution, and that is quite a change in only a few years of the use of politics against infanticide.

It's worth remembering the attitude of nearly all the press during the debate about Baby Jane Doe and other Baby Does (see Chapter 5). Contrast it with the conclusion of a December 4, 1984, editorial in the *Washington Post* ("Protecting Handicapped Infants"):

Some objective guidance must be provided, for just as we do not leave other life-and-death decisions to families and physicians alone, the society has a responsibility to the child concerned and a communal obligation to provide an orderly mechanism for the protection of his life and rights.

We are becoming a little bit more civilized.

11

Civil Rights for Disabled Americans: The Foundation of a Political Agenda

Harlan Hahn

Among the issues that form the current agenda of political debate, perhaps few offer as much promise for achieving significant political change as the development of public policy affecting disabled Americans. Emerging from a legacy which commonly regarded disability either as a depressing topic to be avoided whenever possible or as a minor component of other policy issues, public leaders now have the opportunity to acquire a new understanding of this subject which embodies the viable prospect of resolving crucial problems that confront disabled citizens. Most existing policies appear to be based on erroneous assumptions about the nature and meaning of disability. A reevaluation of the question, therefore, offers a rare chance not only to correct prior mistakes but also to establish the foundation of a society adapted to the concerns of disabled as well as nondisabled persons.

A major basis of the hope for changes in public policy can be traced in an important shift in prevalent definitions of disability (Hahn, 1982). In the past, disability was defined almost exclusively from a *medical* perspective that focused on functional impairments. Disability was considered a defect or deficiency that could be located within the individual, and primary emphasis was devoted to the etiology or causes of organic conditions that permitted persons with different types of disabilities to be placed in separate diagnostic categories. From the clinical perspective of medicine, efforts to improve the functional capabilities of individuals were regarded as the exclusive solution to disability, and policy changes were essentially excluded from consideration as a possible remedy for the difficulties confronting the disabled. As a result, the issue of disability not only was depoliticized, but the preoccupation with etiological diagnosis also fragmented the disability community by stressing the functional traits that divided them rather than the external obstacles that they faced as a common problem. Groups representing the interests of disabled persons were organized around separate diagnostic categories, and few attempts were made to form alliances or coalitions that might facilitate the emergence of a broad social and political movement of citizens with various types of disabilities.

Subsequently, as a result of legislative decisions, disability was viewed primarily from an *economic* vantage point that concentrated on vocational limitations. This approach implied that disability was defined as a "health-related inability" or limitation on the amount or kind of work that a person could perform (Berkowitz, Johnson, and Murphy 1976, pp. 7-8). Although the assumptions of this orientation appear more appropriate to an economy based on manual labor rather than on the delivery of services or on sophisticated technology, the economic definition has been widely adopted in income maintenance and support programs that seem to equate disability with unemployability, or an "inability to engage in substantial gainful activity." By focusing on the capacity to work almost at the expense of other life activities, this approach not only is unidimensional, but it also makes some unwarranted and untenable assumptions about the linkage between impairments and productivity. Hence, policies founded on an economic perspective have been criticized (Hahn 1985b, p. 13) for transforming disabled people into an "economically managed but politically vulnerable segment of the population."

Increasingly, however, laws and regulations adopted in the 1970s permitted the formation of a sociopolitical approach that considers disability as a product of the interaction between the individual and the environment. Whereas both prior orientations regard disability principally as a personal misfortune or limitation, the sociopolitical view stresses the role of the environment in determining the meaning of this phenomenon. Thus, disability cannot be defined simply by functional capabilities or by occupational skills. A comprehensive understanding of disability requires an examination of the architectural, institutional, and attitudinal environment encountered by disabled persons. From this perspective, the primary problems confronting citizens with disabilities are bias, prejudice, segregation, and discrimination that can be eradicated through policies designed to guarantee them equal rights.

The disparity between these concepts underscores the fundamental fact that disability is ultimately defined by government policy. In other words, disability is essentially whatever public laws and programs say it is. Policy can be informed by research based on medical, economic, or sociopolitical understandings of disability; but responsibility for deciding the definitional issue eventually must be vested solely in elected officials. The relatively broad discretion provided political leaders in choosing among alternative means of conceptualizing disability yields an important opportunity to introduce major changes in public policy. Yet, since politicians are accountable for their actions, the success of these efforts eventually may be determined by the extent to which researchers and the general public also are able to reach agreement about these definitions.

Perhaps the most generally accepted definition of disability is Nagi's (1979, p. 3) concept of "a form of inability or limitation in performing roles and tasks expected of an individual within a social environment." Yet, each of the prevalent theoretical perspectives seems to stress different terms within this definition. Whereas the medical orientation emphasizes inabilities in individual performance, the economic approach focuses on individual limitations in performing the roles and tasks associated with work available in the labor market, and the sociopolitical view devotes primary attention to the social environment and to the notion of "expectations," which can be adapted to fit the capabilities of the individual rather than requiring all persons to adjust and conform to the demands of the economic or built environment.

Policymakers have a relatively wide range of research traditions from which they can select the definition of disability that is incorporated in public policy. But these decisions cannot be divorced from normative considerations. In fact, common acceptance of the values implicit in the medical and economic viewpoints has appeared to have detrimental effects on disabled Americans. A major purpose of this chapter, therefore, is to develop a case for the benefits that can be derived from policies founded on a sociopolitical understanding of disability and to demonstrate the advantages of this approach to problems facing citizens with disabilities.

The differences that must be resolved before important contributions can be made to the formulation of disability programs, however, extend beyond mere definitional controversies. Fundamentally, the analysis of disability appears to be divided by competing paradigms (Hahn, 1984b). The traditional framework for assessing the problems of disabled persons, which might be called the "functional limitations model," centers on restrictions imposed upon an individual by the loss of personal capabilities. Both the medical and economic definitions appear to be compatible with this approach. Although research has increasingly demonstrated that the employment opportunities available to disabled people are determined more by the state of the economy than by their vocational talents (Howards, Brehm, and Nagi, 1980), for example, emphasis in vocational rehabilitation programs still focuses primarily on the individual rather than on the environment. The principal solution to the difficulties encountered by disabled individuals is sought through programs to improve their physical and work skills rather than by attempts to secure changes in the society with which they must cope.

Recently, however, the conventional orientation has been challenged by a new theoretical perspective that builds on the sociopolitical definition. This framework could be described as the "minority group model." This approach views prejudice and discrimination as the major issues confronting citizens with disabilities. Although the new paradigm is consistent with a sociopolitical understanding of disability, there appear to be some fundamental incompatibilities between the "minority group model" and medical or economic conceptualizations. Since the primary source of the problem can be traced to defects in what might be termed the attitudinal environment of society rather than to personal deficiencies, the solution cannot be achieved solely by seeking continuous improvements in the functional and occupational capacities of disabled individuals. Instead, the eradication of bias and segregation requires extended efforts to secure equal rights for disabled citizens and the rigorous enforcement of antidiscrimination measures.

There are obviously many issues that divide the "functional limitations" and the "minority group" models. While the former paradigm reflects the emphasis of medical and economic perspectives on individual performance in employment or in other activities of daily life, the latter model focuses attention on the extent to which the environment is a product of collective decisions or nondecisions by the public and political leaders that have a different impact on the members of society. Basic to the "minority group" approach is a recognition that all aspects of the external world—including architecture, communications, and social organizations—are shaped by public policy and that policies are a reflection of pervasive cultural values and attitudes. Structures are built, messages are transmitted, and institutions are created, primarily because laws, ordinances, and regulations permitted them to be constructed in that manner. As a result, governments bear an inescapable responsibility for those facets of the environment that have a discriminatory effect on persons with disabilities. Furthermore, evidence of widespread aversion to the presence of disabled individuals cannot be separated from the values and feelings that have contributed to the formation of social policy. Hence, if institutions allow the nondisabled majority to avoid and to exclude people with disabilities, that result cannot be attributed to mere happenstance. This realization also imposes a corresponding duty on policymakers to protect the civil rights of disabled citizens by eliminating this form of segregation and inequality.

Major responsibility for the emergence of the "minority group model" probably can be ascribed both to increased studies of disability, especially in the social sciences, and to the growing strength of the social and political movement of disabled persons. Although the recognition that disabled citizens comprise a minority group in American society has been acknowledged by researchers for several decades, the concept did not become a focal point for the appraisal of disability until recent years. By failing to explore the theoretical assumptions that formed the basis of their investigations, academicians and activists often have found it difficult to engage in a meaningful dialogue about disability. Perhaps the basic discrepancies between the "functional limitations" and the "minority group" models must be resolved before additional progress can be made.

The adoption of the "minority group model" has important judicial and constitutional implications. In the legal tradition spawned by the "equal protection" clause of the Fourteenth Amendment to the U.S. Constitution, courts have been loath to uphold the constitutionality of laws that require differential treatment for separate categories of persons when at least one of those groups has been subjected to a history of invidious discrimination. Hence, legislation that mandates unequal status for black and white citizens would be declared unconstitutional; and a similar conclusion might be reached concerning policies that treat women and men in a different manner. Yet, despite the fact that numerous statutes and regulations impose significant burdens on disabled Americans and corresponding advantages for the nondisabled majority, judges have been reluctant to arrive at a comparable finding when they are confronted with cases involving disability. Much of this reticence undoubtedly can be ascribed to a widespread failure to acknowledge that disabled persons form a minority group in American society and to the relative absence of a substantial body of research literature that examines their problems from this perspective. Even though members of the judiciary often hesitate to admit that their opinions are influenced by studies in the social sciences, there is little reason to doubt that their decisions are affected by the information they receive about issues such as disability not only in the mass media but also during their academic training. Thus, educational efforts that seek to explain and to clarify the analogies between the status of other minorities and the treatment of disabled citizens can contribute significantly to the struggle of the latter group for freedom and equality. While studies founded on the "functional limitations" paradigm have not appeared to result in major advancements in the civil rights of disabled Americans, research based on the "minority group model" offers the promise of strengthening the position of the disability rights movement in the courts as well as in other branches of the political process.

There are many different groups that must be involved in the process of seeking agreement about solutions to the major problems of people with disabilities. Disabled persons may not always agree among themselves about these questions. Similarly, important sources of disagreement might be discovered among professionals and other nondisabled individuals interested in disability. While the general public still appears to regard disability primarily as a personal misfortune rather than as the basis of a new struggle for civil rights, major modifications of these attitudes and of the provisions of public policy seem to depend upon gaining some consensus between significant participants in the decision-making process. In the past, discussions of this subject frequently have been clouded by paternalistic expressions of sympathy and support by the nondisabled for the aspirations of disabled persons.

This chapter examines some of the major dimensions of the new paradigm that views the problems facing disabled citizens as an equal rights issue. The clarification of this alternative seems essential to fulfillment of the hope for significant advances in laws and programs affecting persons with disabilities. Although the endeavor is admittedly speculative, it is hoped the analysis will contribute to an enhanced understanding of major issues that must be resolved before an agenda for the reformulation of disability policy can be developed.

DISABILITY AND THE ENVIRONMENT

Perhaps one of the most critical issues that separates the contrasting paradigms is the role played by individual and environmental characteristics in shaping the problems facing disabled persons. Since concern about disability originated primarily in the health sciences, many early studies of this subject in medicine and rehabilitation displayed a clinical orientation that reflected an almost exclusive preoccupation with improving the functional capacity of an individual. The surrounding environment was considered either fixed and immutable or beyond the legitimate purview of investigation. Gradually, however, many professionals have begun to recognize that environmental changes such as the removal of architectural barriers or modifications of the worksite can contribute to an amelioration of the difficulties of people with disabilities. As a result, the sociopolitical definition of disability as a product of interactive features of the individual and the environment has gained increasing support from nondisabled observers as well as among disabled persons who experience the restrictions imposed by an unyielding environment in their own lives. Examples of the growing consciousness of environmental constraints by people with disabilities could be enumerated almost endlessly. Many persons who use wheelchairs have begun to realize that they habitually follow routine paths in their everyday lives and that they are compelled to forego the choice of visiting locations that are inaccessible or blocked by architectural barriers. Similarly, individuals with vision or hearing impairments are seeking alternatives to an exclusive reliance on written or oral communications as a means of obtaining the information necessary to perform their jobs and to pursue a satisfying life. As computers and sophisticated technology permit meaningful activity even for people with severe functional limitations, the recognition of the role of the environment in the definition of disability seems almost certain to increase significantly. Perhaps the principal controversies concerning this issue, however, continue to revolve around the relative importance of the environmental or individual attributes in problems associated with disability and the type of environment which is the primary source of the difficulty.

The respective weight attached to individual and environmental characteristics in the assessment of disability can be arrayed across a broad spectrum. At one end of this range, environmental configurations might be perceived as a relatively minor aspect of the problem. While studies guided by the "functional limitations model" of disability sometimes acknowledge the need for changes in the environment, for example, this objective usually is treated as secondary to the goal of improving personal capabilities. At the other extreme, the environment could be considered as the principal or even the sole determinant of disability. From this perspective, the difficulties encountered by disabled persons may be viewed as arising not from functional losses sustained by an individual but from the attitudinal and physical constraints created by a disabling environment. While supporters of the "minority group" paradigm generally ascribe greater significance to environmental than to individual traits and the followers of the "functional limitations model" display opposite proclivities, the precise value to be assigned each of these considerations probably reflects some as yet unspecified point between the two poles that can only be identified through further research.

The notion of a "disabling environment" encompasses both physical and attitudinal obstacles to full participation in society. Attitudes restrict opportunities even more blatantly than physical barriers. There is a link between the two types of obstacles; if evidence demonstrates a deep-seated and pervasive antipathy or aversion toward people with disabilities, the restrictions imposed by the built environment and by social institutions cannot be considered simply accidental or coincidental.

The controversy over individual versus environmental attributes may be shaped both by the theoretical orientations of different observers and by the limits of human imagination (Hahn, 1985a). Some find it difficult to conceive of an environment adapted to the needs of everyone, including people with a variety of disabilities. For others who glimpse the vision of a future that encompasses vast technological change and a massive restructuring of human habitats, the design of such physical surroundings might seem possible and even feasible. Still others are able to foresee a potential world of this nature, with some exceptions made for functional capacities which cannot be ameliorated through environmental modifications. Perhaps many others at least can envision a society that might accommodate a broader range of human capabilities than the present environment. As noted elsewhere (Hahn, 1984b, pp. 24-25), even these variations may be associated with the extent to which thinking has been affected by "functional limitations" or "minority group" paradigms:

> The two competing models which evolved in research and disability have seemed to yield distinctive emphases on "service delivery" or "disability rights" as the primary solutions to the problems of this segment of the population. These differences also appear to represent contrasting estimates of the potential for environmental change. Whereas the "functional limitations" perspective views the provisions of extensive services as the most appropriate means of assisting disabled persons in surroundings which cannot or will not be adapted to satisfy their needs and desires, proponents of the "minority group" orientation refuse to abandon the prospect of a world in which these modifications are treated as a right rather than as a privilege or a special concession. Obviously, until these alterations are made, the need for a broad range of social services must be given a high priority. Yet, the vision of a society in which environmental adaptations will be viewed as part of a basic commitment to values such as freedom and equality must not be sacrificed to an inordinate concern with meeting the immediate functional requirements of disabled persons in the existing environment. Programs and policies which regard the delivery of services as the sole, exclusive or principal means of aiding disabled individuals may ultimately prove to be incomplete and even self-defeating.

The distinction between these perspectives becomes important in assessing the extent to which individual and environmental characteristics contribute to the problems of disabled people. If it is theoretically possible to plan an environment that can meet the requirements of almost every inhabitant, for example, the prevalent tendency to equate disability with individual limitations would be seriously undermined. Such a finding may form the basis for a need to adopt compensatory measures to ensure disabled persons are provided with opportunities that would otherwise be available in an environment designed to fit the needs of everybody. Similarly, if there is some type of upper limit on the extent to which human settlements can accommodate persons with various disabilities, then this standard might replace the conditions of the existing environment as a appropriate benchmark for evaluating the support granted this segment of the population. Although observers may differ in their capacity to imagine a world without serious artificial obstacles, discussion of these hypothetical alternatives may promote an increased recognition of the contribution of environmental characteristics to the difficulties posed by a disability.

In general, there appears to be an emerging consensus among both disabled and nondisabled observers about the need to alter the *built environment*. Although architectural barriers have not yet been widely recognized as a fundamental constraint on personal liberty, the simple fact that many disabled people are virtually imprisoned in a vast range of circumstances has produced increased interest in accessibility. Yet even this concern has usually been limited to new construction and to buildings that are thought to be most appropriately frequented by persons with disabilities. The major objection to an expanded plan to modify the existing configurations of the landscape is, of course, cost. In a society truly committed to the principle of providing freedom and equality to all its citizens including those with disabilities, financial consideration might be considered secondary to guarantees of civil rights.

Perhaps much of the resistance to a comprehensive restructuring of the architectural environment also can be ascribed to the continued prevalence of the "functional limitations model." As long as disabilities are perceived primarily as individual traits rather than as characteristics produced by interactions with the environment, the restraints imposed by pervasive architectural obstacles may be viewed as unfortunate but unavoidable. By contrast, the "minority group model" permits an assessment of the extent to which the confines of the built environment represent a denial of civil rights that could be remedied by changes in public policy.

There does not yet appear to be much agreement about the control exerted upon disabled citizens by *social institutions* in American society. People with disabilities, however, have frequent contact with a diverse group of public and private agencies that reflect conflicting objectives and inconsistent programs. Perhaps many of the problems that they encounter in this environment can also be attributed to the prevalent influence of the "functional limitations model" of disability which seems to imply that the provisions of social services is the only appropriate method of assisting this segment of the population. A major consequence of these assumptions is reflected in the fact that there is simply no coherent disability policy in the United States. Current laws and programs are replete with contradictions and disincentives which, for example, often encourage disabled persons to seek employment while denying them the medical support they need to sustain their lives. Moreover, public and private groups serving disabled children and adults have spawned vested interests that might be even more difficult to combat than pervasive reluctance to modify the built environment. The tendency to organize around separate diagnostic categories reflecting different impairments also has inhibited the formation of a unified social and political movement of disabled citizens.

In surroundings that have been designed with little regard for their needs, people with disabilities obviously require many types of services. But corresponding or equivalent emphasis also should be focused on efforts that would grant them independence rather than perpetuating their dependency. The realization that disabled citizens form a minority group in American society may compel public and private organizations to engage in programs of social, political, and legal advocacy comparable to their activities in the delivery of social services. In addition, increased attention must be devoted to the relationship between disability and the social structure. Statistics indicating that three-fifths of disabled Americans are in a financial position which places them below the poverty line (Bowe, 1978, 1980), for example, cannot be dismissed as happenstance. There are undoubtedly many as yet undiscovered structural and institutional inequalities that consign disabled persons to a status incompatible with their rights.

Perhaps the core of the controversy about disability and environmental attributes can be found in the assessment of public attitudes. Few persons acquainted with research on this subject would deny that the nondisabled majority holds--either consciously or subconsciously—unfavorable perceptions of people with disabilities. In analyses of disability founded on the "functional limitations model," however, these sentiments often are considered merely another unfortunate burden that must be borne by disabled individuals. From this perspective, the task of restoring functional capacities to meet the demands of the existing environment has seemed so compelling and the goal of changing public opinion has appeared so unattainable that attention has been diverted from this problem. The study of attitudes concerning disability has never occupied a prominent or critical position in research guided by a theoretical interest in functional impairments. Nevertheless, for the "minority group model," investigations of the so-called attitudinal environment surrounding disabled citizens seems fundamental.

The realization that prejudicial attitudes comprise the source of the unfair disadvantages and inequalities bestowed on racial, ethnic, and other minorities has been widely accepted by political leaders and the American public. Yet the predominant emphasis on individual functioning seems to have impeded the accumulation of similar conclusive documentation about the origins of the treatment accorded disabled citizens. There does not yet appear to be a widespread consensus regarding the barriers imposed on disabled persons by public attitudes. For nondisabled professionals and researchers who appear to be preoccupied by the issue of functional loss, the impact of such opinions might seem minor in comparison with the consequences of physical or behavioral restrictions. To the extent that perceptions of disability are viewed as a problem by the nondisabled, the prescribed solution usually consists of public relations or educational campaigns to promote a more positive image of people with disabilities. For large numbers of disabled persons themselves, on the other hand, the recognition that prevalent attitudes comprise the foundation of many subtle forms of bias, prejudice, and discrimination seems to be an essential prerequisite to their struggle for equal rights.

The focus on attitudes as a central issue in the analysis of disability also provides a means of developing a unified approach to the subject. In evaluating both the architectural and institutional environment, many observers might argue that the needs of people with different types of impairments are so diverse that they could not possibly be accommodated by a comprehensive design or that separate organizations must be maintained to serve their distinctive interests. However, while the present classification of disabled persons in separate diagnostic categories provides some information about the causes of their disabilities, it does not reflect an assessment of the functional effects of various impairments. Perhaps, even to preserve the traditional paradigm for the study of disability, a revision of present disability classifications may be necessary so that they more accurately represent different functional capacities rather than unique medical conditions.

Fundamentally, however, conceptualizations of disability must be designed to permit a careful examination of the possibility that the treatment of disabled people depends more upon the sentiments they elicit from others than upon the restrictions produced by their functional impairments. Moreover, this aspect of the "minority group model" facilitates a recognition of the difficulties shared by persons with sensory, mobility, and other types of disabilities. The emphasis on attitudinal responses to disability focuses on problems that they have in common rather than on impairments that seem to divide them. Although an appraisal of the independent effects of attitudes in an environment that also imposes severe functional restrictions on disabled people obviously represents a complicated endeavor, an important initial step might be taken by acknowledging that hypotheses derived from the new paradigm appear to be as worthy of investigation as the implications of the "functional limitations model," which previously precluded this type of study.

Perhaps one of the most serious obstacles to the progress of disabled citizens is related to widespread presumptions of biological inferiority. Ironically, these are the same assumptions that have been used to oppress other minorities. Just as racial or ethnic groups were once considered genetically deficient and women were regarded as weaker than men, the subjugation of people with disabilities often appears to be implicitly justified by individual limitations or inabilities. In a culture that places an extraordinarily high premium on physical agility, strength, and appearance, the subordination of disabled people might even appear to be natural. Moreover, they live in a world that was planned and constructed almost exclusively for the nondisabled.

The existing configurations of architectural and institutional environments are the products of public policy. Buildings can be erected to accommodate persons with greater or lesser functional capabilities. Even the structure of society is shaped by the distribution of rewards and costs contained in policy decisions. These observations must alert public officials to two possibilities: The deprivations imposed upon disabled citizens by present environmental features might have been prompted either by the political neglect of their interests and needs or by a deep and unrecognized aversion to this segment of society. Perhaps the "functional limitations model" has also contributed to incorrect assumptions about the physical and behavioral imperfection of disabled people. Presumptions of biological inferiority or superiority are antithetical to the competing paradigm that regards disabled citizens as a minority group.

The ethical and moral implications of these problems deserve further exploration. Attention must be devoted to the relationship between the problems of disabled persons and basic democratic values such as equality and liberty. For observers accustomed to the familiar paradigm of functional limitations, this topic might provoke unfamiliar and even disturbing questions. In a culture that usually regards disability as personal misfortune, few have been willing to identify it as a characteristic that results in deprivation and the denial of constitutional guarantees supposedly granted to every citizen. Yet the realization that an environment molded by public policy also can be altered to meet the needs of people with a wide range of functional capabilities may promote a corresponding awareness that the inequalities and restrictions plaguing disabled Americans are primarily the products of political decisions rather than of personal impairments. Perhaps the most obvious contradictions between the problems facing this group and the principles of freedom and inequality can be found in the built environment that not only imposes severe constraints on individual choice but that also places disabled persons at a competitive disadvantage with their nondisabled peers. But major constraints are also evident in social institutions that limit the opportunities available to people with disabilities, and in the so-called attitudinal environment, that yield frequent rejection and exclusion. Furthermore, both the built and the institutional environments are based on prevailing public attitudes. Applying the concepts of liberty and equality to the circumstances of disabled persons, therefore, seems indispensable to a comprehensive effort to secure improvements in disability policy.

Although freedom has been variously defined by concepts of autonomy and by the availability of alternatives, evidence that a disability has a profoundly constricting impact on the exercise of liberty in the present environment seems almost undeniable. An understanding of the full extent to which environmental barriers impinge on personal freedom might require an intimate knowledge of the everyday lives of many disabled citizens. Nonetheless, few nondisabled individuals would tolerate the curtailments of individual options that become part of the daily experience of people with disabilities. Many disabled persons are continually denied access to public accommodations, barred from common organizational activities, and subjected to discrediting interactions with the nondisabled majority. Some disabled individuals may become so accustomed to habitual, safe, and predictable routines that they might not be completely aware of the autonomy and choices they are compelled to surrender in an environment that is poorly adapted to their interests and needs. Although constitutional guarantees of freedom of movement have been extended to international travelers, similar rights have not been granted to persons who use wheelchairs in their own neighborhoods. In countless ways, the liberty of disabled citizens is restricted in an environment implicitly designed by official acts to be reserved almost exclusively for the nondisabled.

Comparisons between disabled and nondisabled of the population fail to disclose indications of relative equality in almost any area of society. In an environment that provides advantages to the nondisabled and disadvantages to disabled individuals the assumptions of a meritocracy may not be sufficient to fulfill the promise of equality. Compensatory efforts also might be needed to ensure that disabled citizens are granted civil rights consistent with this basic democratic principle. Mastery of the existing environment does not seem to be an appropriate prerequisite for exercising the rights of citizenship. Freedom and equality are legal guarantees that must be extended to all citizens, including those with disabilities. A full recognition of the importance of these standards seems to depend upon the realization that disabled citizens form a minority group—with all the ramifications of that term—in American society.

THE IDENTIFICATION OF A MINORITY GROUP

There appear to be several different means by which deprived and disadvantaged segments of the population may qualify for designation as a minority group. Initially, for example, they might be considered a minority if others are willing to use that phrase in describing them. By this criterion, the status of citizens with disabilities appears to be somewhat ambiguous. Although the concept of minority group often has been involved in prior studies of disability, it has been relegated to a relatively minor role. Hence, the aspirations of disabled citizens have not yet been widely understood as a quest for civil rights.

Second, the minority status of a group can be determined by comparing their position with dominant portions of the population on crucial social and economic indicators. According to this standard, despite the flaws in available statistics, there seems to be little doubt that disabled people deserve to be considered a minority. Persons with disabilities experience the highest unemployment rate and the most prevalent levels of welfare dependency in the country. They have been disproportionately exposed to persistent poverty and inadequate schools, housing, transportation, and other services. Even the exclusion of disabled individuals from voting booths, juries, and political meetings seems to parallel the barriers impeding other groups that have struggled to gain equal rights.

Finally, almost all minority groups have been subjected to similar experiences which include ascriptions of biological inferiority, segregation, stigmatization, stereotyping, bias, prejudice, discrimination, and overt bigotry. Most people are reluctant to identify disabled citizens as a minority because they fail to examine the relationship between these concepts and the problems associated with disability. While numerous prior studies of disability have contained a reference to disabled people as a minority group, the use of this phrase frequently has seemed tentative or uncertain.

Perhaps nowhere is this ambivalence more clearly evident than in the discussion of segregation. Even the language employed to describe this issue seems permeated by doubt and reservations. Features of the built environment that prevent interactions between disabled and nondisabled portions of the population, for example, are called "architectural barriers" rather than instruments of segregation. Similarly, the abolition of separate schools for disabled students is characterized as "mainstreaming" rather than integration or desegregation. And the release of disabled persons from restrictive confinement is termed "deinstitutionalization" or a project of "independent living." Much of this vocabulary probably can be ascribed to a focus on functional restrictions that has inhibited an awareness of the extent to which ordinary architectural configurations, institutional arrangements, and public attitudes result in the separation and exclusion of disabled people from the remainder of society. By contrast, the opposing paradigm recognizes that the combined effects of these environments may produce a pattern of segregation that is even more extensive than the most rigid apartheid policies of racist governments.

The interpretation of attitudes concerning disability, however, seems especially fundamental to the evaluation of the competing models. Ironically, while there appears to be general agreement that disabled people comprise a stigmatized group, this perspective has not become a major focal point for research. Just as the analysis of disabled persons as a minority group has been overshadowed by an interest in functional limitations, the concept of stigma has appeared to suffer a similar fate. These developments have had a crucial impact on the understanding of public attitudes about people with disabilities. Without a clear acknowledgment that the status of disabled persons might be based on prejudicial attitudes, for example, environmental segregation and the denial of liberty and equality seemed to escape significant notice as pressing social issues. As a result, important components of the theoretical foundations of the "minority group model" have not yet been firmly established.

Perhaps even more significant than the treatment of the concept of stigma is a lack of agreement about stereotyping. People with disabilities have not become the targets of the same type of hostile and vicious preconceptions that have been directed at other minorities, but there is controversy about the extent to which they have been the victims of a tendency to impute the unfavorable images of a group to an individual member. Many employers who refuse to hire disabled personnel justify their decisions by asserting that an individual with a disability simply would not be able to perform the work. Similar rationalization is used to support the development of physical or functional requirements for a wide range of jobs. These assertions, however, may cloak an unacknowledged tendency to underestimate the capabilities of this group of applicants or a deep-seated aversion to disability. Most nondisabled persons, including physicians as well as personnel officers, do not possess enough information to make a knowledgeable judgment about the capacities of disabled individuals or about their potential effectiveness in a modified environment.

Disabled persons themselves are not permitted to challenge the myths and misconceptions that prevent them from securing an impartial evaluation in the pursuit of employment. Programs stressing the abilities of disabled people or urging businesses to "hire the handicapped" have not been notably successful. While the traditional paradigm for the study of disability seems to provide implicit support for the legitimacy of functional requirements as qualifications for jobs and other resources, the "minority group model" approaches the issue with considerable skepticism. The task of unraveling stereotyped perceptions of disabled individuals and those that reflect a careful appraisal of personal competence is difficult but crucial to an objective analysis of this problem.

The results of such an investigation are essential to an even more fundamental task of determining the extent to which the treatment of disabled citizens is determined by prejudice. This issue also is likely to provoke disagreement. In the research tradition supported by the "functional limitations model," there seemed to be little opportunity for serious exploration of the possibility that prejudicial attitudes might be an underlying problem for disabled Americans. The focus on developing the physical and other capacities of disabled individuals to meet the standards prescribed by the present environment appeared to detract from these issues. Hence, persons familiar with the conventional approach to the analysis of disability might find the notion of prejudice alien or strange. Alternatively, for the "minority group model," this concept is central. Decisions based on stereotypes of disability could be readily dismissed unless they reflect prejudice or bias about disabled people. Such prejudice—the kind that stems from fear, hatred, and ignorance— cannot be easily disregarded. Development of the new paradigm for the study of disability seems to depend upon intensive analysis of prejudicial attitudes.

Although an attempt to separate the effects of discrimination from other restraints imposed on disabled persons is a complex undertaking, there appear to be several means of approaching this task. One relatively direct method would be to assess attitudinal change according to the extent to which various disabilities are perceptible or visible. Most groups that have been previously recognized as minorities possess some type of physical characteristic such as skin color, gender, or age that permits them to be distinguished from the rest of the population. While the focus on functional impairments has obscured the significance of personal appearance as an identifying attribute of disability, the presence of a distinguishing trait that is either immediately obvious or detectable by close scrutiny can have a crucial impact on how others perceive disabled persons. From this perspective, concepts such as visibility and permanency might replace functional limitations as the defining features of disability. A possible means of testing this approach might be provided by developing a "disability continuum," which suggests a relationship between the visibility of a permanent disability and the prejudice it evokes from others (Hahn, 1984a). This type of investigation not only could assist in sorting out the distinctive effects of responses elicited by physical, mental, and other kinds of disabilities; but it also might elevate theories of prejudice to a prominent position in research on perceptions of people with disabilities.

In some critical ways, discrimination against disabled persons differs from that directed at other minorities. The prejudice imposed on disabled persons usually has assumed a more subtle form than the displays of overt bigotry and even violence that have been inflicted on other groups. Perhaps this pattern can be attributed to the pervasive feelings of paternalism that permeate relationships between disabled individuals and the nondisabled. In an atmosphere in which disabilities are commonly regarded as signs of weakness, helplessness, and biological inferiority, open expressions of malevolent intolerance have been relatively rare. As a result, the social and political movement of persons with disabilities seldom has experienced dramatic acts of discrimination that might arouse the conscience of a nation. In addition, this group has been compelled to contend with a nondisabled majority that claims to be sympathetic and supportive of their aspirations. In many respects, difficulties in gaining recognition as a minority group probably are exacerbated by the relative absence not only of blatant manifestations of bigotry but also of an admitted adversary who might otherwise stimulate increased dialogue about disability rights. But neither of these factors seems indispensable to an understanding that citizens with disabilities often have been the victims of discrimination.

The struggle to define disability as an equal rights issue requires an intense commitment by disabled persons. As a group that is estimated to encompass more than 36 million Americans, the potential persuasiveness of a unified demand for civil rights by disabled persons is substantial. And yet people with disabilities never have been able to organize a constituency comparable to other voting blocs in U.S. politics. Many disabled persons are reluctant to identify themselves or to recognize disability as an issue that requires the expenditure of political energies. In a crucial sense, the disability rights movement is asking disabled citizens to concentrate on that aspect of their identity which is most negatively stigmatized by the remainder of society and to mobilize around it. The demand is admittedly imposing, but the ultimate test of any minority group is self-identification. Although disabled persons are increasingly prepared to acknowledge their membership in a disadvantaged minority and to admit that they have been the target of discrimination, this consciousness has not yet become a sweeping force for social and political change. Perhaps there is a need for additional sources of strength to fulfill the promise implied by the mounting awareness of the status of disabled people in American society.

Deprived of a cultural heritage that might otherwise be an important source of political as well as psychological support, a growing proportion of disabled persons are searching for a new understanding of the nature and meaning of disability. The discrepancy between positions on this issue seems to be enormous. While many of the nondisabled still appear to be wrestling with an image of disability as an indication of biological inferiority, a significant number of disabled individuals seem prepared to enter what might be termed the "black-is-beautiful" phase in the development of a minority culture. Some disabled people are seeking a positive source of identity as a focal point for their political struggle (Anspach, 1979).

Although there has been little direct mention of the topic, many people with disabilities are beginning to realize that they share important values that might eventually become recognized elements of a subculture. A complete enumeration of common themes in the lives of disabled people obviously would be premature at this stage. Yet mention might be made of several significant experiences that contain positive as well as negative implications for the formation of a unified perspective on policy issues.

One of the most unpleasant features of the lifestyles of many disabled individuals, for example, is the pervasive sense of physical and social isolation produced not only by the restrictions of the built environment but also by the aversive reactions of the nondisabled that often consign them to the role of distant friends or even mascots rather than to a more intimate status as peers, competitors, or mates.

While the sheer energy necessary to surmount artificial barriers undoubtedly has detracted from the cohesion of this community, the unyielding nature of their surroundings also has sparked an anger that many people with disabilities are learning to express and to channel in political directions. Emerging from a background that is often overprotective and permeated by perception of disabled people primarily as the recipients of help, many have gained a spirit of independence that not only spawns occasional feistiness but also supplies a strong motivation for social action. Many who have been taught that the existing environment is a place to be mastered primarily by "overcoming" their disabilities also have acquired an adaptability that may give them a problematic view of medical authority, a realization of the need for continuous planning, and an unusual capacity to develop ad hoc solutions to the obstacles they encounter. The simple ability to survive in a society poorly adapted to the needs of disabled people seems to bear implicit testimony to the superficiality of physical standards that society seeks to impose on its members.

In addition, persons with disabilities may have acquired means of accepting and adjusting to the inevitability of aging and bodily decline that exceed the anticipations of their nondisabled counterparts. Although many people with disabilities have grown tired of gaining acceptance by the nondisabled majority only when they can be viewed as inspirational or courageous, important aspects of their lives can be identified as crucial sources of dignity and pride. Despite the unfavorable images of disability which have been widely adopted by the nondisabled community, the mutual experience of disabled people seems to embody valuable resources that might support a prolonged and intense struggle for equal rights.

The eventual goal of the social and political movement of disabled persons is, of course, to persuade the American public that citizens with disabilities should be granted freedom and equality. The objective may not be fulfilled without extensive support from other segments of the population. In the formation of coalitions and alliances, nondisabled professionals and others interested in disability could play an especially critical role. For many who have been familiar with the "functional limitations model," the prospect of adjusting to an alternative approach is not likely to be greeted with enthusiasm. Traditional ideas seldom disappear without a struggle, and battles fought over academic theories are often vicious and destructive. Yet, without at least the tacit support of many disabled persons, the political credibility of professionals who seek to preserve programs and policies based on the conventional paradigm could be seriously undermined. Nondisabled professionals and people with disabilities appear to be joined by an uneasy relationship. Probably a major responsibility of this association is a realization that the "minority group model" represents an alternative to an earlier theoretical framework that deserves at least equivalent support and respect.

POLICY IMPLICATIONS

Perhaps one of the most obvious implications of the tension between different paradigms of disability is the need for additional research. There are obvious gaps, especially in the "minority group model," that require exploration before major policy questions can be decided. A comprehensive attempt must be undertaken to examine the separate effects of functional, environmental, and attitudinal characteristics upon the status of disabled Americans. Much of this work might be performed by disabled researchers, some of whom are seeking to develop a network known as the Disability Forum to develop new policy proposals and to promote a reconceptualization of disability. In the past, studies of this subject have been conducted primarily by nondisabled investigators who subscribed to the "functional limitations model." These developments reflect a marked contrast to the trends that have affected other segments of the population. Since the analysis of problems facing women is no longer dominated by males, for example, similar efforts must be made to facilitate the growth of innovative approaches to the study of disability that reflect the experience and perspectives of disabled people.

The recognition of disabled persons as a minority group also contains important implications for the resolution of a wide range of pressing political issues. One of the most troublesome controversies that has arisen in recent years, for example, centers on what might be termed "life or death questions" involving people with disabilities. These topics range from the "Baby Doe" cases of disabled infants to the so-called "right to die" request of Elizabeth Bouvia, a 26-year-old woman with cerebral palsy, to ethical dilemmas about terminating or sustaining the lives of older persons with severe disabilities. From a vantage point that emphasizes the difficulties posed by functional limitations in the existing environment, seemingly legitimate concerns might be expressed about the "quality of life" available to disabled individuals at every stage of the life cycle.

By contrast, from a minority group perspective, these arguments might be interpreted differently. Along with the prevalence of telethons and the massive resources allocated to medical research, the prevalent values of the nondisabled majority seem to denote a widespread belief that the principle solution to the problem of disability is to eradicate it. As witnesses to a historical tradition that has included the widespread practice of genocide as well as the extermination of 1 million disabled persons in Nazi Germany, people with disabilities are understandably loath to grant others the power to determine their fate. Although this group has lacked the sense of generational continuity provided minorities that are defined primarily by genetic characteristics, disabled persons may possess a valuable though previously unrecognized culture that can inform these complex moral questions.

Similar considerations might contribute to educational policies affecting disabled students. Although the "minority group model" clearly supports the integration of schools, this perspective also suggests that the scholastic performance of disabled youngsters cannot be promoted solely by programs designed to meet their functional requirements or "special needs." Disabled children are not raised by parents who belong to the same minority or in homes influenced both by a legacy of oppression and by a tradition of protection against assaults by the outside world. As a result, both disabled and nondisabled students might be provided appropriate instruction that would allow the former group to develop a sense of dignity and pride in themselves and in the minority community of which they are a part. This orientation is consistent with evidence indicating that positive labeling is often a critical factor contributing to academic achievement. The introduction of ideas designed to promote feelings of competence and confidence in disabled young people may require extensive curricular changes in higher education as well as in elementary and secondary schools. Individuals entering careers that involve frequent contacts with disabled persons also need to become acquainted with civil rights issues and the cultural values of this segment of the population.

Perhaps the most fundamental change implied by the assessment of disabled persons as a minority group, however, is the rigorous enforcement of antidiscrimination laws. The provisions of Pub. L. No. 94-142, the Education of All Handicapped Children Act of 1975, and section 504 of the Rehabilitation Act of 1973, which prohibits discrimination against disabled persons in programs receiving federal financial assistance, have never been conscientiously implemented. The Office of Federal Contract Compliance Procedures in the Department of Labor, which has major responsibility for the administration of laws prohibiting employment discrimination, has even expressed reservations about the cost-effectiveness of these measures. But cost-benefit ratios must not be confused with legal rights. While some have thought it reasonable to ban discrimination against disabled persons only when these measures are financially acceptable, the new paradigm of disability is based on different assumptions. Recognizing that government policy bears a primary responsibility for determining the extent to which society is adapted to the needs of disabled people and that mastery of the environment is not necessarily an appropriate prerequisite for achieving equality and freedom, the "minority group model" asserts that laws and regulations must be guided by a respect for human rights rather than by economic calculations.

The demands imposed on disabled people by the present environment have been shaped primarily by public attitudes rather than by historical coincidence. There is presently no empirical basis for rejecting the contention that the core of the problem can be found in stereotypical perceptions of disability as well as in prejudice and aversion toward disabled persons. Public leaders are hardly in a position to ignore the desires of disabled citizens for equal treatment in employment, transportation, housing, and public accommodations. Consideration also might be given to the enactment of several measures suggested by European experience such as an effective program of employment quotas, which would guarantee disabled workers a percentage of the jobs available in the labor force, and a disability allowance, which would offset the costs incurred by disabled individuals in their efforts to cope with an unaccommodative environment. Additionally, in a move that might help to break the current stalemate in the development of a national health program, disabled people might become the next group to be included in a government-sponsored plan of medical care. These proposals need not be viewed as substitutes for the vast system of social welfare programs that now dominates disability policy in the United States. As long as the existing environment remains relatively unchanged, the need for social services is not apt to diminish. And yet, by seeking a society in which constitutional guarantees of freedom and equality are offered to disabled citizens as a right rather than a privilege, the struggle for civil rights may lift a burden from the national conscience which would far exceed the economic sacrifices that might be required to implement these measures.

The political agenda of the disability rights movement extends beyond proposals which have been advanced by other minorities. A massive restructuring of the environment and of social institutions seems to represent only an initial step toward even more crucial change. Perhaps even more fundamentally, this movement appears to be seeking a revolutionary shift in the way that people think and perceive other human beings. Too often, in our everyday interactions with other members of the same species, we engage in a process that might be called "short-circuited" thinking. We tend to look at other persons and assign them to a category or "pigeonhole" in our minds based on their physical or behavioral characteristics. We seldom take time to appraise the value or qualities of others and to develop a bodily image of them consistent with their inner properties. Many persons with disabilities, who have endured the effects of stigmatizing and prejudicial attitudes, are asking a predominantly nondisabled world to reverse the usual processes that shape their perceptions. By participating in the struggle for civil rights in an environment that is not adapted to their needs, disabled citizens are seeking recognition as valued members of society. Their aspirations represent a request that nondisabled Americans can deny only at the expense of profound national shame.

NOTES

Anspach, R. R. 1979. From stigma to identity politics: Political activism among the physically disabled and former mental patients. *Social Science and Medicine, 13*, 765-73.

Berkowitz, M., W. G. Johnson, and E. H. Murphy. 1976. *Public Policy Toward Disability.* New York: Praeger.

Bowe, F. 1978. *Handicapping America: Barriers to Disabled People.* New York: Harper and Row.

Bowe, F. 1980. *Rehabilitating America: Toward independence for disabled and elderly people.* New York: Harper and Row.

Hahn, H. 1982. Disability and rehabilitation policy: Is paternalistic neglect really benign? *Public Administration Review, 42,* 385-89.

Hahn, H. 1984a. *The issue of equality: European perceptions of employment policy for disabled persons.* New York: World Rehabilitation Fund.

Hahn, H. 1984b. Changing perceptions of disability and the future of rehabilitation. Unpublished paper presented at the Ninth Mary Switzer Memorial Seminar. New York, New York.

Hahn, H. 1985a. Disability policy and the problem of discrimination. *American Behavioral Scientist* (forthcoming).

Hahn, H. 1985b. Toward a politics of disability: Definitions, disciplines, and policies. Unpublished paper. University of Southern California.

Howards, I., H. P. Brehm, and S. Z. Nagi. 1980. *Disability: From policy problem to federal program.* New York: Praeger.

Nagi, S. Z. 1979. The concept and measurement of disability. In E. D. Berkowitz (ed.) *Disability policies and government programs.* New York: Praeger.

12

Conclusions

Alan Gartner and Tom Joe

This book has shown the ways in which disability and the disabled are portrayed in the society—the "images of disability"—which play themselves out in the programs designed to serve the disabled. In effect, the programs are the societal expression of the "disabling images." Harlan Hahn's piece confronts this situation, not with specifics about programs, but with a call to reconceptualize the way we think about disability and the disabled. We agree. It is our belief that the fundamental changes needed in the disability field can come only as part of a basic change in ways of thinking. Here, we offer some brief thoughts as to the direction of the needed changes and some ideas as to the processes of getting there.

At bottom, the first change must come in the inappropriate expressions of the medical model, the characterizing of disabled people as sick, helpless, invalid. The doctors who find disease and the psychologists who find deficits are the agents of that model. While descriptions are important, the ever finer subcategorization (labeling) of people becomes an end in itself. Indeed, it is more than that because the categorization as to handicapping condition becomes the basis for service provision. For example, in special education, students with the same handicapping condition generally are grouped together for instruction. While an orthopedic handicap may be a basis for adapting the physical education program, it offers no basis—except administrative convenience—for grouping students for spelling instruction. What happens here is that the particular—the disability—comes to be seen as the whole person, namely, the crippled child, the blind man, the deaf woman.

What is called for, whether in education or other human service fields, is a recognition of the range of humankind, the awareness that all individuals possess both strengths and limitations, in varying mixtures and to different degrees, and that services can best be developed which build on those strengths and address the limitations as matters to be coped with or overcome, not as defining characteristics. The narrow definition of categories of disability serves little function, too often either becoming the sole basis for identifying an individual or as a convenient basis for lumping together people according to a criterion too often irrelevant to the task at hand. To be clear, we are not suggesting the silly formulation that denies the fact of the disability, or uses cutesy language to dispel reality. As Dai R. Thompson says, "Being disabled is not a 'challenge' we voluntarily undertake. Nor is it that we are merely 'differently abled.' We are disabled; there are just some things we can't do, at least not as quickly or easily as other people" (Susan E. Browne et al., eds., *With the Power of Each Breath: A Disabled Women's Anthology.* Pittsburgh: Cleis Press, 1985).

Along with a recognition of the individuality of persons within what Robert Funk calls the "caste of the handicapped," and the need to respond to individual needs with individually appropriate provisions, there must also be a recognition that in the present society there is a movement among people called "disabled." Thus, in a sense, the very process of mobilizing to break the shackles of caste involves coming together within its bounds.

Whatever the agenda items, given the nature of American society, the disability community is going to need allies to win its case. Sometimes it will be those close at hand—the advocacy of parents for the needs of their children. In other cases, it will be the topical intersect with another group's priorities—the coalition with "Right to Life" groups concerning the rights of high-risk newborns. And there are potential alliances with those other groups for whom the society—still dominantly white, male, youth-oriented—has also seen biology as determinant—women, older people, blacks.

There are tensions in alliances, as the (potential) partners have (or perceive) differing interests: between those of the disabled persons and those of the able-bodied family of which that person is a member, between the rights of a woman to decision making as to an abortion and the rights of the newborn with severe disabilities, or between that newborn and the family into which he or she was born. And while there may be points of common interest between two groups, for example as noted above between the disabilities community and the right-to-life groups, it is important that there be congruence, if not total agreement, on broader issues. For example, an alliance with the right-to-life groups would not serve well the interests of high-risk newborns if, as Nat Hentoff notes, the groups' support ended with the critical care nursery and did not carry through the life of the person with disabilities.

More complex than alliances between groups of the disabled and the nondisabled are alliances between and among disabled. While it would be politically good, that is, effective, for *the* disabled, all 36 million, to come together, this likelihood, not surprisingly, is slim. And, more than not, this is for ample reason. Just as it is erroneous and an act of stereotyping to lump all persons with disabilities together—which is why in language we urge "persons with disabilities" and not "disabled persons" —so, too, it is mistaking the diversity of persons with disabilities to expect or desire that they all will have the same views or values. Some are Yankee fans, others favor the Mets; some are men, others women; some are black, others white; many are poor but some affluent; some politically liberal, others conservative; some see gains won primarily from individual efforts, others from group action. On many, indeed most, issues, it will be these (and other) factors, not the fact of the person's disability, which will have most salience.

Yet, in many areas, disability will be an important unifying factor. On some issues, groups among the disabled will find common interests and, thus, common cause, while on other issues their interests will diverge. Where this happens, the differing groups may take opposite sides or, as occurs in alliances, one group may defer to the interests of the other in the desire to build an ongoing alliance. Clearly, on some issues, most disability advocates will make common cause. For example, the extension of civil rights protection (as in the issuance of the 504 regulations and now in the overturning of *Grove City*); inclusion in public education of all students and the assurance that school programs meet individual student needs; full access to employment and to training programs, not just those "for" the disabled; environments that are barrier free (or better yet access enhancing), whether that be curb-cuts and ramps for those who are mobility-impaired, gates between subway cars for the vision-impaired, closed captioning for the hearing-impaired; full access to the political process, which means all polling places are barrier free and ballots and key political documents are available in braille, and televised debates are captioned and signers are present at public meetings; overcoming the prejudices and stereotyping behavior with which so many of the able-bodied (and some of the disabled) are afflicted.

The use of government as the primary instrument for changing social institutions affecting disabled people is a relatively new development. Historically, each disability group has relied on private charity and volunteerism for help in coping with the material, social, and economic deprivations imposed by law and social practice—for example, the March of

Dimes for polio research and rehabilitation; free summer camp for crippled children sponsored by civic clubs; religious "homes" for the handicapped, and so on.

As long as disability groups relied on these simple, established private sector relationships, it was not necessary to consider the claims of other, nondisabled groups or to develop strategic agendas for fundamental change. The move to the public arena promises much greater impact, but also poses risks and challenges which have not yet been fully appreciated. The early victories were won in a time of economic prosperity and political liberalism. It was not necessary for the disabled to set priorities among desired public policies and expenditures; it was not necessary to consider the demands of others—the poor, blacks, women, and other disadvantaged groups—when promoting policies to meet the needs of disability groups; nor was it necessary to sacrifice some objectives in order to form more encompassing policy alliances with such groups to compete with other organized interests for scarce resources.

In today's economic and political climate, it is no longer possible to avoid setting priorities among policy demands. Threats to existing antidiscrimination laws and federal funding for basic income support programs affecting all disadvantaged people must be countered by building coalitions between and among the disabled and other affected groups. And this, in turn, requires disability groups to make choices between holding out for policies of benefit only to themselves or devoting their efforts to more inclusive, and vital, common interests.

In the absence of strategic priorities, which encompass the needs of others who are victimized by poverty and discrimination, disabled people will win some and lose some in the political arena—but the wins may be inconsequential and the losses devastating in the long run.

We come back then to the matter of image, of the interaction between disabling images of people and the places they occupy in society. Persons with disabilities are not treated seriously because they have limited power and are seen as neither whole nor equal. And they are seen that way because they have limited power. Work then needs to be carried out on both sides of the equation: in changing the images and in changing the opportunity structure. At present, the disabling images constrain opportunities and the resulting limited achievements confirm the images. It can be different. Changed images lead to new opportunities and the achievements resulting from such opportunities will alter images. It is time, then, to work on both, to transform the reciprocal relationship between image and opportunity from an engine of oppression to a motor of liberation.

INDEX

"ability to work," 121
able-bodied, 118
acceptance, 87
accessibility laws, 70
accident, 34
accountability, for resources, 111
"active vigorous treatment," 169-70
activism, 17, 19; disabled Vietnam
    veterans, 154
"Act of Love, An" (TV movie), 69, 73
adjustment, portrayals of, 70-72
Adventures of Augie March, The
    (Bellow), 40
American Academy of Pediatrics, 80,
    171, 173, 176
American Association on Mental
    Deficiency, 138
American Cancer Society, 12
American Civil Liberties Union
    (ACLU), 164
American Coalition of Citizens with
    Disabilities, 15, 171
American College of Obstetricians and
    Gynecologists, 174
American College of Physicians, 174
American Heart Association, 12
American Hospital Association, 171
American Medical Association (AMA),
    174
American Nurses Association, 174
American Pediatric Surgical Association,
    Ethics Committee of, 170
American Psychological Association,
    138
American Speech-Language-Hearing
    Association, 138
amputation, psychosexual significance
    of, 67
anti-abortion groups, 91
antidiscrimination, 70
architectural barriers, 25, 189, 195
ARROYA, 153

artificial arms, psychosexual significance
    of, 67
Association for Children and Adults with
    Autism, 138
Association for Persons with Severe
    Handicaps, 138
Association for Retarded Citizens, 138,
    171
Association for the Severely
    Handicapped, 172
atonement, 60
attitudes: accessible mass transit, 155; as
    central issue in disability analysis,
    191; conflicting, 120; discriminatory,
    26 (*see also* discrimination); inter-
    pretation of, concerning disability,
    195; opposing, on employment, 120;
    prejudicial, 191; restriction of oppor-
    tunities, 187; study of, 190

Baby Doe(s): as human beings, 178;
    privacy of, 161-79; prominent de-
    fenders of, 164; right to live, 163-64
Baby Doe squads, 80
Baby Jane Doe, privacy of, 171
Baby Jane Doe case, 80, 83-86, 91-92,
    166
Barriers to Excellence, 105
benefits, 117; as "buying off" disabled,
    120; as "dumping ground," 123;
    eligibility, 119, 121, 125
Benito Cereno, 36
Best Years of Our Lives, The (movie),
    71, 73
bias, 194
bigotry, 194, 197
biological inferiority, 192, 194, 197,
    198
birthmark, 52
Black Bird, The (film), 72
blackness, psychosexual significance of,
    67

Bleak House (Dickens), 56
Bleeding Heart, The (French), 54
blindness, 49-51, 53-54, 57, 59, 60;
    special insights, 71
*Board of Education of the Hendrich
    Hudson School* v. *Rowley*, 22, 98
Bouvia, Elizabeth, 80-81, 83-86, 90,
    200
braille, 106
"broken person" concept, 134-35
Brown v. *Board of Education*, 16
Brown v. *Topeka*, 155
built environment, 189, 193, 195
bus, lift-operated, 156

Califano, Joseph, 18
California Foundation on Employment
    and Disability, Media Access Office,
    75
cash benefits, 122, 125. *See also*
    benefits
"caste of the handicapped," 206
caste status, 24
castration complex, 34
Center for Independent Living (CIL), 15,
    90, 149
cerebral palsy, 73
"champions of the heart," 82
charitable care, 10-14
Charity Cripple, 33, 35-37
child abuse, 173; redefining, 174
child abuse laws: Amendment of 1984,
    176; violations of, 171
Child Abuse Prevention and Treatment
    Act, 172, 174
child neglect, 166
Children of a Lesser God (Medoff), 55,
    56
Children's Memorial Hospital (Chicago),
    163
Choate v. *Alexander*, 21
Christmas Carol, A (Dickens), 36
City of Hope National Medical Center,
    Department of Pediatric Surgery at,
    170
Civil Liberties Union, New York, 171
civil rights, for disabled Americans, 181-
    203; goal of, 24

Civil Rights Act of 1964, section 601,
    172
civil rights protection, extension of, 207
civil rights reform, 14-17
classroom, application of technology in,
    129-40
Cleburne v. *Cleburne Living Center*, 1
coin identification, 132
collective bargaining agreements, and
    employment of disabled, 123
Coming Home (movie), 73
compensation, 71
communication: aids, 24; barriers, 25;
    devices, 131
communications access, 24
community-based facilities, 151
community-based independent living
    support services, 24
computerized voice recognition systems,
    132
computers, 187; research and
    applications of, 133
Confidence Man, The (Melville), 36
Congress of Physically Handicapped
    Organizations, 13
consciousness raising, 138
Consolidated Rail Corporation v.
    Darrone, 20
consumerism, 14
Council for Exceptional Children, 138
county poor farms, 9
couples with disabilities, 57
courage, 45
creative thinking, 106
Cricket on the Hearth (Dickens), 49
criminality and disability, 66-70
cripple(s): in literature, 31-45; problems
    of, as human problems, 37
cultural activities, 152-54
cunning, 45
Cuomo, Mario, 155

day schools, expansion of, 16
deafness, 55-56, 57, 58; technology
    applications, 131
death: by dehydration, 161; as manage-
    ment option, 165, 167; as preferred
    management option, 168; by star-
    vation, 171

Death Kit (Sontag), 53, 59
"Death in the Nursery" (TV series), 168
decision making: effective process of, 138; formulation of professional standards, 139; informed, 137
decisive technology, 146
dehumanization, 134, 135
deinstitutionalization, 14, 90, 149, 195
demedicalization/self-care, 14
Demonic Cripple, 33, 34-35
demonstrations, for enactment of section 504 regulations, 18
dependency, 55
depression, 60
Diamond, Sondra, 167-68
Disabled in Action, 138, 172
disabled children: increase in numbers of, 103; normalization of services, 99
disabled people: care of, in early years of U.S., 9-10; changing views of, 75-78; housing of, 11; humanization of, 8-23; integration of into economic mainstream, 23; maladjusted, 71; as minority group, 7-8, 22, 25
disabled women: relationships with men, 51-57; writers view of, 48-49
disabling images, 1
disability: activist groups, 75; and criminality, 66-70; definitions of, 121, 181; depiction of, 31-45; as fate worse than death, 60; variable definitions of, 119
"disability continuum," 197
Disability Forum, 200
disability policy: from human rights perspective, 11; policy reform, 15
Disability Rag, The, 92, 165
disability rights, 7-27; activists, 91; equality in, 23-27; political agenda of movement, 202
Disability Rights Education and Defense Fund, 138, 172
Disability Rights Union, 172
disability-specified organizations, formation of, 13
discrimination, 69, 74, 126, 194; in employment, 75-76; separation of from other restraints, 196; withholding treatment as form of, 172

double-amputee, 67
Down's syndrome, 76, 79, 161-66

"Early Management and Decision Making for the Treatment of Myelomeningocele," 169
Eastern Paralyzed Veterans Association, 155, 157
Easter Seal Society, 10, 12
economic resources, effect on disability adjustment, 144
education: for deaf children, 59; discrimination in, 75, 77; enrollment of handicapped children, 97; improvement in quality of, 98; on needs of disabled people, 10; policy, 90; principles for primary state and local responsibility, 101; programs, expansion of for disabled children, 16; for severely disabled, 90
educational services, clarification of lines of authority, 101
Education of All Handicapped Children Act of 1975 (P.L. 94-142), 21, 97, 201; provisions of, 98
Education Testing Service, study by, 103
electronic speech synthesizers, 131
Elephant Man, The, 70, 76, 77
Elizabeth Alone (Trevor), 52
employment of disabled, 117-26; affirmative action in, 18; appropriate and adequate, 24; barriers in, 25-26; discrimination in, 75, 76; labor force participation statistics, 122
emotional adjustment, 70
emotional education, 71
emotionally disturbed, 105
endurance, 39, 40
environment: attitudinal, 191; barriers, 25-26; disability and, 186-94; restructuring, 202
epilepsy, 58
equal citizenship, 23
equality, 23-27, 156, 199
equal opportunity, 103-4; defined, 27
equity, 156
ethics, codes of, 137-38
evaluation, special education, 105-6
exploitation, dehumanizing, 76

extended family, responsibility for disabled persons, 9
eyetyper, 131

Face of the Deep (Twersky), 57
facial disfigurement, 56, 67, 68
"Facts of Life" (TV series), 73
failure, 118
Falwell, Reverend Jerry, 164
family resources, effect on disability adjustment, 144
family responsibility, for disabled, 146-47
fear, 68
federal financial assistance (*see* federal funds)
federal funds, 20-21, 101, 208
federal government investigations, handicapped infants, 172
federal statutory reform, 16-17
Ferraro, Geraldine, 173
fiction and drama, disabled women in, 47
financing, special education, 102
Fletcher, Joseph, 165
flexibility of resources, 110-11
freedom, 199
friendships: disabled women, 49-50; intimate, 50; with women peers, 49
"Fugitive, The" (TV series), 67
Functional Electrical Stimulation, 130
functional limitations model, 138, 185, 188, 189, 192, 196, 199, 200; need for environmental changes, 187
funding formulas, 110

Glass Menagerie, The (Williams), 33, 37, 51
Goddard Space Flight Center, 130
Goffman, Erving, 68
government, as primary instrument for changing social institutions, 207
Grove City College v. *Bell*, 21
Growth of the Soil, The (Hamsun), 58
guidelines, for identification of disability, 100
guilt, 60

halfway houses, 151

handicapped infants: entitlement of due process and equal protection under law, 174; neglect of, 173; section 504 enforcement for, 171; subsequent life, 177
handicapped people (*see also* disabled people): three common prejudices against, 67
Hazard of New Fortunes, A (Howells), 33, 38
Health, Education, and Welfare, Department of, 18; Office of Civil Rights, 170
Health and Human Services, Department of, 177
health-related inability, 182
hearing-impaired, 103; technological advances, 130
helplessness, 53, 62, 197; learned states of, 122
"Highway to Heaven" (TV series), 73
home, application of technology in, 129-40
home health care services, 147-48
homicide, 166
housing, 149-52; adequate, 24; affordable, 149; government subsidized, 150; special, 151
Housing and Urban Development, Department of (HUD), 150
human interest stories, 74, 75
humanity, loss of, 68, 69
humanization, defined, 8
Hunchback of Notre Dame, The (horror classic), 68
hydrocephalus, 79, 84

identification, special education, 105-6
images of disease and disability, social and psychological consequences of, 33
incentives, 123; modification of, 125
incompetent persons, 1
Independence Trail, 153
independent living, 90, 195
independent living centers, 149; community-based, 18
independent living movement, 15, 120

Individual Education Program (IEP), 97-98, 111

individualization, 113; of services, 99

Ineraid, 131

Infant Bioethics Committees, 177

infanticide, 58, 162, 165; lawsuits, 177; legislation to end, 178

infantilization, 50

inferiority, 53, 61, 62

inservice training, 101, 104

insurance companies: as alternate sources for financing, 148; disability compensation and rehabilitation, 126; view of disability, 123

integration, of disabled children, 27, 104-5; in our classrooms, 98; vs. segregation, 156

International Games for the Disabled, 82

In This Sign (Greenberg), 57

Introvoice, 132

Irving Independent School District v. *Tatro*, 22, 98

isolation, 49, 52, 62, 71, 87, 198

Issues in Law and Medicine, 176

Jernigan, Kenneth, 1-2, 81

"Jewel in the Crown, The" (British miniseries), 67

job placement, 125

John Hopkins Hospital, Birth Defects Treatment Center at, 170

Keller, Helen, 50, 51

King's General, The (du Maurier), 47, 58

Koch, Ed, 155

Koop, Everett, 88, 89

Kurzweil Reading Machine, 132, 153

labeling, 113, 205; positive, 201

lameness, 51-52, 60

language, technology applications, 130

law reform, 15-16

learning disabled, 103, 105

least restrictive environment (LRE), 135, 137

legislation, early development of, 13

Lesch-Nyhan syndrome, 162

Let Us Now Praise Famous Men (Agee), 42

"Letter From a Vegetable" (Diamond), 165

lip reading, 106

literature: cripples in, 31-45; disabled women in, 47

"Little House on the Prairie" (TV series), 74

Lloyd v. *Regional Transportation Authority,* 26

loneliness, 87

long-term care facilities, 151

Long Walk Home, The (Kriegel), 42, 43

mainstreaming, 102, 106-7, 137, 195; researching on, 107

mainstreaming models, studies of, 112

marriage, disabled women and, 52-57

Mask (movie), 77

mass transit, accessibility of, 154-57

mathematics skills, teaching of, 132

"maxitaxi," 156

mechanization, 134

media: awareness of disability community, 75; power of, 81

Medicaid, 21, 147

medical care, appropriate, 24

medical rehabilitations, 121

Medicare, 147

Memoirs of a Midget (de la Mare), 50, 61, 63

Men, The (movie), 71

mentally retarded, 103, 105; toileting skills, 132

Meridian (Walker), 60-61

Metropolitan Transportation Authority (MTA), 155, 157

microcomputer-controlled interactive videodisc system, 132

minority group, 188; equal opportunities, 126; identification of, 194-99

minority group model, 184-86, 189, 195-96, 199-201; judicial and constitutional implications, 185; policy implications, 200-3

mobility aids, 24

mobility-impaired, 26, 156

mobility training, 106

Moby Dick, 34

Monday After the Miracle (Gibson), 50

monster, depiction of disabled person as, 68

motion pictures, images of disabled people in, 65-78

motivation, improving individual, 125

Muscular Distrophy Association, 10, 12

National Association of the Deaf, 13

National Association of Retarded Citizens, 10

National Association of Social Workers, 138

National Environmental Policy Act, 21

National Federation of the Blind, 2, 13, 81

National Legal Center for the Medically Dependent and Disabled, 177

National Organization on Disability, 165

national rehabilitation policy, 90

National Spinal Cord Injury Foundation, 10

natural endowment, 170

Nevis Mountain Dew, 69, 73

newborns, 76; severely disabled, treatment of, 91

Night Mother (Norman), 58

nondisabled society, acceptance in, 57

normalization, 136, 137

Notes for the Two-Dollar Window (Kriegel), 43

Not in the Calendar (Kennedy), 50-51

Office of Federal Contract Compliance Procedures (Dept. of Labor), 201

Of Mice and Men, 68

Oklahoma Life Science Center, 91

Older Americans Act, 147

On Men and Manhood (Kriegel), 44

"Ordeal of Bill Carney, The" (TV movie), 75

ordinariness, 38

Orphan Drugs Bill, 76

orthopedically impaired, 103

Other Side of the Mountain, The (movie), 75

paraplegia, 71, 73; technological advances, 130

Paraplegia News, 155

paratransit systems, 156

parent groups, 19

Pastoral Symphony, 60

patience, 45

personal care, for disabled, 146-48

personality disfigurement, 68

personnel development, comprehensive system, 101

Phantom of the Opera, The (horror classic), 68, 72

"physically challenged," 74

physically disabled categories, 144

pity, 53, 59

policy implications, 200-3

political action committees, 18

Powers That Be, The, 81

prejudice, 26, 74, 91, 194; social, 70

preservice training, 101

President's Commission for the Study of Ethical Problems in Medicine, 164

print journalism, treatment of disability issues, 79-93

private rehabilitation agencies, 124; disability compensation and rehabilitation, 126

professionals, in disability services, 10; increase in number of, 12

programs: current, as work disincentive, 118; effectiveness, 112-13; and school organization, 111-12

Project Access, 153

public education, rights to, 21-22, 99

public entitlements, to persons with severe disabilities, 11

public facilities, access to, 16-17

Public Law No. 94-142. *See* Education for All Handicapped Children Act

public policy: development of, affecting disabled Americans, 181; environment and, 192; restructuring, 124-25

public rehabilitation agencies, 124

public transportation, accessible, 24

quadriplegia, 69, 73, 76; technological advances, 130, 132

quality of life, 165, 176-77, 200; decisions, 173; formula, 170; minimally adequate, 162

"Quincy" (TV series), 76

rage, 60
reading skills, teaching of, 132
Reagan, Ronald, 82, 88, 164, 172
Reagan administration, 80, 88; changing
    federal role, 19
Realistic Cripple, 33, 37
recreation, 152-54
referral, special education, 105-6
Rehabilitation Act of 1973, 16, 145;
    1978 amendments, 13; section 504,
    17, 18, 171, 172; Title VII, 18
rehabilitation benefits, 12. *See also*
    benefits
rehabilitation programs, 124
Rehabilitation Services Administration,
    90
rejection, 53, 57, 71, 118
Remote Control, 81
Research Triangle Institute, 105, 130
resourcefulness, 45
resource-neutral allocation formulas, 111
resources, availability and flexibility of,
    110-11
revulsion, 53, 54
Reynolds, William, 88
Richard III, 31-32
Rights of the Critically Ill, The
    (Robertson), 166
right-to-die, 92, 200
right-to-life advocates, 91, 92
right-to-life organization, 164; coalition
    of, 206
robots, use of, 147
romantic rejection, 77
Rowan, Carl, 89
Russell Pathsounder, 131

school services, scope of, 100
school organization, program and, 111-
    12
Section 504 case reviews, 20-23
segregation, 10-14, 194, 195
self: creation of, 45; dimensions and
    boundaries, 61; existing within
    geography, 43
self-acceptance, 58; lack of, 73;
    psychological, 70
self-assurance, 73
self-care skills, 106

self-contained classrooms, 113
self-contempt, 61
self-control: loss of, 68; moral, 69
self-determination, 144
self-esteem, enhancing, 120
self-feeding, technological advances, 132
self-help, 14
self-help groups, 149
self-identification, 198
self-loathing, 58
self-pity, 70, 76
self-realization, 61
self-sufficiency, 120; economic, 125
seriously emotionally disturbed, 103
services, access to, 103-4
severe disability, 69; overcoming, 75
severely emotionally disturbed, 109
severely intellectually impaired, 109
sexuality, and disabled people, 72-75
Shadow/VET, 132
Shaw, Dr. Anthony, 170
sheltered workshops, 11, 122
Siamese twins, 91, 166
sign language, 106
sign language interpreters, 24
skills training, 24
Smart Wheelchair, 130
Smith v. *Robinson*, 22, 98
Snowdon v. *Birmingham Jefferson
    County Transit Authority*, 26
social discrimination, 92
social function of disability images, 74-
    75
social integration, 69, 74
social interactive skills, 106
social movements, 14-17
social ostracism, 77
social reform, organization for, 14-15
Social Security Act of 1935, 11; 1956
    amendments to, 12
Social Security Disability Insurance
    (SSDI), 121
Social Services block grant, 147
society, assumptions about disability,
    107-9
Southern Community College v. *Davis*,
    20
special-care institutions, 9
special-care nursery, 163, 165

special education, 205; access to, 103;
   risk students in, 104
special education programming,
   effectiveness and quality, 106-7
special gifts, 71
Special Olympics, 83, 153
Speech Autocuer, 130-31
speech impaired, 103
spina bifida, 79, 84, 162-63, 169
staffing and training of personnel, 101-2
standards of practice, 137-38
starvation, death by, 161
stereotyping, 194, 195, 196
stigma, fundamental nature of, 68
stigmatization, 194
student programs, for disabled, 14
stuttering, 74
suicide, 58, 69, 70, 73; through
   starvation, 80
Supplemental Security Income (SSI),
   121
"supportive care only," 169-70
"substantial gainful activity" (SGA),
   121, 182
supportive therapy, 146
Survivor Cripple, 33, 38-45

Targeted Jobs Tax Credit, 123
technological aids: designing and
   applying, 135-36; resolution of
   ethical issues, 139
technology: defining, 145-46; for physically disabled, 143-59
technology applications, 129-40; current
   developments in, 130-36; ethical,
   137-39; underlying premises and
   ethical issues, 133-36
television, images of disabled people in,
   65-78
Tender Mercies (Brown), 60
time telling, 132
Titticut Follies (classic film), 90
"T. J. Hooker" (TV series), 76
total-care institutions, existence of
   massive, 11-13
training, emphasis on, 125
training institutions, 11
treatment, handicapped infants,
   withholding of, 165

Transbus, 156, 157
transportation, 154-58; access to, 16-17
Transportation, Department of, 156

Ulysses (Joyce), 49
United Cerebral Palsy, 10, 12, 138
Urban Mass Transportation Adminis-
   tration demonstration grant, 156
Urban Mass Transportation Act of 1964,
   154

"vegetable like" existence, 69
victimization, 34, 37; of women, 60
victims, blaming the, 68
villains, disabled, 67-70
visually handicapped, 103
visual impairments, technological
   advances, 131-32
vocational training, 10

Waiting for the Barbarians (Coetzee), 54
warehousing, 149
weakness, 197
Westport Transit District, Mobility
   Advisory Group of, 156
wheelchairs: major improvements in,
   158; redesign, 153
White House Conference on Handicapped
   Individuals, 145
wholeness, lacking sense of, 39
Whose Life is it, Anyway?, 69, 73
"Why I Write" (Orwell), 41
"Wild Wild West" (TV series), 67, 72
Wilson, Edmund, 32
Winespring Mountain (Ogburn), 53, 58
woman, accepted as herself, 58-59
Women and Disability Awareness
   Project, 92
Wood, Michael, 65
work place, application of technology in,
   129-40
Wound and the Bow, The (Wilson), 32-
   33
writers, intimate personal experience, 61
writer's attitude, character's attitude as
   expression of, 59-62, 63

Yale-New Haven Hospital, 165, 167

About the Editors and Contributors

ALAN GARTNER is the director, Office of Sponsored Research, Graduate School and University Center, City University of New York, and, formerly, executive director, Division of Special Education, New York City Public Schools. He is author or editor of some 20 books concerning public policy, education, and other human services.

TOM JOE is the founder and director, Center for the Study of Social Policy, Washington, D.C., and, formerly has held high administrative positions in state and federal government. He is coauthor of the recent *By the Few, For the Few: The Reagan Welfare Legacy.* In 1986, he was selected as a MacArthur Fellow.

ROBERT FUNK is the director, Disability Rights Education and Defense Fund, the national legal arm of the disability rights movement.

LEONARD KRIEGEL is professor and director of the Institute for Labor Studies, The City College, City University of New York, and author of four novels.

DEBORAH KENT is an author of novels for teenagers and young adults and writes on issues related to disability.

PAUL K. LONGMORE is program specialist, Program in Disability and Society, University of Southern California. He is by training an historian and author of a forthcoming biography of George Washington.

DOUGLAS BIKLEN is director, Division of Special Education, Syracuse University and author of several leading texts concerning special education and rehabilitation.

LISA J. WALKER is vice-president, Institute for Educational Leadership, Washington, D.C., and formerly, as a congressional staff person, had major responsibility for drafting both Section 504 of the Rehabilitation Act and PL 94-142, "The Education of All Handicapped Children Act."

CHERYL ROGERS is a senior research associate at the Center for the Study of Social Policy. She is coauthor, *By the Few, For the Few.*

AL CAVALIER is director, Bioengineering Program, at the national headquarters of the Association for Retarded Citizens of the United States.

GEORGIA L. MCMURRAY is deputy general director, Community Service Society of New York, and, formerly, director, Agency for Child Development, City of New York.

NAT HENTOFF is a columnist for the *Village Voice* and author of books on civil liberties, race, and jazz.

HARLAN HAHN is founder and director, Program in Disability and Society, University of Southern California. He is by training a political scientist and is the author of several books on government, race relations, and urban affairs.